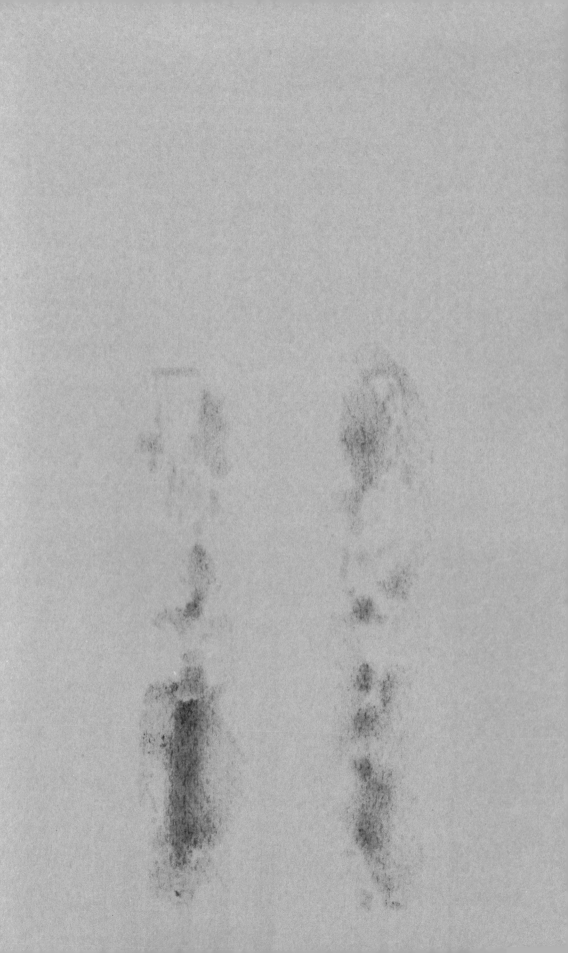

Sign
Systems
for
Libraries

Sign Systems for Libraries

Solving the Wayfinding Problem

Compiled and Edited by
DOROTHY POLLET and PETER C. HASKELL

R. R. Bowker Company
New York & London, 1979

To Michael, and to Sid and Ben

Cover design by Alice
Text design by Edward A. Butler

Published by R. R. Bowker Company
1180 Avenue of the Americas, New York, N.Y. 10036
Copyright © 1979 by Xerox Corporation
All rights reserved
Printed and bound in the United States of America

Library of Congress Cataloging in Publication Data
Main entry under title:

Sign systems for libraries.

  Bibliography: p.
  Includes index.
  1. Library signs. I. Pollet, Dorothy.
II. Haskell, Peter C.
Z679.57.S53   025.5   79-11138
ISBN 0-8352-1149-5

Contents

page v

Contents
vi

Foreword

My concern with wayfinding in libraries was heightened by an event some years ago at Cornell University in Ithaca, New York. A graduate student in architecture had requested permission to scrutinize, as part of his thesis research, the difficulties that first-time visitors to the Olin Library encountered in finding their way from the building entrance to the material they needed on the shelves. Permission was granted, although we felt that the project was probably a bit naive. After all, the Olin Library, which was then relatively new, had enjoyed the fullest planning expertise the profession could provide, and it had been designed by an excellent architectural firm. Moreover, it had been uniformly and highly praised by many of the best-informed library building experts in the land. What impediments could there possibly be to its effective use?

When we sat down later, however, to view the student's videotapes of frustrated first-time visitors misunderstanding our simplest graphics, looking in vain for signs where we had concluded that none were needed, and turning logically but fecklessly into blank walls, we were startled and chagrined. Then we were, I think, a little wiser. Olin was a *good* library. If there were confusing elements in this building, the same was probably true for all library buildings.

Upon reflection, it did seem that we librarians had been less attentive to the wayfinding problems of our users than we might have been. Some of us had avoided using signs altogether. Others had put up the wrong kinds of signs, admonishing patrons not to waste call slips, instructing dogs to wait outside (usually placed too high for dogs to see), or banning on-site sleeping. Indeed, probably the only signs that library patrons could find uniformly throughout the English-speaking world were "Men" and "Women."

In recent years, increasing numbers of library building programs have called attention to the need for graphics. Where this has happened, designers have sometimes created very effective and handsome signs. This had long been the case with airports, department stores, and shopping malls, where the profit incentive had inspired their clients to call for signs. With our encouragement, designers have now begun to do as well for us, as the signage systems in a number of recent library buildings attest. Even where budget limitations prevent the employment of professional designers, our increased awareness is helping us to do better for ourselves.

Recent years have also witnessed a resurgence of concern among librarians for enhancing the library skills of their patrons. According to homely wisdom, however, there is more than one way to skin a cat. Perhaps we can attain some of the same end by making the library easier to use, and that is what this book is all about. Dorothy Pollet and Peter Haskell have assembled a symposium of specialists who address the matter of making libraries more accessible, particularly to the first-time or unskilled library patron.

The chapters, it will be noted, proceed from the theoretical to the practical. There has not before been a book about library signage in the United States, and it is to be hoped that the availability of one will contribute to facilitating library use. If noted librarian Jesse Shera is correct that the function of libraries is "to maximize the social utility of the graphic record," then the subject of this book is central to our business.

David Kaser

Introduction

Finding a title for this book was not easy. The central concept, although a logical and useful one, did not lend itself to a concise label. Signs are central to the idea, but the concept goes further to include building directories, wall graphics, printed library guides, maps of the building, space arrangement, displays, even information stations—in short, all visual means of helping readers find and use the services of a library. To be truly helpful to users, it is crucial that these components be planned and organized as a system. Our somewhat cumbersome term "visual guidance systems" expresses this central idea.

Those who have written on closely related topics have also grappled with problems of terminology. In the foreword to *Signage: Planning Environmental Visual Communication* (Institute of Signage Research, 1976), Karen Claus and R. James Claus describe the absence of scholarly material when they first began to investigate the nature of visual communication in the environment.[1] The Clauses coined the term "signage" to identify the phenomenon and explain their area of interest to academic colleagues. Although still unfamiliar to many outside of design and architectural circles, signage has become an accepted term to describe a systematic approach to signs and related components of the visual environment that convey information. "Environmental communications" and "environmental graphics" are also frequently heard. The first newsletter of the Society of Environmental Graphic Designers defined the role of the designer who specializes in this area in the following manner: "to plan, program, design and specify graphic elements within an environment. Typically included are signage systems which identify, direct and inform within complex facilities [such as] cities, hospitals, universities, offices [and] airports. Additionally, architectural graphics which visually enhance a space . . . murals, super-graphics, flags, banners, kiosks, etc., are elements of the discipline."[2]

Throughout the book, we often use "wayfinding," a self-explanatory term employed in navigation, survival training, and geography, to express our central concept from the user's point of view. Users unfamiliar with a library engage in wayfinding behavior, and this process can be either aided or frustrated by the environment they encounter. By studying user reactions to the visual environment of libraries, librarians can do a number of things to make that environment more understandable to users. The thesis of this book is that libraries can be made legible.

Why are visual guidance systems important to libraries?

> . . . libraries are formidable places at best . . . People who use the library are immediately aware of their shortcomings and very few like to expose the fact that they do not know the answer to the question they want to look up . . . With this situation it is much better for the shy reader (and there are many of them) to be able to go to the catalog and look up his own information. He will be more likely to come again if he can help himself.[3]

Even when library users are not particularly shy and would prefer to have help rather than finding things on their own, it is still important to apply the concept of a visual guidance system. Service points must be placed so that they are logically related to the entrances and spaces of the library. In addition, since most libraries cannot fully staff all service points during all hours of operation, some signs or other means of visual guidance will always be required. These must be intelligently placed if they are to fulfill their intended goal of helping users. More than one commentator has expressed the view that library patrons should always have the option of self-guidance in libraries where this is possible.

> If all the library staff were propped up dead at their posts, like the legionnaires in *Beau Geste*, it should still be possible for a student on his first visit to find his way to the books he needs.[4]

J. L. Thornton, in an article entitled "Too Few Libraries Are Organized for Readers," states his idea of a library as a place "in which readers are helped to help themselves, are encouraged to browse, and can find their own way around."[5]

Whenever people enter an unfamiliar environment, they experience disorientation and stress. Libraries are no exception. They intimidate potential users through their size, complexity, ambiguity, and unfamiliar tools and equipment. A prominent designer has speculated that much user frustration is a result of knowing that all the necessary information is available in the library, but not knowing how to get to it. Even experienced library users are baffled by unfamiliar space arrangements, catalogs, procedures, and equipment. For an example of what a well-planned visual guidance system can do to index the library environment for users, contrast the image of a library totally devoid of signs—or one with a plethora of confusing, poorly placed or illegible signs—with that of the "well-signed" libraries shown in Chapter 20. For the first-time user, it can mean the difference between success or failure, between a positive attitude toward libraries and a negative one. Library signage systems help to complete the process that begins with the acquiring, organizing, and storing of materials: they supplement the services of library staff in helping users gain access to the collections of the library. In addition, a good guidance system sets a tone for the library, subtly conveying that this library has a friendly, welcoming atmosphere, and that it is a well-organized, efficient place.

The design of a signage, or visual guidance, system begins with an analysis and definition of user needs, their characteristic approaches to the library, and their potential points of decision and stress. Successful systems provide orientation (what services are available), direction (how to get to your goal), and identification (how to know when you have arrived there). These systems have in common the characteristics of consistency, hierarchical arrangement of information (from general to specific), updating capability, and responsiveness to audience needs. The last point is of particular significance: the focus of a guidance system should be on functions and behavior, not on walls and spaces. Improved service to users should be the ultimate test of the system. In the last analysis, good design will be judged by its accountability to human needs.

Perhaps within the next few years the book that is needed—the one that reflects the results of thoroughgoing research on wayfinding in libraries—will emerge from studies yet to be done. In the meantime, this book is meant to serve as a stimulating source book, a state-of-the-art symposium on visual guidance systems in libraries. Its objective is to bring together experts from various fields relevant to the topic—library science, psychology, optometry, geography, design, and space planning—and writers portraying different types of library experiences with signage systems. This interdisciplinary perspective is designed to provide a definition of problems as well as propose creative solutions; to offer practical, specific advice as well as discussions of underlying theory.

Part 1 lays the groundwork for the design of a visual guidance system by presenting theories and research relevant to user behavior in public service environments. The results of research on user orientation needs, mental mapping, and the human vision system are applied to the library setting. Part 2 covers the specifics of planning and designing a visual guidance system, from defining the needs of a particular library, to engaging a consultant, to producing signs, to evaluating the system as a whole. Practical solutions developed by real libraries are covered in Part 3. Ideas and/or case studies are presented for school media centers, public libraries, special libraries, and academic libraries. Here also a user tells what it is like on the other side of the information desk. Part 4 suggests ways in which library building planning and space arrangement can assist the wayfinding process. Chapter 20 in this section presents the state of the art of library guidance systems through pictures.

In all, with the help of contributors and many others, we hope we have made the complex problem of wayfinding in libraries more understandable, relevant, and solvable.

D. Pollet
P. C. Haskell

ACKNOWLEDGMENTS

Sign Systems for Libraries would not have been possible without the help of many people who care about bringing good design to the library environment. In addition to the contributors who lent their expertise and creative energies to the topic of wayfinding in libraries, we wish especially to thank the many libraries that provided photographs; the entire staff of the Institute of Signage Research; Lois Kazakoff, formerly of Perkins & Will; and William R. Myers of the Department of Transportation.

We wish to acknowledge Franklin and Marshall College, which provided a grant for the completion of the manuscript. We would particularly like to thank the staff of the Library for their support, and Dean Richard Traina and Secretary of the College Richard Kneedler for sharing the vision of the library as a legible, accessible place.

For their encouragement, we wish to thank Carol Nemeyer, Pauline Atherton, Helen Gunn, Carolyn Snyder, Carl Jackson, Monty Maxwell, Ivor Davies, Ron Swanson, Evan Farber, Stephen Guynn, Keith Cottam, Mark Robbins, and Hal Espo.

Mike Gray, Bill Myers, Chris Huemer, Susanne Owens, Robert Schlossberg, Doris Gallion, Fran Hopkins, Robert Case, Madeleine Oakley, and Robert Zich read early versions of the chapters and made helpful suggestions.

Barbara Coons and Nancy Mitchell prepared the index, and Linda Danner provided valuable typing and organization assistance. Thanks also to Howard White, editor of *Library Technology Reports*.

We are grateful for the assistance of Corinne Naden and Iris Topel at R. R. Bowker.

NOTES

1   Karen E. Claus and R. James Claus, *Signage: Planning Environmental Visual Communication* (Palo Alto, Calif.: Institute of Signage Research, 1976).

2   *Society of Environmental Graphic Designers Newsletter* 1 (January 1977): 2.

3   Margaret Mann, "What It Means to Catalog," *Library Notes and News* 8 (1927): 288.

4   Nick Childs, "Do Students Have to Use Libraries?" *Times Higher Education Supplement* 85 (June 1, 1973): 24.

5   J. L. Thornton, "Too Few Libraries Are Organized for Readers," *Library Association Record* 78 (1976): 255.

Part
1

Finding One's Way in the Library:
Theory and Research

1

Orientation Needs and the Library Setting

ROSS J. LOOMIS   MARGARET B. PARSONS

Unfamiliar environments make special demands upon us. Even the simplest of settings can involve a jumble of information that has to be sorted and processed before it becomes meaningful. Environmental psychology is one discipline that has recognized the importance of visual information in enabling people to adapt to a wide range of environments.[1] In recent years, other investigators have become interested in understanding how humans process information about their surroundings. Urban sociologists, for example, have studied how residents view the city or neighborhood they live in,[2] and geographers have examined how individuals use mental imagery or mapping to describe physical spaces.[3]

In this chapter the term *orientation* refers to the processing of environmental information for two purposes: to locate one's position in a physical setting and to determine a course of action for coping with the demands of a particular environment.[4] The concern here is with orientation involving public-access environments in general, and libraries in particular. Public-access environments are simply places that are open to the public, such as parks, airports, shopping centers, and museums. They are designed to meet particular needs such as recreation, shopping, travel, education, and aesthetic enjoyment. The physical features of these public settings may constitute one source of orientation information, but there are other cues that exist in the setting, as illustrated in the following example.

Imagine a patron entering a library in search of a particular book or reference work. What sources of orientation information are available? A complete list of cues might be endless, but we can identify at least three sources. For instance, basic architectural features of the building can serve as cues. Stairs, doorways, and halls all suggest passage to other parts of the building. Service desks and counters, catalogs, and open stacks also help to orient the visitor by prompting such specific behaviors as consulting the card catalog, asking for assistance, or searching for a book in the stacks.

Another cue is graphic material and printed aids. Signs, symbols, color cues, brochures, and maps are examples of orientation aids.

As a third source, people can give information about the library setting. At a most direct level, the patron can ask for assistance from staff members or other patrons. Observing others coping with the environment and imitating their behaviors assists orientation in an indirect manner. An even less direct social cue comes from previous learning associated with the concept "library." Most people have learned, for instance, that a library is a place where one is supposed to be quiet—an expectation that helps guide behavior, but at the same time may inhibit questions and the use of orientation aids that require talking to others.

From this array of architectural cues, prepared orientation materials, and social orientation aids, patrons must select relevant information to locate themselves and choose the next course of action. Obviously, library users have another very important aid that they bring with them—memory. The role of memory in mediating expectations about the library environment has already been suggested. As a patron uses a library on repeated occasions, he or she relies more heavily on memory and develops a mental map showing the physical layout of the building, a subject discussed in more detail in Chapter 2.

In this chapter, we will look at orientation from four different perspectives: (1) the general interest in relating physical environment design to human behavior, (2) patron orientation needs, (3) psychological concepts that provide insight into the mental activity involved in perceptual orientation and may serve as reference points in thinking about the orientation needs of library users, and (4) a review of selected research examples on the use of such public-access settings as museums and parks for possible implications in library orientation planning.

PHYSICAL ENVIRONMENT
AND HUMAN BEHAVIOR

The current interest in helping patrons better use the library environment is only one example of a growing interest in relating behavior to architectural design. Sommer,[5] among others, has called attention to the importance of involving users or consumers more directly in the development of building design, and Mitchell[6] has urged the establishment of a viable working relationship between the professionals who create environments and those who must live and work in them. This awareness of the importance of user needs and behavior has spanned a number of different disciplines. In fact, involving the user more directly in environmental design requires the combined skills of several professions[7] and even the possible creation of a social science language that can be used jointly by social scientists and design professionals such as architects and planners.[8]

What do we mean by user needs? A discussion by Zeisel[9] helps to answer this question. *User needs* are those characteristics required of an environment to permit the completion of activities planned or typically undertaken in a specific setting. The idea of user needs can be made clearer by distinguishing it from *user wants*, which refer to characteristics that might be desirable but are not absolutely necessary for successful adaptation in a particular setting. Providing basic orientation at critical points through such vehicles as signs and information personnel are related to user needs; the use of color and other design elements that add visual interest, but do not constitute essential information, are more closely tied to user wants.

One benefit of directing attention to user needs is that these needs can be identified and made more explicit. In fact, the current interest in providing more effective graphics and signage to guide people through public-access environments is a good example of identifying a specific user need. At the present time, however, most library user studies[10] focus on audience description, and patterns in the circulation and handling of library materials[11] and are limited primarily to academic libraries.[12] Although knowledge of audience characteristics and circulation trends is indeed important, patron needs that are related specifically to orientation in the use of the library is one category that could be defined more explicitly. There is little research on library user orientation (as defined here) available at present, but some behavioral aspects could serve as a starting point in defining patron orientation needs for future research.

Once the category of user needs has been defined, it can be included in a larger system of environmental design criteria. For example, Murtha[13] has organized a classification system of behavioral criteria to be considered in evaluating architectural designs for public places. One essential category is *perceptual maintenance*, which refers to planning the environment to provide the kinds and levels of stimuli necessary for performing perceptual tasks. Orientation can be thought of as a perceptual task important for adapting to the physical features of a particular setting. Emphasis on user orientation needs and wants is one example of the growing interest in stressing behavioral criteria in environmental design.

PATRON ORIENTATION NEEDS

Orientation is defined above as the perceptual process of determining one's location in the environment and deciding where to go next. Breaking down that definition, orientation can be considered in terms of: (1) a general response to the environment, (2) creating images or mental maps about the geographic properties of different environments, and (3) making a series of decisions about the environment.

The general response aspect of orientation is familiar to anyone who has ever taken an introductory course in psychology, for it was first defined by Pavlov in his famous studies on the conditioning of responses in animals. Increased sensitivity, greater muscle tension, changes in brain activity to produce greater arousal or attention, increased tension in specific skeletal muscle groups that control sensory organs such as the eyes, and changes in visceral activities such as blood pressure and heart rate are characteristics of the general response to new environmental stimuli. These activities enable a living creature to reach its maximum potential for processing information about the environment, in particular about any specific stimuli that triggered the general orientation pattern responses.[14]

What kinds of stimuli evoke a general orientation response? Complex or novel stimuli, environmental conditions that produce conflict or uncertainty, and stimuli to which the perceiver attaches special or significant meanings, such as the sound of his or her name, can trigger increased responsiveness.

How can this general responsiveness, sometimes called general orientation, be related to user orientation needs? For one thing, minimizing distractions, such as unnecessary noise, can reduce the likelihood of disrupting attention from the task at hand. Thus, the long-standing practice of keeping library environments quiet can help the user to focus on reading or other information-gathering tasks. It also can be concluded that features such as novelty or environmental change could be incorporated into orientation aids (e.g., signs, logos) to help draw patron attention to important sources of orientation information. On the other hand, complexity or novelty could compete with orientation materials for user attention, and thus produce unintended confusion.

One of the most fundamental orientation needs is to find one's location

FIGURE 1-1 A simple sign can be strategically located in anticipation of a question—in this case, where the stairway is located—that patrons are apt to have in mind at a particular point in the building.

within the total space of the library by forming a mental map that can serve as an environmental organizer. Architectural features of buildings should be used where possible to assist in the mapping process. An open courtyard, for example, when shown graphically on a map, can provide an overall sense of the symmetry of a building.

A third kind of orientation need involves making a series of decisions about the environment. Kaplan[15] has described this functional process in the form of a series of rather simple questions. Adaptation or orientation to a setting involves locating oneself within a geographic space, correctly anticipating what will happen next, evaluating the setting and any events in terms of good or bad outcomes, and deciding on a course of action. In practical terms, we must remember that since the patron is going to be making a series of decisions about the environment, orientation aids should be located so as to anticipate the information needed at any particular point in the library. For instance, finding and using the card catalog and starting a search for a specific book in open stacks entail going through the decision-making sequence several times. Patrons must locate themselves, anticipate environmental structures or events that will occur, evaluate the results of their search, and continually decide on the next course of action. Signs, instructions, staff, and other aids situated in areas that invite interaction can provide help at each of these decision-making points. Figure 1-1 is an example of a sign intended to anticipate decision making by the user.

So far, orientation has been emphasized as a perceptual task related to successful coping with the environment. However, it is also useful to think of disorientation, or the failure to handle environmental information effectively. Disorientation can occur as distraction at the level of general orientation response, such as noise in a normally quiet library reading room. As noted earlier, patrons are distracted from reading and other concentration tasks in order to look for the source of the noise. Perhaps the most common disorientation experience is feeling lost when mental images fail to correspond to the real world. The result can be fatigue, loss of enjoyment in using an environment,[16] frustration,[17] irritability, and even panic. If patron needs are stressed from the perspective of avoiding disorientation, the emphasis would be on anticipating problem areas in advance, and then designing solutions into orientation aids and even into the architectural space itself.

Unfortunately, orientation aids can sometimes contribute to the feeling of disorientation, as noted in an example from Porteous.[18] Only through careful evaluation and pretesting can we be reasonably sure that signs, maps, and other guides, as shown in Fig. 1-2,[19] do not disorient patrons, however unintentionally.

PSYCHOLOGICAL CONCEPTS
IN PATRON ORIENTATION

Some psychological factors, such as arousal, information overload and stress, social variables, and overconfidence in decision making, may influence orientation behavior.

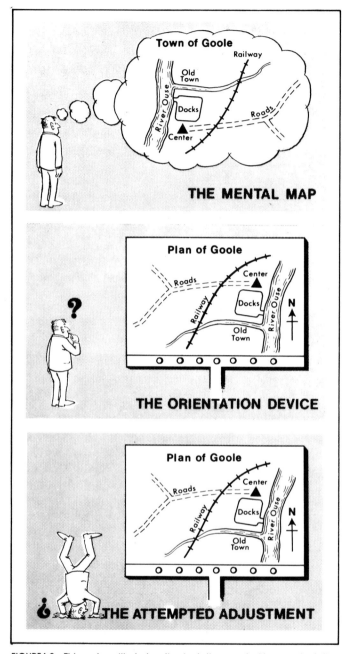

FIGURE 1-2 This cartoon illustrates disorientation created by an orientation device that was inverted in relation to the mental map people had of the geographic area. Illustration reprinted from Porteous, J. D., *Environment and Behavior* 3, No. 2 (June 1971), by permission of the publisher, Sage Publications, Inc.

Arousal and Orientation

Almost everyone has had the experience of rushing through an airport or train station to catch a plane or train that is about to leave. At such a time, orientation aids take on great importance. Signs, numbers, and letters must supply critical information to guide one to the appropriate gate as fast as possible. It is especially distressing to discover that in rushing about the airport or station, information was read incorrectly and a wrong concourse or gate was selected. The excitement generated by being in a hurry and feeling the pressure of running out of time results in an ineffective processing of information and a growing sense of disorientation, which may heighten the feelings of excitement. It is not likely that patrons using a library will experience the same level of excitement as a traveler rushing for a plane, although college students looking for resource materials to use in an overdue term paper are certainly apt to feel pressured. Actually, the opposite is also true—low levels of tension or excitement also may cause inaccurate processing of environmental information.

Psychologists call this sense of excitement "arousal," a term that has been used to refer both to the emotional excitement and to the underlying increased brain activity.[20] States of arousal range from a low level near sleep or unconsciousness, often characterized by feelings of boredom, to a highly excited feeling that could be associated with panic behavior. In general, very low (boring) or very high (exciting) states of arousal are less pleasant to experience than are moderate levels,[21] especially if one understands that he or she has very little control of the situation. From the standpoint of orientation needs, what is significant about the psychological arousal theory is that information is processed most effectively at a moderate or middle-range level. If arousal is very high or very low, a person's attention to environmental cues is apt to be impaired (see Fig. 1-3). Orientation aids should evoke these middle ranges of arousal by using some complexity or novelty in their design and by avoiding schemes that are overly complicated or ambiguous.

Information Overload and Stress

Modern urban environments notably provide more stimulation than one can comfortably process or organize. This "information overload" can cause a high level of arousal, and it constitutes a form of environmental stress.[22] One's reaction to such an overload is to channel or focus one's attention more narrowly, thus tuning out peripheral stimuli.[23] Too many signs arranged in an incoherent fashion may be less instructive than too few, since patrons may entirely ignore signs that are crowded together.

By the same token, settings may have insufficient stimulation, or "information underload," resulting in low arousal, boredom, and fatigue. Such monotonous settings as a quiet reading room can also be stressful, and lowered levels of attention can make orientation cues less effective.

Social Variables

As mentioned earlier, other people can serve as a source of orientation information, and such socially based data can be direct or indirect. This same distinction can be used in talking about the social variables of direct interaction

FIGURE 1-3 These simple and easily visible letter graphics anticipate the possible decline of perceptual accuracy under states of high or low psychological arousal. In addition to the large size of the letters, color is used to attract attention in an otherwise rather monotonous environment.

with others, the influence of crowding, and socially determined expectations about the library environment. These social sources of orientation information parallel the three variables discussed in this section.

The presence of other people can provide orientation information through direct social interaction. Patrons can ask each other or staff members on duty for orientation help. However, the presence of others, particularly of official attendants, does not necessarily mean that they will be used, and in fact there may be a tendency to avoid them.[24] Just why people avoid asking attendants for help is not clear.[25] Perhaps having to deal with a stranger adds more complexity to an already overloaded environment. It may be that people feel embarrassed about seeking help and prefer to find their own way around. And, generally, men seem more hesitant to ask for help than women, who are also inclined to be less bothered by crowds than men.[26]

Crowding or the close proximity of others can serve as a guide to movement behavior.[27] Studies in shopping malls and exhibitions show that crowds can model or influence individual behavior.[28] One way that a patron can handle the orientation decisions of where to go and what to do next is to follow the lead of others. Crowding, however, can be a source of disorientation. Other people can create distracting stimuli that continually evoke general orientation responses, and crowds can contribute to information overload in a setting.

Orientation may also occur through the social expectations that people have about a setting. In fact, Barker[29] concludes that behavior in a particular setting will be a function of both the physical features of that setting and socially learned norms and expectations about how to behave there. Past learning of features related to a particular environment may come into play in helping patrons become oriented to a building. For example, patrons learn that a library is a place with features such as book stacks and reading desks. Remember that stimuli that are meaningful or significant to the individual evoke the general orientation response. Orientation aids can be made more effective if they build on meanings and expectations the patrons bring with them. For instance, a survey of library users could attempt to find the more commonly used words for parts of a library, and then build some of these words into orientation aids.

Overconfidence in Decision Making

One factor that can be important in anticipating the orientation behavior of library patrons is the general tendency of people to overestimate their ability to make decisions. Evidence of this overconfidence comes from various studies in human decision making under a variety of situations and for a range of problems.[30] It is possible that overconfidence in orientation situations may encourage people to avoid aids altogether. For example, if people overestimate their ability to locate the various areas within a library, they may give only scant attention to signs, maps, and other information aids regardless of the care that has gone into designing them. They may also resist asking for assistance from library staff.

RESEARCH ON USER NEEDS
IN PUBLIC-ACCESS SETTINGS

The importance of obtaining accurate knowledge about users and their needs has already been noted. Now let us examine some of the ways in which user needs may be determined for a particular setting. Although the emphasis is on user orientation, the examples are applicable to a wide range of user needs.

The aim of any research on user behavior should be to build a body of knowledge about the ways in which people do or do not use the library: how they retrieve information, how they interpret and carry out instructions, how they get from one place to another, how they apportion their time, how they judge the overall quality of their visits. This body of knowledge should allow for change and should be fed continually by new data from a responsive staff. There must be, furthermore, a desire to incorporate information and ideas culled from this knowledge into new strategies for improving the effectiveness of existing formats.

How do we obtain information about user needs? The first step is to establish baseline data on how visitors perceive their surroundings and orient themselves under existing conditions.[31] Which signs do they heed? Which do they ignore? How effective are written instructions for using library services? Where do patrons make decisions and how do they pick up information about what to do next? What areas of the building cause disorientation? How and where do patrons interact with library personnel? Such questions focus attention on typical behavior patterns within particular areas of the library. Once these patterns are identified, needed improvements in the existing conditions will suggest themselves.

Simple but fruitful techniques may be borrowed from the social sciences and adapted to public settings, such as museums, parks, and libraries, to establish baseline information.[32] Although it is true that these research tools are most responsive in the hands of professionals who have been thoroughly trained in their operation and limitations,[33] it is also true that professionals from other fields can develop sensitivity to and knowledge of their uses.

The staff of the Brooklyn Museum in New York, for example, developed a straightforward, effective method for eliciting visitor reactions to an exhibition of Egyptian art, and then was able to turn the data into an informative and useful research document.[34] The museum encouraged visitors to express their ideas about the exhibition in a comments book, which was placed on a stand at the rear of the gallery. Comments ranged from simple expressions of enjoyment to criticisms of content and format. The outcome of the project was a final document, later published, containing a great deal of information about the way in which visitors related not only to the exhibition but to the museum in general, about their preferences for certain kinds of instructional materials, and about their sensitivities to such factors as lighting, noise, and comfort levels.

Research in public-access settings requires a multimethod approach.[35] A combination of talking with visitors, observing them, and testing them, as well as mapping the distribution of activities throughout the building and maintaining patron-monitored diaries to record the sequential nature of visits, all contribute to a more complete and reliable understanding of what goes on.[36]

Loomis, Hummel, and Cervone[37] found that multiple methods were absolutely necessary in learning about museum visitor orientation. Recall that people tend to be overconfident in their decision making—exactly what the investigators found. Visitors' responses to one survey question indicated that they did not have any orientation problems in the museum; however, observational studies showed that they did, in fact, have difficulties in specific areas. For example, disorientation was obvious at the front entrance, near stairways and elevators, and at entrances to exhibit halls. In addition to the observations, spot interviews were helpful in learning about the completeness and accuracy of visitor mental maps of the museum, as well as the difficulties that visitors experienced in determining what floor they were on.

Researchers[38] have found that one of the more effective ways to learn about the problems patrons experience is simply to stop and question them.[39] A patron's ability to give orientation information to another patron (or, in this case, a staff member posing as a patron) is one test of that person's ease or difficulty in getting around. Furthermore, the language used by patrons under such circumstances can provide significant clues for the wording and location of signs and other aids.[40] A study of visitors to the Boston Museum of Fine Arts[41] revealed that pictorial maps of the exhibition areas were most useful if they presented the museum environment and collections in the way that laypeople would naturally perceive the setting, i.e., without labels and other prompts, which suggests that information overload may occur in many orientation aids.

Once empirical evidence about orientation problems has been established, it is time to test solutions in the form of signs and other aids. It is best to experiment with proposed solutions on site before the final versions are installed.[42] Even slight misjudgments about size, format, wording, or placement can mean that the whole effort has been wasted. Better to spend time pretesting solutions in their real settings than to risk missing the goal.[43]

Examples of the importance of using the right words for successful orientation can be drawn from museum visitor studies.[44] In one case, visitors had grown accustomed to using the family name of a benefactor when referring to a planetarium located within a museum. After a period of time, a large sign was placed in the museum lobby area informing visitors of the planetarium entrance. However, the sign referred to the planetarium by its official name, which had never been used publicly. The result was that visitors were confused about the location of the planetarium—even though it was the only one in the museum—since the name on the sign had little significance for them. As would be expected from the discussion of social variables in orientation, visitors were relying on information they had brought with them to locate the planetarium.

If it becomes necessary to provide lengthy or detailed instruction, as in the case of orienting the patron to the use of the main catalog or the computer terminal, library staff would do well to consult the literature of exhibit evaluation and educational technology. Nicol[45] summarizes the approach by saying that instructional exhibits should utilize the systems-design model by clearly specifying the objectives for the total system, analyzing each component, and developing a feedback loop to ascertain whether objectives have been met. Screven[46] organizes this process in a sequence of tasks: define the intended audience; define the educational goals; develop reliable measures or tests of visitor knowledge and attitudes; pretest a sample of the intended audience so that comparisons can be made after the instructional exhibit has been installed; plan the potential content and design for the exhibit; try out these plans in the form of a mock-up exhibit on site; construct and install the final version; and, through observation, interviewing, and further testing, evaluate the final exhibit so that further improvements may be made.

CONCLUSION

The ability to find one's way in a setting and to accomplish desired goals not only satisfies an immediate need; it also deepens one's appreciation for the setting and strengthens one's relationship with it.

Ways in which library staff can utilize information about users of public-access environments in considering the orientation needs of the library patron have been suggested. Two key ideas should be noted: (1) certain fundamental principles—such as the tendency to engage in a continual decision-making process vis-à-vis the environment and the need to create an overall image of the setting—must be at the heart of orientation planning; and (2) a priori assumptions about the relative effectiveness of orientation aids such as brochures, maps, color codes, instructional graphics, slides, and video programs are apt to be inadequate without investigating the requirements for a particular space and a particular audience.

Whatever orientation aids are provided, they should relate logically to one another and to the major architectural features of the building. The user requires reinforcement as he or she moves through the setting, and the orientation system should remind patrons at appropriate places that they are proceeding in the right direction. Consideration of the user needs discussed here can help ensure that the orientation features of a library environment are effectively used by library patrons.

NOTES

1. S. Kaplan, "The Challenge of Environmental Psychology: A Proposal for a New Functionalism," *American Psychologist* 27 (1972): 140-143.

2. H. J. Klein, "The Delimitation of Town Centre in the Image of Its Citizens," in *Urban Core and Inner City*, ed. by Sociological Department of University of Amsterdam (Leiden: Brill, 1966), pp. 286-306.

3. R. M. Downs and D. Stea, eds., *Image and Environment: Cognitive Mapping and Spatial Behavior* (Chicago: Aldine, 1973).

4. J. D. Porteous, *Environment and Behavior* (Reading, Mass.: Addison-Wesley, 1977).

5. R. Sommer, *Design Awareness* (San Francisco: Rinehart, 1972).

6. H. E. Mitchell, "Professional and Client: An Emerging Collaborative Relationship," in *Designing for Human Behavior: Architecture and the Behavioral Sciences*, ed. by J. Lang et al. (Stroudsberg, Pa.: Dowden, Hutchinson and Ross, 1974), pp. 15-43.

7. I. Altman, *The Environment and Social Behavior* (Monterey, Calif.: Brooks-Cole, 1975).

8. D. Conway, *Social Science and Design: A Process Model for Architect and Social Scientist Collaboration* (Washington, D.C.: American Institute of Architects, 1973).

9. J. Zeisel, *Sociology and Architectural Design* (New York: Russell Sage, 1975).

10. R. W. Burns, "Library Use as a Performance Measure: Its Background and Rationale," *Journal of Academic Librarianship* 4 (1978): 4-11.

11. K. Wilson-Davis, "The Center for Research on User Studies: Aims and Functions," *ASLIB Proceedings* 29 (1977): 67-76.

12. M. Stevenson, "Progress in Documentation: Education of Users of Libraries and Information Services," *Journal of Documentation* 33 (1977): 53-78.

13. D. M. Murtha, *Dimensions of User Benefit* (Washington, D.C.: American Institute of Architects, 1976).

14. P. G. Zimbardo and F. L. Ruch, *Psychology and Life*, 9th ed. (Glenview, Ill.: Scott, Foresman, 1975).

15. Kaplan, "The Challenge of Environmental Psychology."

16. M. Borun, *Measuring the Unmeasurable* (Washington, D.C.: Association for Science and Technology Centers, 1977).

17. K. Lynch, *The Image of the City* (Cambridge, Mass.: MIT Press, 1960).

18. J. D. Porteous, "Design with People: The Quality of the Urban Environment," *Environment and Behavior* 3 (1971): 155-178.

19. Porteous, "Design with People."

20. D. E. Berlyne, *Aesthetics and Psychobiology* (New York: Appleton, 1972).

21. D. E. Berlyne, *Conflict, Arousal and Curiosity* (New York: McGraw-Hill, 1960).

22. S. Milgram, "The Experience of Living in Cities," *Science* 167 (1970): 1461-1468.

23. S. Cohen, "Environmental Load and the Allocation of Attention," in A. Baum and S.

Valins, eds., *Advances in Environmental Research* (Hillsdale, N.J.: L. Erlbaum Associates, 1977).

24. M. S. Cohen et al., "Orientation in a Museum: An Experimental Visitor Study," *Curator* 20 (1977): 85–96.

25. R. J. Loomis, C. F. Hummel, and J. Cervone, *Sample Visitor Orientation Problems in the Denver Museum of Natural History*, Working Papers in Visitor Studies, no. 2 (Denver: The Denver Museum of Natural History, 1978).

26. P. A. Bell et al., *Environmental Psychology* (Philadelphia: Saunders, 1978).

27. P. S. Weiss and S. A. Boutourline, *A Summary of Fairs, Pavilions, Exhibits and Their Audiences*, mimeographed (Seattle, Wash.: 1962).

28. W. F. E. Preiser, *Analysis of Pedestrian Velocity and Stationary Behavior in a Shopping Mall*, Research Report (Blacksburg, Va.: Virginia Polytechnic Institute and State University College of Architecture, 1973).

29. R. G. Barker, *Ecological Psychology: Concepts and Methods for Studying the Environment of Human Behavior* (Stanford: Stanford University Press, 1968).

30. P. Slovic et al., "Behavioral Decision Theory," in *Annual Review of Psychology*, ed. by M. R. Rosenzweig and L. W. Porter, vol. 28 (Palo Alto, Calif.: Annual Reviews Inc., 1977), pp. 1–39.

31. Cohen et al., "Orientation in a Museum."

32. E. Webb et al., *Unobtrusive Measures: Nonreactive Research in the Social Sciences* (Chicago: Rand McNally, 1966).

33. Burns, "Library Use as a Performance Measure."

34. E. F. Wedge, *Nefertiti Graffiti: Comments on an Exhibition* (Brooklyn, N.Y.: The Brooklyn Museum, 1977).

35. *Lost in Art: Evaluation of the Visitor Information Center, Boston Museum of Fine Arts*, mimeographed (Southworth and Southworth, Architecture and Planning, 1974).

36. T. Shlecter and D. Campbell, *Ecologically Oriented Methods in Evaluation: An Illustrated Example*, mimeographed (Lawrence, Kans.: 1978).

37. Loomis, Hummel, and Cervone, *Sample Visitor Orientation Problems*.

38. Cohen et al., "Orientation in a Museum."

39. R. J. Loomis and R. Cooksey, *Visitor Orientation to the American Museum of Atomic Energy*, mimeographed (Oak Ridge, Tenn.: 1977).

40. Loomis and Cooksey, *Visitor Orientation*.

41. *Lost in Art*.

42. H. Spencer and L. Reynolds, *Directional Signing and Labelling in Libraries and Museums: A Review of Current Theory and Practice*, mimeographed (London: Royal College of Art, 1977).

43. T. J. Brennan, *Elements of Social Group Behavior in a Natural Setting*, mimeographed (Chicago, Ill.: 1977).

44. Loomis, Hummel, and Cervone, *Sample Visitor Orientation Problems*.

45. E. Nicol, *The Development of Validated Museum Exhibits* (Washington, D.C.: U.S. Dept. of Health, Education, and Welfare, Office of Education, 1969).

46. C. G. Screven, "Exhibit Evaluation: A Goal-Referenced Approach," *Curator* 19 (1976): 271–290.

Mazes, Minds, and Maps

ROGER M. DOWNS

The maze is a pervasive and enduring motif. In tracing the history of mazes and labyrinths, Matthews points to their role in religious art, landscape architecture, and mythology.[1] The maze is a powerful metaphor for the confrontation between people and their world. It evokes images of travail, of the struggle against mysterious forces, of the curious repulsion of and yet attraction to convoluted and serpentine forms.

In daily experience, the motif has become a cliché: one speaks of tangled bureaucratic mazes and of seeing light at the end of the tunnel. But the maze motif retains its literal meaning in the everyday confrontation with the built environment. The intertwined curves and culs-de-sac of suburbia, the back alleys of the older parts of downtown, and the workings of mass transit systems all display a labyrinthian quality.

On an architectural scale, no structure comes closer to the maze experience than does any reasonably sized library. Each library has its own distinctive physical ambience, and yet *all* libraries seem to induce common feelings and behavioral responses that reinforce the maze metaphor. Consider the image of "the stacks": repetitious shapes and arrangements of shelves;

low ceilings; poor lighting; the leaden, dusty atmosphere imparted by the over-heating system; the closing thud of fire doors; the catacomb feeling of the subterranean levels; and the detached sensation due to infrequently washed windows above ground. The entrance hall is a scene of confusion as those who know where they are going separate themselves from those who do not know and are, therefore, hesitant. The card catalog area is equally confusing as people try to match call numbers with storage locations and storage locations with maps and lists of the physical layout. In the stacks, passersby avoid physical or eye contact with each other, and spatial behavior by some people is often a perfect illustration of the "random walk concept," a patternless, although not aimless, wandering in and out of the shelves.

No one would deny that these images are exaggerated and overdrawn, but it is also true that they reflect a valid and common reaction by library users. As a convenient literary device, the library-as-maze metaphor is an expression of the frustrations of everyday encounters with libraries. The problem of way-finding—of being able to start and finish plans for getting to and from places—is of genuine concern to librarians and library users alike. But is it so great a problem that it really demands a solution? At first sight, it seems insignificant in contrast to the immediate fiscal problems that libraries must solve in order to survive. And, if libraries are like mazes, then is the wayfinding problem not merely an annoyance, something to be regretted but tolerated?

It is unfortunate that the magnitude of the wayfinding problem cannot be expressed in terms of a cost. There is no agreed-upon and direct means of assessing such costs either to the library or to its users. The situation is scarcely parallel to the problems of wayfinding on roads; in that situation the Federal Highway Administration found that lost travelers are prone to somewhat erratic driving, which imperils others on the highway. It may be closer to the situation in the London Underground system as described by Raffle and Sell: "Although they [lost passengers] are a minority of the total passengers carried, they can cause delays out of all proportion to their numbers if they cannot understand the system."[2]

The idea of delay does not apply in the same way to libraries, but it is obvious that to the extent that people are intimidated by repeated wayfinding problems, the effectiveness of library use will be diminished in the short run. In the long run, the frequency and volume of use will decline. But how can one arrive at reliable estimates of behavior that has not taken place? Even surveys of actual behavior are not as straightforward as they might appear. People can be asked about wayfinding, about how "lost" they feel in a building. Gordon Best followed such a strategy in a study of wayfinding behavior in the Manchester Town Hall in England. He reported that "the feeling of 'lostness' varied widely from one town hall user to the next. Some people who were interviewed after spending nearly 30 minutes wandering around the buildings insisted that, at no point were they lost, [while] others appeared to find their way without trouble [yet] complained that they had felt 'lost' while doing so."[3]

So, without direct empirical studies, to assess the extent of the problem, one must resort to personal experience, anecdote, and inferences drawn from surveys of library users. All of these sources point to a widely accepted belief that libraries are, indeed, like mazes and that finding one's way in them is difficult and frustrating. This belief is most commonly voiced in the form of the disparaging and mistaken remark that "libraries are places where they hide books." The mistake lies not in the sentiment itself but in the assignment of responsibility. Architects and designers, *not* librarians, should be substituted for "they," although, as will be seen later, librarians must share some of the blame.

Of necessity, the physical design and layout of a library do pose problems of wayfinding, as is the case with any complex built structure. Moreover, some of the artistic effects that architects and designers strive for exacerbate the magnitude of the wayfinding problem. In their concern for the sculpturing of interior spaces, they use slight level changes, avoid long interior vistas, and break up space to avoid monotony and to provide an element of visual "surprise." Yet, in considering the design and arrangement of interior spaces, they never explicitly include behavioral considerations of wayfinding. This omission is not surprising in the light of the prevailing conception of architecture as an artistic process. As Robert Sommer has argued, to the extent that architects are concerned with developing an empirical, scientific basis for their discipline, they have achieved considerable success from an engineering-technological perspective, "but in the behavioral realm, the way buildings affect people, architects fall back on intuition, anecdote, and casual observation. Consultants flourish in the design fields because there is no body of information assembled in such a way that it is useful to architects and other design professionals."[4]

At best, therefore, the wayfinding system is viewed as but one part of the interior decorating process, as something to be pasted on, as unobtrusively as possible, after construction is completed and the design etched in stone.

But the solution to wayfinding problems is *not* just a case of designing "better" signs, or of a focus on perceptual problems of sign legibility and graphics. Such information is necessary but not sufficient. As highway traffic engineers have discovered, better signs do not necessarily speed traffic flow and reduce the number of accidents. It is the comprehension of the sign's meaning that is important, the ability to relate the information that one reads to the information and plans that one already knows in order to make decisions about what to do next. In the case of the library, it is the user's understanding of the library as a complex system that is important. The library system encompasses card catalogs, specialized indexes, interlibrary loan services, and more, all within a physical layout. The *process of wayfinding* depends on how one understands this physical layout and then organizes his or her spatial behavior within it. The *wayfinding system* must assist the wayfinding process by providing signs, maps, color codings, and information desks. So, the design of an efficient wayfinding system depends on an understanding of:

1 wayfinding as a cognitive process for solving problems of movement in space,

2 the process of learning in a spatial context, and

3 the design of physical environments that support both wayfinding and learning.

THE PROCESS OF WAYFINDING

The attempt to link wayfinding, cognition, and design depends on a particular approach to the understanding of human spatial behavior. Incredibly, although physicists have achieved great success in explaining the spatial behavior of minute particles, and astronomers with massive galaxies, there is no similarly satisfying explanation of human spatial behavior. The key idea in this statement is a *satisfying* explanation.

Human spatial behavior, as the movement of people between locations, can be recorded in terms of origins, destinations, volumes, speeds, directions taken, and routes followed. But as Reginald Golledge has argued, two very different explanations for the patterns of recorded spatial behavior can be offered. On the one hand, library users could be viewed as "physical particles" whose spatial behavior is controlled by the physical properties of the library. One could measure the relevant physical properties by the attractiveness of various destinations, the capacity of reading rooms and corridors, or the physical distances that separate the destinations. These measures can form the basis for a variety of models that depend on physical analogs such as gravity or statistical mechanics. When applied to traffic flows over time, for example, such models give reasonably accurate quantitative predictions of patterns of spatial behavior.[5]

Another approach views movement as the result of psychological processes that are goal directed and deliberately adapted to the surrounding spatial environment. This psychological approach, focusing on the individual decision maker, seems the only satisfying way of explaining spatial behavior. Teleological questions must be asked about motives, goals, and knowledge to elicit information that is useful to architects and environmental designers. Unfortunately, the answers to such questions are a long way off. Much of everyday behavior is taken for granted and thus mistakenly regarded as intuitively self-evident; wayfinding is no exception. In fact, despite the ever-present need to control movement across the earth's surface, there is no commonly accepted term to describe the process itself. One speaks of knowing a place like the back of the hand or of being able to make trips blindfolded. However, speaking is not the same as understanding. The term "wayfinding" is as good a choice to describe the ability as "navigation" or "orientation." It does not, however, lead us into a rich body of literature.

Given some of the more salient characteristics of the wayfinding process, it is not surprising that it has escaped systematic study by the social sciences. The most striking characteristic of human wayfinding is its extraordinary effectiveness. Detailed records of human activity patterns reveal complex, interlocking sequences of movements linking home, work, shopping facilities, recreation facilities, and so on.[6] Despite this volume of movement, it is rare for wayfinding to break down, for a person to become lost. Moreover, individuals are generally unaware of the thinking processes by which they organize and control patterns of spatial behavior.

This lack of awareness or consciousness of a highly efficient process accounts for the fragmented and distorted popular beliefs that surround wayfinding. For example, there is a suggestion that wayfinding is an innate ability. Some groups have maintained it, others have not. These beliefs are intertwined with the idea that it is "primitive" peoples who have maintained a superior wayfinding ability and "civilized" peoples who have lost it.

Two errors are compounded in this popular misconception. First, the detailed processes that control wayfinding are learned and taught, not innate and inherited. Despite the frequent suggestion that some people "have," via some mysterious endowment, a good sense of direction, there is no innate, special, or sixth sense that guides wayfinding. It does not come naturally, and if some people are more efficient than others, that is a direct result of superior learning strategies and knowledge, not different or special capacities. Second, the supposed difference between primitive and civilized peoples is a misreading of the empirical evidence, a perhaps excusable misreading fostered by a romantic image of prelapsarian societies. Much of the available evidence on wayfinding has been gathered by anthropologists who have tracked the spatial movements of Australian aborigines,[7] Saulteaux Indians,[8] and Micronesian islanders.[9] Successful navigation across apparently trackless desert, tundra, or ocean is an impressive achievement. But appearances are deceptive. The environment is not trackless; it can be "read" for wayfinding clues, and the reading process can be taught to and learned by almost anyone with time and effort. As Gatty demonstrates, there is nothing to stop a civilized person from learning to cope with wilderness navigation and survival.[10] One rapidly growing sport—orienteering—originated in Scandinavia and combines running with wayfinding through the natural environment.[11]

Current understanding of the process of wayfinding must draw on two bodies of literature. The first, the literature on wayfinding itself, is of relatively little use. Much of it is anecdotal, with few rigorous empirical studies. From the perspective of library design, studies of such esoteric contexts as wildernesses or deserts give little specific guidance. Studies of wayfinding in the man-made environment are rare. Kevin Lynch's *The Image of the City* offered the first extensive review of the orientation literature, and his empirical analysis considered questions of movement and environmental legibility at the citywide scale.[12] The studies that imitated this work essentially confirm Lynch's findings. Two volumes that discuss wayfinding and signs at the scale of city streets— Stephen Carr's *City Signs and Lights*[13] and the Venturi, Brown, and Izenour study, *Learning from Las Vegas*[14]—provide useful parallel situations. Within buildings, wayfinding has been almost totally ignored as a problem to be discussed. There is scattered work on the problems of wayfinding in airports and in hotels, and four works that analyze the links between architectural design and wayfinding: Best,[15] Corlett et al.,[16] Garling,[17] and Passini.[18]

The second body of literature derives from psychology and geography and views wayfinding as one expression of the more general process of *cognitive mapping*.[19] This is the process whereby one makes use of representations of the spatial environment as it is believed to be (or cognitive maps). These representations act as the basis for everyday spatial behavior. They underpin decisions on where to shop, where to live, where to visit, and how to get there. Beyond such utilitarian considerations, cognitive maps organize personal experience, providing a sense of place that links events with time and space. Unfortunately, work on cognitive mapping is also recent and fragmentary. It is ironic, for example, that we know more about the psychological and physiological mechanisms behind the wayfinding process in nonhumans than in humans. There are superb studies of movement around home sites and seasonal migrations of wasps, bees, rats, salmon, pigeons, and chimpanzees. Even the rare studies of human wayfinding tend to focus on the physically handicapped[20] or on such unusual contexts as underwater orientation.[21] The irony is reinforced by the psychologist's use of spatial maze-learning experiments and by the development of map-drawing tasks to determine genetic damage and physiological malfunction. Space, movement, and wayfinding have become convenient avenues to follow in tackling other problems. Only recently have they become problems to be studied in their own right.[22]

Any process is of necessity integral in nature and continuous in operation. But by considering wayfinding in segments, as four linked operations, points at which environmental design may be crucial to the successful solution of a wayfinding problem can be highlighted. The four operations are: (1) orientation, (2) choice of a route, (3) keeping on the right track, and (4) recognition of the objective.

Being oriented and being lost are opposite expressions of the relation between a person and the spatial environment. If the person can tie together an understanding of current location with an understanding of locations (destinations) that are out of immediate perceptual range, he or she is oriented. The inability to make such a tie is what we mean by being lost. The state of being oriented permits the following type of inferences: If I am in the card catalog room, then the microfilm viewers are down that corridor to the left and the BF section books are over there in the east wing up on the third floor.

Orientation as the expression of spatial relationship is the key to the wayfinding process and to the design of a wayfinding system. Three points are significant. First, one must consider both the nature of the existing representation of the library and how it is formed or learned. Second, the surrounding physical environment must provide information about directions and locations. Third, a language is needed to tie the cognitive representation to the surrounding spatial environment. The inferences above show a variety of ways of expressing the spatial relationship: down, left, over there, east, and up on. Each expression is the result of using a coordinate system to link current location with other parts of the library that are out of immediate perceptual range.

The choice of a route follows directly from the idea of orientation. It demands a connection between the current location and the desired destination(s) in the form of a plan of action. The plan involves an ordered sequence of directed movements, which are built around and hinge on a series of decision points. In the case of the person in the card catalog room, the plan for getting to the microfilm room might require following a particular corridor, taking the third turn to the right, and going through the red door at the far end of the corridor.

Plans are expectations about the relation between movement and the spatial environment, and *keeping on the right track* is a continuous process that monitors the execution of the plan. For routes with which one is familiar, the monitoring process may go on "outside" the normal conscious awareness. The comfortable feeling of knowing where one is going is the result of overlearning. In the case of regular passengers on the London Underground system, it produces a particular style of wayfinding behavior: "Having travelled on the new line for a few occasions, they can proceed in a semi-automatic fashion in tune with the system philosophy."[23]

Thus, people can think about other things while moving along, and often arrive at the destination without any specific recollection of that particular journey. Experiences of this "semiautomatic" type lead to the idea that wayfinding comes naturally and that journeys can be made blindfolded. However, a continuous process of monitoring is actually occurring. A person looks ahead, both literally and figuratively, for the decision points at which a turn is to be made or a door is to be entered. One can just as well make the monitoring process something that dominates the conscious attention and thus look for information and signs at which to make a turn and so forth. Reassurance signs can help maintain a sense of orientation. The *recognition of the objective* is the fourth and final step in the monitoring sequence, and it depends either upon prior knowledge of what the destination looks like or upon finding some specific identifying sign.

The role of environmental design in successful wayfinding is clear from this analysis of the wayfinding process. The four component operations enable users to adapt their goals and objectives to the physical layout of the library by a directed sequence of spatial behavior (the process of wayfinding). The success and ease of adaptation depend, in turn, on the original design of the physical layout and on the design of the wayfinding system. Both steps of the design process must provide a spatial environment that is in tune with the underlying cognitive processes of forming and executing plans for spatial behavior, and learning spatial environments. Therefore, wayfinding in libraries must be seen as the result of a mutual adaptation between users, via the process of wayfinding, and designers, via the design of the physical layout and the wayfinding system. All too often the burden of adaptation is placed on users because designers make decisions about the physical layout without any consideration of the problem of wayfinding. Also, designers lack an understanding of the wayfinding system as it is experienced by the library user. The solution to the wayfinding problem falls on the library user by default, and the goal of mutual adaptation is not achieved.

Learning in a Spatial Context

Wayfinding and learning are entangled processes. Consider the ways in which a person comes to know a library. For the most part, the learning experience is unsystematic, disjointed, intermittent, and unintentional. In the ideal case, the user may be taken on a brief guided tour of the building and its facilities, and then given a package of written instructions and diagrams. Beyond this, learning is incidental; it occurs while the person is doing something else, such as finding a book or the interlibrary loan office. On rare occasions, some people may browse and thus intentionally explore parts of the library. How do people use these fragmentary experiences as the basis for developing cognitive representations of the library that will help in forming plans and guiding spatial behavior?

There are two basic learning processes that operate simultaneously and that give rise to two types of cognitive representation. Each type, in turn, can be related to aspects of the spatial environment, and thus each can generate particular design solutions. One process, nondimensional or response learning, generates sequential or route maps and suggests a "linear" design style for the wayfinding system. The other process, dimensional or place learning, produces a spatial or cognitive map and encourages a "spatial" design style. (The terms linear and spatial are adapted from Passini.)[24]

Nondimensional learning is perhaps more familiar as classic stimulus-response or contiguous association learning. The description "nondimensional" emphasizes that the serial order underlying the learned sequence of material has only the most limited and trivial character, that of precedence. The initial learning of a spatial environment necessarily involves nondimensional learning. A sequential or route map can be likened to a path and provides a specific plan for connecting two locations. The plan contains a chainlike series that connects decision points, to which are attached appropriate behavioral actions.

Verbal directions in response to a wayfinding question are frequently given in this form: "Go down to the end of that corridor, take a left turn, and walk until you come to the third door. Then you're there." The final statement characterizes this wayfinding system. The person does not need to know where "there" is in relation to the spatial structure of the library of the whole. The route map can successfully control the wayfinding task: choice of route, keeping on the right track, and recognition of the objective are built in. What is lacking is orientation in the sense of an understanding of the relation of the route to other parts of the library. Unless the person "sees" a connection to other known parts of the library, all he or she can do is reverse the route from "there" back to the original "here."

It is the particularity of route learning in this nondimensional fashion that presents limitations. Knowing the route from the card catalog to the interlibrary loan office and from the card catalog to the microfilm room does not necessarily allow one to work out the route to go directly from the microfilm room to the interlibrary loan office and vice versa. With repeated use, a particular route is learned and overlearned until a feeling develops of being able to make the journey blindfolded.

Dimensional learning involves the gradual acquisition of spatial information—information that derives at least part of its meaning, and hence usefulness, from the inherent dimensions of spatial relationship. Two dimensions, distance and direction, provide built-in properties of order and meaning that must be appreciated during the learning process. The appreciation follows from the integration of experience, especially the integration of sequential or route maps that share either origins, destinations, or decision points. The cognitive representations that emerge from this integrative process function as if they are maps; hence, the term "map" is used to describe them.[25] Cognitive maps are more than the purely quantitative addition of existing knowledge about routes within the library. The integration produces an understanding of the library that is qualitatively different.

Perhaps the easiest way to distinguish between sequential and cognitive maps is to think of the former as knowledge of "how to get there" and the latter as knowledge of "where things are." Cognitive maps offer some important advantages over sequential maps, such as flexibility in solving wayfinding problems. Not only can one generate alternative ways of getting to a particular destination, but one can also generate a plan for connecting places never before visited in sequence.

The two types of learning and the two forms of representation are stages in a general process. They are not mutually exclusive, nor does anyone use only one type of learning. Graduation from nondimensional to dimensional learning takes place as a direct result of time and repeated library use. In developing a "feel" for a place, one acquires a qualitatively different form of knowledge of it.

The transition from one type of learning to another is not irreversible or inevitable. Infrequent experience will not lead people to form cognitive maps; neither will extensive but sporadic use. Some environments, because of physical design, do not lend themselves easily to cognitive mapping and dimensional learning. Passini studied the wayfinding processes of pedestrians in some of the building complexes in Montreal.[26] These complexes are multilevel mixtures of offices, stores, hotels, and subway stations; the maze or labyrinth is an appropriate metaphor. In finding specified destinations, people tended to rely on a particular style of wayfinding wherever possible. Approximately half of the group used a linear style and looked for specific signs that would guide them in sequence to the destination. The other group, using a spatial style, sought information that would produce a spatial understanding of the physical setting. Their wayfinding depended on relating their own location in the setting to their destination. If the people who used a spatial style could not develop and use the cognitive map, they would try to solve the wayfinding problem by turning to the linear style. Although these findings are tentative, they suggest important links between the learning process and the design of a wayfinding system.

Environmental Design and Wayfinding

In the ideal case, the wayfinding system should be considered as an intrinsic part of the original building design. More commonly, however, the design for a wayfinding system occurs in an already existing building complex. Understanding that wayfinding is a cognitive problem-solving process, the designer must consider two issues: the problems posed by the physical layout of the library and the demands generated by different types of library users.

The image of the library as a maze is often an inevitable result of the physical evolution of the library. Growth by accretion is the typical pattern. Not only does this form of growth lead to a complex, segmented physical structure, but, given the engineering problems of joining buildings, corridors are rarely available at all levels. Thus, it is all too often true that "you can't get there from here," and the advice that "if I were going there, I wouldn't start from here" is well taken. Multiple levels pose a three-dimensional wayfinding problem, exacerbated by several entrances/exits. Moreover, many of the "public" parts of the library were not originally intended for such use, and hence are not closely tied into the original traffic circulation pattern.

Users vary in needs and experience. Clearly, for example, the one-time or infrequent user has a different view of the wayfinding design problem from that of the frequent researcher. Similarly, the browser may approach the problem of learning the library differently from the user who generally needs the card catalog and reference section.

The design of the wayfinding system must link the physical layout with the user's needs. At present, it would be fair to say that these links are made on the

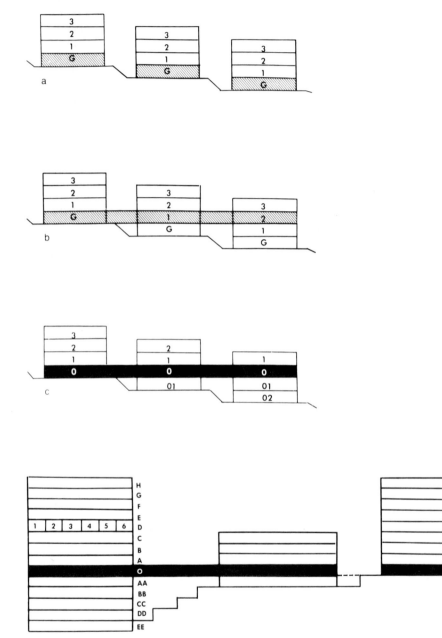

d

FIGURE 2-1 Numbering of floors. (a) The conventional method of describing floors in relation to ground level, (b) the problem that arises with this method on a sloping site if a circulation route independent of ground level is introduced, (c) and (d) two possible solutions to this problem. (Color coding may be used as a visual reminder of the pedestrian circulation level.) From *Directional Signing and Labelling in Libraries and Museums: A Review of Current Theory and Practice*, by Herbert Spencer and Linda Reynolds (London: Royal College of Art, 1977).

basis of unsystematic, intuitive approaches, depending heavily on trial and error, accumulated experience, and "rule of thumb." Passini gives designers a method for visualizing and evaluating the wayfinding problems of buildings both while they are on the drawing board and after they have been constructed.[27] Based on the cognitive approach, Passini's method uses a notation scheme for recording and analyzing the ongoing process of wayfinding. It requires that people verbalize their thoughts as they attempt to find a destination, something they seem able to do more readily than one might imagine. It allows designers to anticipate the information demands at decision points by mentally following hypothetical routes through the building before it is constructed. It also allows users to identify deficiencies in the existing wayfinding system. Behavioral analyses of this type are essential if the design process is to become more systematic. But such analyses are lacking; what follows is at best an interpretation, based on the author's professional understanding of cognition and personal experience with libraries.

Given the cognitive approach to wayfinding, the essential quality we seek in the library is *legibility*. Kevin Lynch, in his study of the visual quality of the American city, defined legibility as "the ease with which its parts can be recognized and can be organized into a coherent pattern. Just as this printed page, if it is legible, can be visually grasped as a related pattern of recognizable symbols, so a legible city would be one whose districts are easily identifiable and are easily grouped into an over-all pattern."[28]

A legible environment is one that can be read and comprehended, one that is humane in the sense that people can come to terms with it. In achieving the goal of a legible library, two interrelated aspects of the wayfinding system must be considered:

1 the system for identifying the parts of a library (part identification) and

2 the system for relating the parts (part relationship).

From the user's viewpoint, the library is a mixture of three classes of objects: specialized services (the interlibrary loan office, the microfilm reader room), basic facilities (copying machines, rest rooms, elevators), and shelves of books. The physical layout of the library determines the arrangement of these objects, and the wayfinding system must make this arrangement legible, and hence comprehensible. The first step is a system of division and labeling. The part-identification system is essential for the process of orientation, and it acts as a language for tying the cognitive representation to the surrounding physical environment.

The vertical dimension of a library is readily appreciated by a floor numbering system. In practice, however, even this simple system is complicated by site characteristics (see Fig. 2-1). If there is a slope, where is the ground or first-floor level? Is this baseline level "continued" through all of the buildings, producing a conflict between perception of the level and the signs identifying the level at which one enters? Spencer was confronted with this design problem at two universities in England. He argued that " 'ground' loses its significance as a description of level and the principal pedestrian circulation route assumes importance irrespective of whether this is above, below, or at ground level."[29]

Two of Spencer's solutions to the problem of vertical labeling are shown in Fig. 2-1. Nevertheless, given the potential for confusion, it is not surprising that Best's study indicated that the largest number of wayfinding errors were made when choosing a floor on which to search for a destination in the Manchester Town Hall.[30]

Because of the size of floors and the frequent separation of the library into distinct buildings, a more detailed system is needed to cope with the problem of understanding the horizontal dimension. One clear indication of identity is naming by function (card catalog room, microfilm room, rest room). However, because there is no logical, necessary order to the arrangement of these functions, detailed naming offers no sense of spatial relationship (part relationship). A partial answer to this problem uses compass directions to name parts of buildings: East Wing, North Wing, and so on. Unfortunately, this system has several major drawbacks, because it is less widely understood than might be expected. First, there is uncertainty about the nature of the system. Is the East Wing "east" in terms of the larger geographical space? Or is it simply one of four distinct, orthogonally arranged structures? If it is east in geographic space, many people will have little sense of where that direction is. Second, it is difficult, within a building, to make and maintain the necessary directional relation to the outside world. And third, most of the routes within a building do not permit one to follow simple compass directions while wayfinding. Thus, compass coordinates are not very helpful in answering the wayfinding problem. Over time, people develop a partial answer through the use of such terms as "up," "down," "over," and "through." This is a local language system specific to the particular library itself. It bears no necessary relation to observable reality; up, for example, may not be up in terms of elevation in physical space. Such local coordinate systems cannot easily be designed; they are a function of emerging use patterns and accepted convention. They can be incorporated into the wayfinding system after they have become firmly established.

For many library users, trying to find particular books in the shelves and stacks can be an exasperating experience. This seems puzzling at first because the books and shelves contain an inherent order that is easy to comprehend, and thus contributes to the goal of a legible library. Given the generally accepted classification systems, books about a particular subject are labeled and grouped in one place, and, within this place, the books are arranged in sequence according to letter and/or number.

But the apparent simplicity of this system is vitiated by two common practices. First, many libraries use two (or more) classification systems; the Library of Congress system sometimes exists alongside the Dewey Decimal system, and combinations of these and other systems abound. Second, libraries often mix descending and ascending shelving systems. Practices such as this erase the user's essential feeling of certainty that comes from knowing what to expect and where to find things. As a consequence, people wander around the shelves peering for clues, and, in this sense, librarians themselves complicate the wayfinding problem.

Identification and division can be aided by the use of color schemes for particular sections or floors of the library. Wherever possible, the colors form the basis for the interior decorating scheme and provide an immediate sense of location at a gross spatial scale. Color systems are commonly used with great success in airports, hospitals, and auditoriums. They can be linked with compass direction names to produce a mutually reinforcing name-identification scheme. Such color-direction links are common in the mythology of many traditional cultures; however, as Margaret Mead reminds us, "it is important to insist that there are no universal symbols. . . . There is no color symbolism which is universal. There are no styles of representation of objects—such as profile, silhouette—which are universally understood. There is no universal syntax."[31]

Unfortunately, there is no national syntax for color schemes in the United States. The lack of a standardized color-direction system means that one is forced to learn each one as a specific instance. This lack is characteristic of the current state of wayfinding systems—one cannot take advantage of standard systems to generate expectations about the physical layout and internal arrangement of new buildings. From a wayfinding perspective, there is something to be said in favor of the repetitive arrangement of supermarket shelves and aisles, and the typical locations of products within the stores.

In considering the system for relating the parts of the library, it is necessary to return to the two types of learning and the two styles of wayfinding. Both the linear and the spatial styles must be accommodated in the final design of the wayfinding system.

The linear system is dependent on signs. Since other chapters treat questions of design, the more general questions of sign arrangement and placement will be considered here. The successful wayfinding plan depends on at least two distinct types of signs: direction and identification. Direction signs must be strung along the major route to a popular destination, and should appear at major decision points, perpendicular to the path of movement.[32] From a psychological point of view, it would also be helpful to have reassurance signs located after each of the major decision points. The color, shape, size, and—above all—placement of direction signs should be distinct from that of destination (identification) signs.[33]

Despite appearances to the contrary, signs cannot be *the* solution to the wayfinding problem in libraries. Apart from initial expense and the cost of modifying signs as the location of books and facilities changes, there must be a trade-off between the number of signs and their utility. This is not a problem of obtrusiveness versus aesthetics, but rather a question of comprehensiveness versus comprehensibility. As Passini documents, there can be too many undifferentiated signs, which only confuse the person looking for specific information.[34] There can also be too much information presented at once: Best's study suggested that details relating to successive choices of route, displayed at one location, were often forgotten at later stages.[35]

As a consequence, there must be a necessary minimum of signs for the first-time or infrequent user. Such signs must be keyed to the most frequently used parts of the library. Beyond this base level, design also must be considered in terms of the spatial style of wayfinding. The key to assisting dimensional learning and the emergence of cognitive maps in the user is the development of graphics in the form of maps and models.

The current state of the art for designing wayfinding graphics is rudimentary. Little is known as to why some maps work and some do not. One important consideration is the nature of the cognitive process of map reading and interpretation.[36] In seeking an understanding of the spatial environment, one does not try to reproduce it photographically. This is rather a pattern-imposing process, which, following some of the Gestalt principles, generates simple structures. Cognitive maps simplify the world by omitting detail, by straightening out curves, by changing angles to either 45 or 90 degrees. Such a process is not aided by the typical cartographic map, which emphasizes accuracy and detail at the expense of legibility. Too often, wayfinding maps are architecturally superb, but cognitively useless. In commenting on the success of the subway map issued by London Transport, Arnheim argues that it "gives the needed information with the utmost clarity and at the same time delights the eye through the harmony of its design. This is achieved by renouncing all geographic detail except for the pertinent topological properties—that is, sequence of stops and interconnections. All roads are reduced to straight lines; all angles to the two simplest. . . . The map leaves out and distorts a great deal, and just because of this, it is the best possible picture of what it wants to show."[37]

Even after a decision on what to show is made and an appropriate format is designed, there is the basic question of where to put the map. Maps displayed horizontally can be oriented in an appropriate relation to the surrounding building. Thus, if a person identifies a location on the map, the real location lies in the corresponding part of the physical setting. Maps on walls pose a problem. Two systems of orientation are commonly used. The map may be positioned so that it shows north on the top or in such a way that by projecting the map horizontally (involving a mental rotation of the map along its bottom edge), one can produce a map that corresponds spatially to the setting. Such mental rotations are difficult to perform. People get confused, and this confirms the feeling for some that they cannot read maps. It is unfortunate that wall maps are more convenient than horizontally displayed maps.

Models of buildings seem to work even less effectively than do maps. Many people lack the ability to visualize the three-dimensional relationships necessary to comprehend the cutaways and exploded portions of the model.

Mastery of the library in the form of a cognitive map cannot be guaranteed. The learning process is too idiosyncratic and unstructured. Many people operate successfully as route mappers, and it is only when they wish to travel unfamiliar routes that this system of knowledge is inadequate. At this point, they turn to the sign system for assistance. Legibility, in the sense of an understanding of an overall, coherent pattern, is lacking because the development of the pattern depends on dimensional learning, a process that can be aided but not ensured.

CONCLUSIONS

Seen from the cognitive perspective, two issues stand out. First, there always will be a wayfinding problem in any physical structure as complex as a library. The library always will retain many of the physical characteristics of a maze, and the persistence of the maze metaphor is an acknowledgment of a permanent state of tension between people and their environment. Second, libraries *can* be made more legible by a variety of devices and techniques.

In the final analysis, the wayfinding problem exists as a function of the complex relationships between time, space, and behavior. Learning a spatial environment requires repeated experiences. To the extent that such repetition is impossible, the user is forced to rely on the exigencies of the sign system, on the capacity for route mapping. There is no shortcut to the development of an integrated, coherent cognitive map of the library as a whole. The dimensional learning process can be aided by, but not replaced by, the wayfinding system that is built into the library.

Thus, the arguments in this chapter do not offer any immediate panaceas to the problem of wayfinding in libraries. On the one hand, it is recognized that very little is really known about the problem and that there is much to understand. On the other hand, this lack of knowledge stems from unasked—not unanswerable—questions. Best and Passini both show that with relatively simple research methods and small samples the relationships between the basic elements—the physical layout, the wayfinding system, and the human wayfinding process—can easily be disentangled. The goal of a legible library, of the mutual adaptation of these elements, is attainable.

ACKNOWLEDGMENT

I am grateful for the invaluable assistance of Cordelia Swinton, who provided information about libraries.

NOTES

1. W. H. Matthews, *Mazes and Labyrinths: Their History and Development*, reprint of 1922 ed. (New York: Dover, 1970).

2. A. Raffle and R. G. Sell, "The Victoria Line—Passenger Considerations," *Applied Ergonomics* 1 (1969):5.

3. Gordon Best, "Direction-Finding in Large Buildings," in *Architectural Psychology: Proceedings of the Conference Held at Dalandhui University of Strathclyde, 28 February–2 March 1969*, ed. by David Canter (London: RIBA Publications Limited, 1970), p. 73.

4. Robert Sommer, *Personal Space: The Behavioral Basis of Design* (Englewood Cliffs, N.J.: Prentice-Hall, 1969), p. 6.

5. Peter Tregenza, *The Design of Interior Circulation* (London: Crosby, Lockwood, Staples, 1976).

6. F. Stuart Chapin and Richard K. Brail, "Human Activity Systems in the Metropolitan United States," *Environment and Behavior* 1 (1969): 107–130.

7. Ronald Berndt and Catherine Berndt, *The World of the First Australians: An Introduction to the Traditional Life of the Australian Aborigines*, rev. ed. (Chicago: University of Chicago Press, 1965).

8. A. Irving Hallowell, "Cultural Factors in Spatial Organization," in his *Culture and Experience* (Philadelphia: University of Pennsylvania Press, 1955), pp. 184–215.

9. Thomas Gladwin, *East Is a Big Bird: Navigation and Logic on Puluwat Atoll* (Cambridge, Mass.: Harvard University Press, 1970).

10. Harold Gatty, *Nature Is Your Guide: How to Find Your Way on Land and Sea by Observing Nature* (New York: Dutton, 1958).

11. John Disley, *Orienteering* (Harrisburg, Pa.: Stackpole, 1967).

12. Kevin Lynch, *The Image of the City* (Cambridge, Mass.: M.I.T. Press, 1960).

13. Stephen Carr, *City Signs and Lights: A Policy Study* (Cambridge, Mass.: M.I.T. Press, 1973).

14. Robert Venturi, Denise Scott Brown, and Stephen Izenour, *Learning from Las Vegas* (Cambridge, Mass.: M.I.T. Press, 1972).

15. Best, "Direction-Finding in Large Buildings."

16. E. N. Corlett, I. Manenica, and R. P. Bishop, "The Design of Direction Finding Systems in Buildings," *Applied Ergonomics* 3 (1972): 66–69.

17. Tommy Garling, "Geographical Orientation Ability as Related to Wayfinding in the Designed Environment," *Man-Environment Systems* 5 (1975): 175–176.

18. Romedi Passini, "Wayfinding: A Study of Spatial Problem Solving with Implications for Physical Design" (Ph.D. diss., The Pennsylvania State University, 1977).

19. Roger Downs and David Stea, *Maps in Minds: Reflections on Cognitive Mapping* (New York: Harper, 1977).

20. J. Alfred Leonard, "Studies in Blind Mobility," *Applied Ergonomics* 3 (1972): 37–46.

21. H. E. Ross, D. J. Dickinson, and B. J. Jupp, "Geographical Orientation Under Water," *Human Factors* 12 (1970): 13–14.

22. Ulric Neisser, *Cognition and Reality: Principles and Implications of Cognitive Psychology* (San Francisco: Freeman, 1976).

23. Raffle and Sell, "The Victoria Line—Passenger Considerations," p. 5.

24. Passini, "Wayfinding."

25. Edward Tolman, "Cognitive Maps in Rats and Men," *Psychological Review* 55 (1948): 189–208.

26. Passini, "Wayfinding."

27. Ibid.

28. Lynch, *The Image of the City*, pp. 2–3.

29. H. Spencer, "Signposting," *RIBA Journal 73* (1966): 552.

30. Best, as reported in Corlett, Manenica, and Bishop, "The Design of Direction Finding Systems," p. 66.

31. Margaret Mead, "Anthropology and Glyphs," *Print* 23 (1969): 50.

32. Best, as reported in Corlett, Manenica, and Bishop, "The Design of Direction Finding Systems," p. 66.

33. Passini, "Wayfinding."

34. Ibid.

35. Best, as reported in Corlett, Manenica, and Bishop, "The Design of Direction Finding Systems," p. 66.

36. Arthur Robinson and Barbara Petchenik, *The Nature of Maps: Essays toward Understanding Maps and Mapping* (Chicago: University of Chicago Press, 1976).

37. Rudolf Arnheim, *Art and Visual Perception: A Psychology of the Creative Eye* (Berkeley: University of California Press, 1954), pp. 151–152.

3

Perceiving the Visual Message

SHELDON WECHSLER

A visual communications system is valueless without a sensory organ that can react to light energy emanating from the system's parts. In humans, the sensory organ is a complex one. It takes the light energy through a series of optical components, focuses it on photosensitive nerve tissue, transforms it into electrical energy, and then transmits that energy to a computer—the brain—that converts it into a conscious message (Fig. 3-1).

Visual communication, then, is dependent on the eye and the brain. The concern here is not with the extremes of visual functioning, but with how visual information can best be transferred within the limits of good design and sound economics for all users of libraries, including those with less than optimal vision.

Proper lighting is one necessity. The eye cannot function without it. Proper lighting is not the same as intense lighting, nor is it a static condition. A sign intended to convey information to an individual entering a library may need different illumination for night use than for use on a sunny day when there is snow on the ground. Shielding the illuminating sources and positioning signs with respect to sources of glare are important and dynamic considerations.

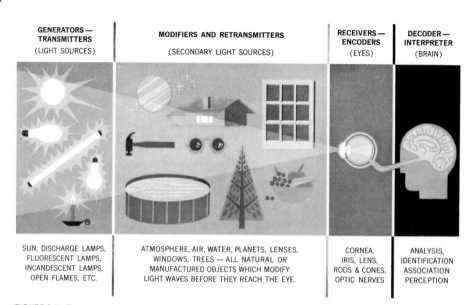

GENERATORS— TRANSMITTERS (LIGHT SOURCES)	MODIFIERS AND RETRANSMITTERS (SECONDARY LIGHT SOURCES)	RECEIVERS— ENCODERS (EYES)	DECODER— INTERPRETER (BRAIN)
SUN, DISCHARGE LAMPS, FLUORESCENT LAMPS, INCANDESCENT LAMPS, OPEN FLAMES, ETC.	ATMOSPHERE, AIR, WATER, PLANETS, LENSES, WINDOWS, TREES — ALL NATURAL OR MANUFACTURED OBJECTS WHICH MODIFY LIGHT WAVES BEFORE THEY REACH THE EYE.	CORNEA, IRIS, LENS, RODS & CONES, OPTIC NERVES	ANALYSIS, IDENTIFICATION ASSOCIATION PERCEPTION

FIGURE 3-1 The act of seeing requires a light source, an eye, and a brain. Most things we see are secondary light sources that reflect some light energy. Some of the reflected light energy from secondary light sources must enter the eye and be transmitted to the brain before sight can take place. Courtesy of General Electric Company.

Contrast is another necessity. Although the tailor may use white thread on white cloth, printing signs or books in "white on white" would be unthinkable—and unreadable. There are times when minimal contrast is a desirable design feature, but there are other times when design concerns must be modified to promote communication.

Visual guidance systems must aid the large percentage of people who have less than normal vision. Ten percent of the American population has some impairment in color perception. It is estimated that more than 10 million people in the United States have a *visual impairment*, which is defined as "trouble seeing with one or both eyes even with glasses."[1] The same study estimates the prevalence of severe visual impairment at almost 1.5 million people in the United States. *Severe visual impairment* includes "inability to read ordinary newsprint with glasses."

People who wear corrective lenses may still need special consideration even though their vision, as corrected, is normal. Glare can be a problem for eyeglass and contact lens wearers. Sign height and distance can create difficulties for bifocal wearers. But proper attention to the needs of all people can minimize or, hopefully, can eliminate any problems with perceiving visual messages.

The chapter will discuss some basic information about the eye and vision as related to environmental communications systems in libraries. The data, of course, must be evaluated against design requirements, space restrictions, and budget concerns. It has been necessary to make some generalizations, which may not be applicable in specific instances. Whenever possible, consult an expert.

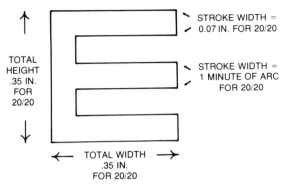

FIGURE 3-2   Snellen letters are designed on a 5 × 5 grid; each letter is 5 units high and 5 units wide. The strokes of the letter are 1 unit wide. Each stroke is designed to subtend 1 minute of arc at the observer's eye for 20/20 vision.

VISUAL ACUITY

Visual acuity, or keenness of vision, is measured by the minimum letter size that is legible to the observer. The test of visual acuity is usually performed at a distance of 20 feet, or 6 meters, and uses a standard design of letters (Snellen letters) of various carefully graded sizes (see Fig. 3-2). The acuity of vision is frequently recorded as a fraction, e.g., 20/20 or 20/40 (if feet are used in the measurement) and 6/6 or 6/12 (for meters). The numerator of the fraction indicates the distance between the observer and the letter chart. It is always recorded as though the eye test is performed at 20 feet, or 6 meters. So, if the test is actually performed 10 feet from the chart, and the observer's vision is normal, the actual result is 10/10, but recorded as 20/20. If the vision is less than normal, it might be 10/30 and recorded as 20/60 (or 6/18). The denominator refers to the size of the letters. Letters of 20/40 size are twice that of 20/20, and 20/60 letters are three times that of 20/20. The letters are larger in height, width, and spacing.

Table 3-1 lists the total letter size and the size of the strokes and spaces of Snellen acuity letters. The letter size and stroke width are determined from angle considerations. Each stroke of the letter subtends 1 minute of arc (1/60 of a degree) at the eye (see Fig. 3-3). Similarly a 20/40 letter subtends 10 minutes of arc and a 20/200 letter 50 minutes of arc. A letter that subtends an angle of 5 minutes of arc is legible to a person with normal vision.

The visual acuity testing method assumes that there are no time constraints, that the letter is designed according to specific standards (Snellen

FIGURE 3-3   A 20/20 Snellen acuity letter subtends an angle of 5 minutes of arc at the observer's eye. If the test is performed at 10 feet rather than the standard 20 feet, the letter that subtends an angle of 5 minutes of arc technically should be recorded as 10/10.

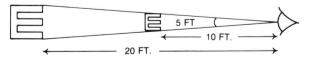

TABLE 3-1. Snellen Acuity Letter Size and Stroke Width for
Visual Acuity Ratings from 20/20 to 20/200

VISUAL ACUITY	LETTER SIZE (INCHES)	STROKE WIDTH (INCHES)
20/20	.35	.07
20/25	.44	.09
20/30	.52	.10
20/40	.70	.14
20/50	.87	.17
20/60	1.05	.21
20/70	1.22	.24
20/80	1.40	.28
20/100	1.75	.35
20/200	3.49	.70

letters), and that the contrast and lighting are optimal. Such conditions are
rarely present in the usual visual communication situation. Therefore, visual
acuity standards should be used only as a baseline when planning visual communication devices. If a sign is intended to be legible to patrons with 20/40 or
better visual acuity and the contrast and lighting are less than optimal, the
letters must be larger than the base size, 20/40. The same is true when there
are time constraints. Contrast, illumination, and time allowances can never be
better than optimal, and, therefore, the letter size should always be larger than
the base size.

How many library users have normal 20/20 vision? Between 1960 and
1962, the Department of Health, Education, and Welfare (HEW) surveyed the
"corrected" visual acuity of 111,000 adults between the ages of 18 and 79.
Table 3-2 summarizes the percentage of those adults with the various levels of
visual acuity. It is evident from these data that guidance systems in libraries
must use a vision standard well below 20/20 if they are to serve the needs of all
patrons.

TABLE 3-2. Percentage Distribution of "Corrected"
Visual Acuity for Adults Between the Ages of 18 and 79
Years*

VISUAL ACUITY	PERCENT
20/20 or better	72.8
20/30	17.7
20/40	4.5
20/50	1.8
20/70	0.9
20/100	1.5
20/200	0.4
less than 20/200	0.4
Total	100.0

*Note that over 25 percent of adults habitually function with
20/30 or less visual acuity and almost 10 percent function
with 20/40 or less acuity (H.E.W. National Health survey,
1960–1962).

Corrected vision as used in the National Health Survey statistics denotes functional acuity; that is, the level at which the adults in the survey are actually seeing with whatever correction (such as eyeglasses or contact lenses) they use. This is the kind of variation in vision performance that can be expected in any group. Among the people using libraries, it might be expected that the 20/100 or less group would be smaller than in the general population. But the fact remains that a large number of people who use libraries have less than normal visual acuity.

Legibility and Readability

We have, so far, been concerned with the *legibility* of letters, defined by Claus and Claus[2] as "the characteristics of letters or numbers which make it possible to differentiate one from the other." The term "readability" much more closely applies to the problems encountered by those interested in visual communication. Claus and Claus define *readability* as "the quality which enables the observer to correctly perceive the information content of letters or numbers grouped together in words, sentences or other meaningful relationships."

The legibility of letters, which must be a precursor to readability, depends substantially on how the letters are grouped together. In addition to other factors, the legibility of letters and numbers is a function of the space between them (see Fig. 3-4). When interletter spacing is increased from 20 to 40 percent of the height of the letter, the speed with which the message can be read will increase as much as 25 percent. According to J. H. Prince,[3] the spaces between letters produce maximum readability when the interletter spaces are half the width of a letter that is 5 units high and 4 units wide. Finally, when the area for a message is restricted, it is best to space the letters properly by filling the area available and leaving only a stroke width or so of margin for maximum readability.

Stroke width also plays an important part in legibility and readability. If the ratio of stroke width to height is varied, the distance at which the letters in a message become visible will vary. The optimal ratio between stroke width and letter height for black letters on a white background is 1:6 to 1:8. Where the letters are white and the background is black, the ratio is 1:8 to 1:10 for optimal viewing (see Fig. 3-5), according to Claus and Claus.[4]

The difference in stroke width to letter height ratio for black on white as opposed to white on black is attributable to the phenomenon of irradiation. Irradiation causes the brighter white characters to "flow" onto the black background. Because this phenomenon relates to the light energy that is given off by the lighter color, it is a function of the contrast between the two areas. A reduction in contrast reduces the irradiation effect.

The relationship between the width of a letter and its height will also affect readability. Although various researchers have determined the width to height ratio for best legibility, there has been no exact agreement. In general, the consensus appears to be in the range of a width of two-thirds of the letter height to a width equal to the letter height for maximal visibility (see Fig. 3-6). This ratio is usually affected by the letter style.

It is important to consider the differences between the groups of letters that make up meaningful words and the groups of letters (or numbers) that are

OVERCROWDING

FIGURE 3-4   The readability of letters is partly a function of the space between the letters. In this example, overcrowding reduces readability. From Claus, R. James and Karen Claus, *Visual Environment* (Don Mills, Ontario: Collier-Macmillan Canada, 1971).

not familiar or meaningful to the reader. The readability of familiar words is greater because the reader does not have to decipher each character. As a result, library signs such as "Reference" and "Periodicals" are more readily appreciated than signs of similar size and configuration that label shelves for volumes RE694.3 to RG723.2.

The style of printing relates to the speed and ease with which a sign can be read. Script and slanted letters are less visible than letters that are straight. Avoid letters that are a combination of bold and light or thin strokes. Helvetica Medium and similar styles have gained wide usage in public buildings because of their clarity, readability, and pleasant modern design.

Helvetica Medium print has the advantage of clarity and readability in both the capital and lowercase letters. In general, lowercase letters are more readable than capitals, although capitals may be preferable at times. One instance is in the case of directions to a portion of the alphabet, e.g., Rows A–H. As a general rule, limit the use of capitals to such instances and to the beginning of sentences and one-word directions (see Fig. 3-7).

Letters should be two to three times larger than the minimal size necessary for a person with normal vision to read the message. This will enable many people with less than normal vision to make use of the printed information—of particular importance in public libraries, where the readership usually includes an appreciable number of people in older age groups.

Periodical
Reading Room
Rest Rooms

AUDIOVISUAL SERVICES – RM 56 BASEMENT

EQUIPMENT

PRODUCTION

MAINTENANCE

PHOTOCOPYING

INFORMATION

FIGURE 3-5   The readability of light-on-dark versus dark-on-light signs is different. This black-on-white sign has larger print than the white-on-black one, and is more readable. But note the great difference in sign size.

Universe No. 49

Universe No.55

Universe No.57

Univers No.59

Univers No.65

Univers No.67

Univers No.75

FIGURE 3-6   The letter height to width ratio affects readability. In general, the extremes are to be avoided. The readability of these examples of Univers print with variations in size, stroke width, and height to width ratio is a good example. Courtesy of Prestype, Inc.

FIGURE 3-7   A good example of proper use of capital and lowercase letters. Note the difference in readability between the word "books" and the all-capitals print in Fig. 3-4.

COLOR AND VISUAL COMMUNICATION

Although the sensation of color is subjective and, therefore, resists a precise definition, visual communication would suffer both esthetically and practically without it. But color can be a burden as well as an advantage, and some understanding of its physical, physiological, and psychological aspects is necessary for efficient visual communication.

White light such as sunlight is a combination of all colors of the rainbow. Of all the radiant energy emitted from the sun, the receptors of the human eye—the rods and cones of the retina—react only to those rays that have wavelengths between approximately 380 and 760 nanometers (one nanometer = one-billionth of a meter). If only a small range of radiant energy wavelengths stimulates the retina, a sensation of a specific color is recognized. For instance, wavelengths in the range around 650 nanometers are called red. Those in the range around 470 nanometers are called blue. In other words, the sensation of blue is evoked from the short wavelength end of the visible spectrum, red from the longer end.

Most objects selectively absorb and reflect various wavelengths of light differently (see Fig. 3-8). A tomato reflects more wavelengths in the red part of the spectrum than in the other parts. A leaf on a tree reflects the green wavelengths and absorbs more of the others. Hence, a tomato appears to be red and a leaf appears green. If a tomato were lighted by sunlight from which the longer wavelengths of light were filtered out, it would no longer appear red. If the green wavelengths were filtered from light striking a leaf, the leaf would no longer appear green. The blue of the sky and the red of a sunset are results of the same phenomenon. At sunset the sun's light energy in the shorter areas of the spectrum is filtered out by the earth's atmosphere, imparting a reddish color to the sun.

These properties of light are quantitative too. A fluorescent light that emits a large amount of radiant energy in the short wavelength part of the spectrum will appear brighter in a green room than in a red one. The green pigment will reflect light into the observer's eye, while the red pigment will absorb the radiant energy and appear less bright. Therefore, light intensity is affected by the color of the light source and the color of the surroundings.

Similar principles apply when light is filtered through tinted windows. Sunlight striking a green window has the radiant energy of all of its wavelengths. However, the light coming from the window is richer in green wavelengths than in others. When this light strikes a red object, little energy is reflected. There-

FIGURE 3-8   The selective absorption and reflection of the wavelengths of light energy enable us to see objects "in color." A tomato reflects very little light energy in the low wavelength part of the spectrum and a great deal in the long wavelength part. Blood or a strawberry would have a similar curve. The curve for a blueberry would be high in the short wavelength end and low in the long wavelength part. Courtesy of General Electric Company.

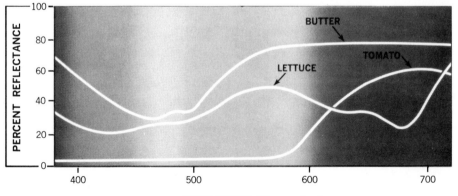

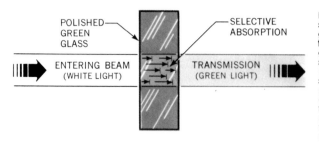

FIGURE 3-9 When white light such as sunlight strikes green glass, the glass selectively transmits the light rays in the green part of the visible spectrum, absorbing the light rays in the other parts of the spectrum. If the absorption in the nongreen part of the spectrum is absolute and the rays coming from the polished glass were to strike a drop of blood, the blood would appear black. Courtesy of General Electric Company.

fore, a red sign indicating an emergency exit may be ineffective in this environment (see Fig. 3-9).

Up to this point, we have considered only the color property known as *hue,* which refers to the color that is perceived, or seen. The hue of an individual drop of blood can be expressed as "red." If a drop of white liquid is mixed with the drop of blood, the hue remains unchanged. But another property of color, the chroma or saturation, would be altered. *Chroma* refers to the purity of a color or the intensity of its distinctive hue. Similarly, if another drop of blood, identical to the first one, is mixed with a drop of gray liquid, it will not be identical to the drop that was mixed with white liquid. The hue of the two drops would remain unchanged (that is, red) because the white and gray additives would not affect the wavelengths of light energy reflected from the mixtures. The chroma would remain unchanged because the original drops of blood were contaminated by equal amounts of fluid. But the *value*—the amount of lightness or darkness—would be different. Color, then, can be accurately expressed in terms of three variables—hue, chroma, and value.

Color Blindness

Although the exact physiological mechanism of color vision remains open to argument among vision scientists, a great deal is known about color confusions inherent in types of color blindness. Monochromatism refers to the totally color-blind individual. The monochromat sees all colors as on a black and white photograph, i.e., in shades of gray. Dichromatism is a condition in which only two of the three primary hues are seen. A dichromat sees colors abnormally because he or she is unable to appreciate the radiant energy in certain parts of the visible spectrum. People with normal color sight are trichromats. Trichromatism indicates that the appropriate mixing of three colored lights will produce a match for any given color standard.

Deuteranopia and protanopia are the most prevalent forms of color blindness. Deuteranopia is complete red-green blindness. The deuteranope sees neutral at the bluish-green and red-purple parts of the spectrum. Blue and yellow appear more normal, but these colors and combinations of them are all that a deuteranope can perceive. The protanope is red blind. Nothing but blues, yellows, and grays are visible to this person, and there is again a substantial reduction in brightness as compared with the normal.

Deuteranopia and protanopia are two classifications of dichromatism. These are classifications of color blindness at least in the sense that the visual

FIGURE 3-10   This is a good example of effective contrast. The white on red combination is very legible.

system is "blind" to certain wavelengths (colors) of light. But the most common form of defective color vision is anomalous trichromatism, which ranges from near-dichromats to nearly normal trichromats. Deuteranomalous trichromats have a diminished sensation of green and require more green light energy than normal when, for instance, they are making a green-red mixture. Prot-anomalous trichromacy is a red weakness, while the rare tritanomalous tri-chromat is blue weak.

The major color deficiencies affect the perception of green and red. Two shades of green may produce no discernible perceptual difference for the deuteranomalous trichromat. Similarly, a bright red arrow on a pink wall may be an ineffective direction indicator for a protanope. Color coding can be an ap-preciable asset or an indecipherable confusion, depending upon the viewer's vision system and the colors used.

The modern world is extremely color oriented. Much of today's visual com-munication makes extensive use of color. The legibility and readability of col-ored print on colored backgrounds are of concern because these factors affect people with normal color vision as well as those whose color vision is less than normal.

In general, legibility of colored print on a colored background is a function of brightness contrast (see Fig. 3-10). As might be expected, such combina-tions as black on yellow, green on white, and blue on white are most legible, while black on blue, yellow on white, and blue on black are least legible.

OTHER FACTORS THAT AFFECT VISION

Adaptation

The human vision system can operate in an extremely large range of light in-tensities. The eye can function outdoors on a moonless night as well as in full sunlight in a snowy field. In fact, when the eye is maximally adapted to the dark, its sensitivity is 100,000 times greater than at the onset of *dark adaptation,* which is the process by which the visual system reacts to decreased illumina-tion.

Reaction to increased illumination is called *light adaptation.* The eye is said to be operating under "scotopic conditions" when it is dark-adapted, and "photopic conditions" when light-adapted. The range between the two is called "mesopic." The mesopic range extends roughly from a little below the illuminance of the sky when the moon is full to the light level 15 minutes after sunset.

When one goes from bright sunlight into a darkened room, such as a movie theater, the eye's ability to function is temporarily impaired. After several minutes, the eyes adapt to the darkness and normal vision returns. When going into bright sunlight after being in a darkened room for a period of time, the adaptation to brightness is much quicker. The speed with which the eye "dark adapts" is much slower than the speed with which it "light adapts." Complete dark adaptation takes about 30 minutes; light adaptation requires approximately 1 minute.

This leads to some interesting visual communication problems. For instance, a sign intended to be seen by people entering a building from a bright environment (such as a day when the sun is shining on untinted concrete) must be illuminated nearly as brightly as is the outdoor environment. The same care must be exercised in planning a visual environment for those who leave a brightly lighted building at night.

Glare

Although glare is popularly known as harsh, bright, dazzling light, it has a more specific meaning. *Glare* is defined in optics as the condition that exists when a bright light is present near the object of regard. Driving into the setting sun, so that the sun shines into the driver's eyes, is an example of glare.

Glare can seriously limit the usefulness of signs. Do not place signs in such a position that the reader has to look toward bright outdoor illumination (Fig. 3-11). But if there is no other suitable place for such a sign, a large border around the printed material may help. If not, it may be necessary to illuminate the sign brightly to counteract the brightness of the glare source.

Aging

At birth, the visual system and other sensory systems of the human body are not fully developed. In the healthy individual, the developing process of vision usually reaches a peak from about ages 20 to 30. Beyond the peak years, the efficiency of the visual system gradually declines, with the effects becoming pronounced around the fifth decade.

The most obvious change occurs in the eye's ability to focus sharply on close objects. A normal-sighted teenager can focus on an object held about 3 inches from the eye. By the mid-twenties, the same person must hold the object approximately 5 inches from the eye for a sharp focus. At age 50 the ability to focus on objects held close to the eye is much reduced. The same person cannot focus clearly at a distance closer than approximately 20 inches.

Presbyopia is the inability to focus on close objects. Bifocal and trifocal lenses are prescribed for this condition. But these lenses, although correcting the focus problem, can create other problems, and people concerned with visual communication should be aware of them.

The small reading portion of the bifocal lens usually allows the wearer clear vision within a range of approximately 10 to 30 inches. This 20-inch range reduces with age. If the printed information designed to be read at that dis-

FIGURE 3-11 Glare is always a problem when a sign is placed in front of a bright light source. Here the sign attached to the ceiling is approximately 15 feet wide and 8 inches high. The left side of the sign directs the reader to "Reference" and the right side to "Interlibrary Loan." The sign is effective only at night.

tance is placed anywhere above eye level, the bifocal wearer will be at a disadvantage. The head must be tipped well back to place the reading segment of the lens between the eye and the print.

This problem affects nearly half of our population, so signs and other printed material placed above eye level need special attention. Such material is most useful in larger size print so that the presbyopic patron can step back and read the material with the larger, upper part of the lens, which is designed for viewing more distant objects. Card catalogs may be particularly troublesome. Both low and high extremes are best avoided. Volume and shelf labeling can be equally difficult if care is not taken to make the print sizes adequate.

Aging also affects the clear tissues of the eye. The eye resembles a camera in the sense that the eye is designed for focusing light rays on the retina, just as a camera focuses light rays on film. With increasing age, the tissues on the surface of and within the eye become less clear. When the crystalline lens within the eye grows appreciably opaque, for instance, the eye is said to have a cataract (see Fig. 3-12).

But virtually all eyes of people who have reached the age of 30 have some opacifications, which scatter and absorb light rays. As a result, the older one is, the more light one needs in order to see. Yet, a great deal of light emanating from the same general direction as the object of regard can also present difficulties.

The problem is similar to that which exists when driving an automobile with

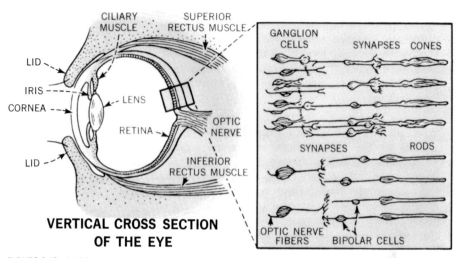

CILIARY MUSCLE
SUPERIOR RECTUS MUSCLE
GANGLION CELLS
SYNAPSES CONES
LID
IRIS
CORNEA
LENS
RETINA
OPTIC NERVE
LID
INFERIOR RECTUS MUSCLE
SYNAPSES
RODS
OPTIC NERVE FIBERS
BIPOLAR CELLS

VERTICAL CROSS SECTION OF THE EYE

FIGURE 3-12 Light energy must pass through the cornea and the lens and focus on the retina. The lens is the part of the eye that becomes less clear with age. If it becomes opaque enough to seriously affect the progress of the light through the eye, the eye is said to have a cataract. In any case, with increasing age the transmission of some wavelengths of light is reduced. The optic nerve fibers are actually a part of the brain. Courtesy of General Electric Company.

a dirty windshield. In daylight when the road is brightly illuminated by the sun, a dirty windshield is a minimal annoyance. After dark, with the road illuminated only by headlights, there may be some difficulty. The difficulty becomes major when headlights from an oncoming automobile light up the opacities on the windshield. For these reasons, it is wise to avoid placing signs close to bright light sources. If signs or other visual information are required in such areas, place large borders around the print. Similarly, printed material is best made with a low reflectance background to avoid having the sign itself become a glare source.

The situation almost seems paradoxical. Eyes with opacities require more light than do clear ones. Yet, more light entering the eye strikes the opacities and obscures the vision. The key is the direction from which the light emanates. A brightly lighted sign made of a low reflectance material is best. But when the sign is surrounded by bright light sources, its readability will be reduced. The challenge is to light the material optimally while reducing other bright light sources.

The pupil of the eye acts like the iris diaphragm of a camera. The larger the pupil size, the more light entering the eye. But pupil size also decreases with age. The smaller pupil size allows less light to enter the eye—another reason to make sure that lighting is adequate to meet the needs of older library users.

Adaptation can also be more difficult for older people than for younger ones. Dark adaptation or glare recovery slows with age. Although people are not all affected equally, glare recovery can be troublesome for older library users. In this respect, changes of illumination should be evaluated carefully, and any bright flash of light should be prevented. A flash, such as the flash of a camera, bleaches the retinal pigment, making large portions of the retina inoperative for a few seconds. Afterimages persist in the visual field, either in positive or negative form, obscuring vision and creating temporary blindness.

Color sensitivity changes with age. As the clear structures within the eye become opacified, they also yellow. This results in a decrease in light energy reaching the retina. The action is similar to the selective filtration of light that takes place when white light strikes a tinted window. As a result, older people see blue and other short wavelength colors with less intensity than do younger people. The very long wavelengths (red and lavender) may be affected as well.

THE MESSAGE

Providing adequate visual guidance in libraries is a difficult and complex task. If all library users had normal vision, the task would be simpler. But if all visual communication is designed for the average or normal observer, the system will fail as often as it succeeds. Fortunately, a good deal is known about the human visual system, and by using this knowledge efficient visual communications can be devised to serve the greatest number of library users.

It is important to realize that devising a visual communication system is a scientific as well as an artistic endeavor. It is not enough merely to design a sign by having two people assess its readability from across the hall. The size, color, type, surrounding colors, lighting intensity and wavelength, and the coordination of one sign with all others in the building are factors that require careful and informed consideration.

It has been said that 80 percent of what one learns comes from vision, a figure that seems reasonable considering the large portion of the brain that is involved with vision and the amount of information processed. The message is clear.

NOTES

1. U.S. National Institutes of Health, *Summary and Critique of Available Data on the Prevalence and Economic and Social Costs of Visual Disorders and Disabilities* (Bethesda, Md.: National Eye Institute, 1976).

2. Karen Claus and R. James Claus, *Visual Communication through Signage,* vol. I, *The Perception of the Message* (Cincinnati: Signs of the Times, 1974), p. 2.

3. J. H. Prince, "Criteria for Word Formation for Maximum Legibility," *Signs of the Times* 148 (January 1958): 42.

4. Claus and Claus, *Visual Communication through Signage,* vol. I, *The Perception of the Message,* p. 2.

Part
2

*Designing a Visual
Guidance System*

Planning Library Signage Systems

KATHERINE M. SELFRIDGE

The need for a more effective presentation of guidance and direction information is evident all around us, in all kinds of buildings and along many roads. Everyone has probably had the experience of following signs until suddenly they vanish before the destination has been reached. Or else we don't see them because there are too many signs to read and sort out. The problem is that to guide people well, signs and other kinds of visual information must be planned with a great deal of logic and some notion of the effective elements of visual presentation—of what makes information visible, noticeable, legible, and understandable, of what makes a positive impact on us.

The goals of visual communication in the library are straightforward—to convey information so that it can be easily absorbed and acted on, and to contribute to the attractiveness of the library and its site. A professional system of signs should be precisely appropriate to both the library's function and the nature of its surroundings, fitting the physical setting while enhancing the image of the library. An attractive sign system really does attract attention in a more positive way than does a poorly designed one.

To be effective, signs and any other forms of visual communication must be coordinated with human perceptions. How humans perceive depends on the total surroundings. All elements of an environment contribute to one's perceptions of it and one's feelings about it.

This chapter is concerned with the many planning and design considerations that contribute to success in conveying information to visitors in libraries. Each library, of course, requires a different solution for signage and other information. The most effective system of information will be the result of logical planning and design that lead to decisions based on the particular conditions of the particular library.

The elements that create a good system of communication may include printed guides, exhibits highlighting collections or services within the library, announcements of public events, and other written material; however, it is mainly the maps, directories, and signs that enable people to circulate through the library in a logical way with ease and assurance. This does not rule out the effectiveness of audiovisual aids in certain situations, but there are no general principles for them that will work in all libraries. Static signs may not call attention to themselves to the same degree as moving lights, flashing signals, taped voices, or other more dynamic methods of communication, but they can be successfully planned, designed, and installed in every type of library.

THE GOOD SIGNAGE SYSTEM

A good system is more than a collection of signs put up as the need arises. Individually, signs can be properly noticeable, legible, accurate and credible, well designed, and having the right kind of information in the right place; but to guide, direct, and inform people as they move through buildings and spaces, signs must be coordinated in a logical progression, with appropriate degrees of emphasis on different kinds of information. The answer is to present information by an interrelated system that integrates messages and traffic patterns and combines them with the architecture in a visually coordinated sequence.

The aim is to present information consistently so that people will learn to look for it in certain places, to recognize it easily, and to follow it with confidence. In general, people need information at decision points, at entrances and exits, along corridors, and at intersections, stairs, elevators, and so on. It also helps to repeat the information at other places to reassure people that, indeed, they are on the right track.

Good signage systems convey a great deal of information. They enable people to orient themselves in unfamiliar surroundings, to find their way to destinations easily and pleasantly, to move without confusion from destination to destination, and to notice and understand all regulations and information about special conditions. This entails a lot of information to be absorbed at different times and in different places. However, as no one wants to be confronted with too many signs, the task is to present the mass of information so that it can be easily, almost unconsciously, perceived and understood. The first aim of the planning and design process is to sort out the information so that it can be presented in different ways and at appropriate times.

Information can be divided into three basic categories: *direction* information to guide and direct people along routes to their destinations; *identification* information to label destinations so that people recognize them when they have arrived; and *instruction* information to inform people about rules, restrictions, special conditions, and procedures. The direction, identification, and instruction categories are in turn separated into major and minor subcategories, often determined by the locations and functions of the information. Not all libraries will require all of the sign categories listed below.

Exterior Signs

Direction
Major direction signs point the way to the library from adjacent streets, the edge of the site, and parking areas.

Minor direction signs either point the way to other places on the library grounds, such as to special, secondary entrances, parking, and handicapped access or parking, or they indicate traffic directions around the library for people in cars, bicycling, or walking.

Identification
Major boundary identification signs give the name of the library at the boundary of the site, perhaps at the street, or near a road leading to the library or parking area.

Major building identification signs name the library, usually near the entrance or the most visible part of the exterior of the building.

Minor identification signs name entrances and places, such as the main entrance, staff or delivery entrance, other special entrances, and parking areas.

Instruction
Major instruction signs describe special conditions or regulations, such as parking and traffic rules or cautions: "stop," words or symbols for no parking and parking permitted, "please do not walk on the grass," "please do not litter," and the hours the library is open.

Interior Signs

Direction
Major direction signs point the way to the main areas of the library at places of possible confusion. Examples are directions (with arrows) to the circulation desk, reference desk, catalogs, and special collections.

Minor direction signs point the way to areas and places within main areas, such as to individual study carrels, stacks, offices, rest rooms, elevators, and stairs.

Identification
Major identification signs name large or important areas such as the library itself, information/circulation desk, general reading room, reference desk and reading room, periodical room, special collections, catalogs, and stack area.

Minor identification signs name smaller areas within main areas, such as the information sign on the general circulation desk, offices, carrels, one catalog case, service desks, floor level numbers, one stack level, rest rooms, and telephone booths. There may be several minor subcategories, but all identification signs mark arrival at destinations, even if they are small places or objects.

Instruction
Instruction signs describe special conditions and regulations about such things as library hours, smoking, eating and drinking, private and restricted areas, how to look up information, and how to use files, catalogs, copy machines, and other equipment.

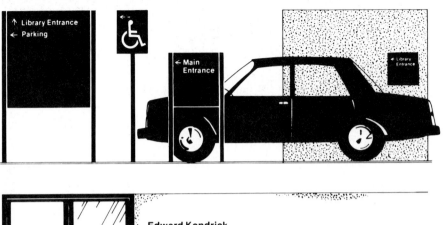

FIGURE 4-1 Exterior signs. Top row shows four direction signs (left to right): major sign, higher and larger than pedestrian signs, to be read from moving vehicles; handicapped symbol on high post to be seen easily by drivers; and two entrance signs of appropriate size and height for pedestrians. Bottom row shows major identification sign, with instruction sign conspicuous and at good reading height, but in a smaller size that does not detract from major sign.

Directories
Major directories list major areas, some minor ones, and their locations by floors and other designations. They are often supplemented by simple floor plans, with "you are here" notations.

Minor directories list areas on one floor or smaller adjacent areas. They are also keyed to the major directory.

Special Graphics
Special graphics include such things as murals, photographic enlargements, hangings, decorative maps, and pictorial symbols. They create mood and color. They can also signal changes in direction or orientation.

The key to good signage is, first, to establish a systematic pattern of major and minor identification, direction, and instruction information so that people will rely on it, finding the data they need at the right place as they go to and through the library, and, second, to present the information with different degrees of visual emphasis so that it can be comfortably absorbed.

Major and minor signs in an exterior and interior sign system separate information by sign size, shape, and placement, and yet also create an identity through similarities of size and shape, layout, type size, and placement. Aesthetically, the shapes and sizes of signs are related to each other to present information in a consistent way. Type should be readable from a distance and yet attractive and readable from a closer view. The typeface should also reflect the style and flavor of the library (see Figs. 4-1 and 4-2).

FIGURE 4-2   Interior signs. Top and middle rows show main directory/map, direction, identification, and room identification signs mounted above entrances and on or next to doors. Bottom row shows minor identification signs.

The underlying principle of good signage is to orient people to the plan and functions of the library, to give them a way of creating an internal map of where they are in relation to where they are going. To provide reassurance, signs and maps orient people first to the broad geographical view, then to specific areas. Each sign cannot do this alone, but an orderly system can create a reinforcing progression of information that gives major orientation and guidance before it presents the next level of information (see Fig. 4-3). For example, orientation maps and directories are placed and made especially noticeable at entrances or where it is helpful to give overall views, but if more specific information is also required at the same location (library hours, smok-

FIGURE 4-3   Major exterior
identification sign for Children's
Hospital in Boston also directs
people up the street to the
emergency entrance and the
main entrance, and across the
street to hospital parking.
Photo by Wayne Soverns, Jr.

ing regulations), it is subordinated visually so that it does not compete with the primary information.

In libraries, the large spaces (such as banks of catalogs, levels of stacks, and large reading rooms) are considered major areas. The smaller places or specific things within them (such as individual catalogs and sections of stacks) are considered minor areas, because people find them after locating the major sites that contain them. In planning, one proceeds in the same manner as in organizing maps. People are oriented first to the major areas, then to the minor, specific ones. In this way, information is conveyed in digestible pieces.

MAKING THE SYSTEM WORK

Planning, designing, and implementing a sign system usually occur in stages during which all the many elements are analyzed and formed into a cohesive whole. Although it is assumed here that a planner/designer is retained by the library for this purpose, the actual work stages and planning and design considerations are basically the same no matter who undertakes the tasks. The processes can be divided into four stages of work, each with presentations, approvals, and budgets: (1) planning and programming, (2) design, (3) documentation, and (4) supervision. In practice, complex processes are rarely linear, and the planning and design stages are apt to overlap.

Planning and Programming

This stage involves three general activities: defining the needs for signage and other visual information, analyzing and classifying signage and related graphics, and investigating signage needs by content and location.

It may sound elementary to point out the necessity for a statement of needs when planning a visual guidance system, but, in fact, essential elements are often missing in completed sign systems. The scope of the work must be listed—the range of exterior and interior signs, maps, guides, posters, announcements, and anything else that the library wants to provide for its patrons.

A list of library resources should also be prepared to make certain that the public will be aware of them. It is obvious to a first-time visitor that few libraries have clear and thorough orientation data near the entrance, or a list of their range of services or resources. Consequently, many visitors remain unaware of the resources offered.

After a list of places and resources that the sign system must identify is made, it should be edited for discrepancies in nomenclature or terminology. Patrons following signs through a building are confused if different terms refer to the same thing. A special collection, for example, may be called by its subject title or by the name of a donor (as in the Map Room or the Thompson Room). Whichever way, it should always be consistent on directories, in direction or identification signs, and in printed instruction aids.

The library staff should also be aware of the special needs of visitors. State codes require different conditions for easy access and barrier-free facilities for the physically disabled. Some list provisions for the elderly, or those with hearing and/or vision difficulties. As much as possible should be done to facilitate library use by people with disabilities. A survey should be made of all hindrances and obstacles, and all conveniences and favorable conditions that will help people with special needs.

In addition, the library staff and the planner/designer should review the characteristics or the special requirements of most of the library patrons. Clearly, visual information will be most effective when it is easily understood and when it appeals to most people. In some libraries, a significant proportion of users might be children, older students, the elderly, foreigners, or members of a local, foreign-language-speaking community. Sometimes the needs of visitors conflict, and compromises must be found. For example, a second language might be thought helpful on library signs in an ethnic neighborhood. That means more signs or many more words per sign will be needed at each location, which might create such an overload of information that people will avoid reading the signs altogether, defeating the use of the two languages. Or, in another example, color is often used very successfully to distinguish different areas, adding warmth and vitality to the surroundings as well, but color coding can be meaningless to the color blind if it is not combined with words. Also, although large, bold typefaces can help people with impaired vision, extra large typefaces might take up so much more space that messages would become too insistent and large. The bold weight of type might create too great a contrast for people with average vision, thus changing the character of the information and people's perceptions of it.

When people's special needs are considered in the planning stage, the library staff and planner/designer can establish the goals and restraints of the system so that the graphics will grow from the true needs of those using the library, as well as from the characteristics of the library itself and the skills of the designer.

Besides defining needs, the library staff should define its wishes for the overall design character of the library—for the image appropriate to the library. Although it is the designer's responsibility to fit the graphic vocabulary to the image during the design stages, the general style must be discussed at the beginning—whether the library is seen as traditional or contemporary; with a subdued and dignified ambience or a bright, friendly one; urban or rural; and so forth. The more these qualities can be expressed, the more likely it is that a good designer will find the most appropriate components to create the desired feeling. This does not mean that an old style of architecture should have an old style of signs, or that a contemporary building should have all contemporary graphics. It means only that the designer should find a way to blend the graphics with the building, keeping them in harmony.

The library staff and the planner/designer should also agree at the beginning on the long-range performance for signs, directories, maps, wall graphics, guides, and anything else in the scope of work. *Performance* concerns the frequency with which signs will need change or reordering, the amount of possible vandalism or theft, the expected ordinary wear and tear, the ease of maintenance, the costs per sign, and the need for availability of new signs. Obviously, new signs are always going to be needed, but often one can predict that certain kinds of signs will change more frequently than others. For example, it might be expected that the exterior identification signs and the interior elevator, stair, rest room, telephone, service, and major-area identification signs will remain the same. Therefore, they can be made of durable materials, perhaps even custom ordered. If it seems likely that smaller area locations may be switched, signs for these (such as offices, desk identification, carrels, call numbers on stacks, catalog and shelf identification) will periodically need to be remade or ordered, and so they might be made initially in less expensive materials or with changeable slots or removable type.

As crucial as performance planning is the question of continued maintenance for the system. Systems fail over the years because the signs change appearance along with their messages: signs are not reordered the same way; typefaces change; direction information changes; new signs are put up as the need arises, which alters the original plan; signs are changed in size and materials and are hung at different heights. Any one of the factors concerning content, design, and placement affects perception. All details of the system must remain the same in order for the system to maintain its impact. The importance

FIGURE 4-4 This major direction sign is combined with a subdirectory listing areas on lower floor of the Cary Memorial Library, Lexington, Massachusetts. Clear and attractive, the sign is made of plastic and vinyl die-cut, dry transfer letters and is well placed next to the stairs to the lower level. Note the simple, distinct arrow, belonging to the same typeface — Helvetica Medium — as the letters.

of consistency, ideally with one person having responsibility over a period of years, must be understood, and this responsibility must be established, or the time and money spent on initiating the system will be wasted.

The planner/designer begins an active synthesis of the preceding information by preparing a program list of all signs and other visual information, which is keyed to the site plan and floor plans of the library. The list is divided into the basic categories of signs to assess the different kinds of information per location. Practically, this means that one number is assigned to identification signs, another to direction signs, another to instruction signs, another to maps, and others to each different category of information. Categories can be divided into major and minor signs of several ranks. The numbers appear on the floor plans and on master lists of signs, which include the wording of the messages for each sign (if possible at this time). The keyed floor plans will thus show the amount and type of information for each location: all direction, identification, and instruction signs, wall graphics, maps, and directories.

It is simplest to mark identification signs first, for the information desk, circulation desk, reference desk, catalogs, stacks, periodical areas, special collections, offices, service centers, nonpublic areas, public nonlibrary facilities (rest rooms, telephones, vending machines, copy machines), and so on. Then, each route to each destination is traced and marked with the identification, direction, and instruction signs that are needed along its length, at points of potential confusion, and where reinforcement is helpful (see Fig. 4-4). In an existing library, it is a good idea to walk the routes to observe where additional signs are needed. This will reinforce the directions already given. There are no rules that will apply to every corridor or large open room. The designer/planner must determine the need in each situation for repeating directions along corridors and in large rooms, without running the danger of oversigning. It will be necessary to make diagrams of sample signs—not facsimiles, but rough signs for content and placement—to test one's judgment.

A curious situation occurs in libraries with poor signs: the unnecessary repetition of signs in one location does not make the message more emphatic, but, in fact, often creates an overload of signage and usually a mixture of typefaces and other graphic elements, which lessen the impact. This is apt to happen in major instruction signage where rules are written out, such as at circulation desks and no smoking areas. In any case, a keyed program list and floor plans should help to eliminate redundancies.

In the planning stage, the planner/designer surveys the physical conditions of the library, noting problems of architecture, lighting, interiors, landscaping, existing furniture, obstacles, and so on. The survey might include the difficulty or ease of orientation and circulation; whether functions are logically placed in relation to each other; difficult angles of vision because of ceiling heights, lighting, or obstacles such as hanging fixtures; and the number of people using spaces or corridors at one time, which leads to the need for particularly conspicuous signs. Sometimes the architecture offers good locations for signs and directories, and, in fact, makes obvious the best shapes for signs and ways of installing them. Sometimes the architecture makes the choices particularly difficult, as when there are no bare walls that will take simple screws or bolts. If lighting is consistent throughout, either fluorescent or incandescent, usually with a mixture of daylight, the choice of colors is easier than if there are various mixtures of lighting in the same building. The survey should also include dimensions for corridor widths and heights; colors of walls, floors, and ceilings; materials already in use or planned; color and style of hardware—in fact, as many environmental elements as possible.

After the program list of direction, identification, and instruction signs is keyed to specific locations on the plans, one can estimate the amount of information anticipated at each location. However, the messages will undoubtedly need to be reviewed and edited for length, clarity, tone, accuracy, and, especially, consistency. Remember that the use of different terms for the same thing is not only a matter of sloppiness; it is potentially baffling to users.

Because their messages are short, it is probably easier to edit identification and direction signs than to edit instructions. People in search of something are not patient about reading paragraphs on signs. Directions are best given in short phrases or lists. The length of text lines should be as short as possible, due to space limitations. The number of words can help to determine the size of type, spacing, layouts, and thus the final sizes of the signs in the system.

Editing for tone is important, too. A pleasant tone is part of the hospitable ambience of the library. Although signs are static, one-way forms of communication, they can make very different impressions through their use of language, as well as by their design. They can scold, command, boast, flaunt, excite, amuse, and encourage. They can be simple and direct. Part of the groundwork is to discuss the right tone to convey information clearly in the library. Establishing these guidelines also serves to discourage departmental librarians from putting up their own signs, which might differ in tone and character of message.

All messages must, of course, be accurate and credible or people will lose faith in the reliability of signs, maps, and other guides. When office or departmental locations are changed, the signs must be changed promptly as well.

At the end of the planning and programming stage, the broad concepts of the system should be evident for the major areas. The major direction and identification signage is specified; minor signs are generally located within the main areas, and general locations for instruction signs are indicated; messages are written out; quantities are estimated; general character is projected and ideas about budgets, costs, and future needs are discussed; and the positive and negative attributes of the architecture are assessed and added to the mix. The planner/designer then begins to assemble the parts.

Design

Design involves the integration of all elements in time and space. These elements consist of: alphabet and typefaces; size and spacing of letters; words and lines of type on sign faces, maps, directories, and other displays; contrast of letters; use of symbols; shapes and sizes of signs, maps, directories, and other displays; use of color; standard placement of signs at locations; and materials and methods of fabrication and installation. In the preliminary design stage, the designer studies the basic concepts and investigates alternative modular components of the system and the individual and collective impact of the graphic design elements.

Typography is an important consideration. Typefaces have very definite characters: they can be bold, refined, dignified, friendly, beautiful, extravagant, simple, ornamental, traditional, contemporary, and much more. Some are easy to read, some are not. Some faces designed centuries ago are perfect for signs today; some of the current ones used in advertising display work poorly in sign systems where legibility from distances is needed. Some alphabets take up more vertical space than others because they have different sizes of ascenders and descenders, which affect the amount of space left open between lines of text. Some alphabets have fat, squat letters that take up more horizontal space per line; some are narrow in proportion. Each typeface has its own proportions, which affect the space around them, which in turn contributes to the final degree of legibility. Some typefaces of the same x height (the body of a letter without the ascenders and descenders, as measured in printer's points) look very different because their proportions differ. Strokes of letters can be upright or slanted. The typeface can be either serif (with end strokes to characters) or sans serif.

Much has been written about the choice of serif and sans serif typefaces (see Figs. 4-5 and 4-6). It is one of the basic design elements that sets the character of the signs. Both can be appropriate in traditional and contemporary settings, depending on other design factors. Helvetica is a sans serif typeface commonly used on signs because it has a heavy enough weight to be read well, with even proportions and strokes for good legibility and spacing, and a straightforward, contemporary quality. However, the use of a serif, more traditional roman typeface may seem more suitable in some libraries. In that

FIGURE 4-5 Serif typeface for major exterior identification sign; black Clarendon capital letters are flush-mounted against concrete. This bolder version of the same typeface used for the church's printed material creates a visible bond between the signs and the literature.

case, the designer may need to space the characters a little more widely because of the variations in the thick and thin strokes in the characters, which reduce the ease and speed of reading the words in lines of text from various distances. If that style creates the right appearance, the spacing elements can be adjusted in mock-ups and by trials on site for legibility.

Remember, however, that all elements affect the ease of reading words on signs from distances. The designer will have to test and evaluate all elements together when making decisions.

The size of typeface characters will also affect the size of the message and the size of the sign. The choice is made by reviewing the longest types of messages per sign category and determining the degree of visual emphasis needed. Instruction signs probably will be longer than major identification signs, but their typefaces should not be as large.

By using a family of typefaces in several sizes for major and minor signs, the designer tries to build visual recognition for all orientation and guidance information, creating the visual distinctions through character size and sign size. In practice then, a designer might choose four-inch letters for the main library identification sign on the building; two-inch letters for major overhead identification and direction signs to major areas, to be seen from, say, 40 feet away as people walk down corridors or cross large rooms; one-inch letters for signs on desks, catalogs, and stacks; and perhaps half-inch or quarter-inch letters for shelf signs and instructions. The choices are broad, so it is wise to test the sizes in context before making final decisions.

There are conflicting opinions about the ease and speed of reading words and lines in either all capital letters or capitals and lowercase letters. In dealing with text on pages, typographers feel that lowercase words are faster and easier to read because the ascenders and descenders create distinctive "coastlines" in words—silhouettes that act as signposts or landmarks to the eye. Words in all capitals are more even, and so take more time to read. Words in caps and lowercase take up less room than words in all caps, an important

FIGURE 4-6   Sans serif typeface for major exterior identification sign; bronze Helvetica capital letters are flush-mounted on warm-colored brick, the bronze matching the window mullions and door frames. The even strokes of the letters make a strong contrast against the brick pattern.

consideration for signs, but the larger x heights of words in all capitals make words more legible from distances than the x heights of the lowercase words in the same typeface. Often the choice is made by the different character of words in all caps and words with lowercase letters. Words in all capitals tend to look more important, more emphatic, sometimes even heavier. This might be appropriate for special emphasis, but not for a continuing body of information.

Spacing and layout are considered concurrently with the choice of typefaces and the sizes of characters. Spacing affects legibility, and it establishes the maximum number of letters that can be used per line. The designer evaluates the length of messages and from what distances they can be read. Most typefaces have guidelines for wide, normal, and tight letter spacing, with predictable degrees of legibility from various distances. The designer chooses a standard for spacing that suits the typeface and each character size, and then tests them in typical situations.

Consistent layouts are the basis for creating a smooth presentation of messages. One can appreciate the value of consistent margins and layouts when looking at signs without them; they seem busy and disorganized. In fact, smooth reading and good design are lost when there is a lack of visual order, whether from too much variation in typefaces, letter sizes or weights or sign sizes, inconsistency of layout or placements, or use of too many colors.

Messages stand out in their context—the words against the sign face, the sign against the wall or ceiling—partly because of clear, empty space around them. Crowded messages discourage people from reading them, but with enough "white space" around them, the same messages seem easier to read. The amount of space between the margins and the text depends on too many factors (particular messages, typefaces, size of characters, contrasts, colors, sign sizes, architecture) to state specific rules, but it can be said that the signs themselves must have adequate space around them to be properly noticed.

The contrast of letters against their backgrounds also affects spacing, legibility, and aesthetics. Light letters on dark backgrounds are usually spaced a little more widely than dark letters on light backgrounds. But, as in all sign system design, choices should be looked at on site to see how well the solution adds to the overall noticeability and harmony of the system in place.

If the library staff and designer wish to use symbols to indicate library services, they should investigate the studies concerning international standards of symbol recognition (see Bibliography), for nothing is less useful than an obscure symbol. Because of their complexity, library services probably are best described in words rather than by symbols, but there are certainly clear and decorative symbols for general public facilities such as rest rooms, telephones, drinking fountains, stairways, elevators, exits, food and beverages, parking, and for regulatory information such as no smoking, no entry, one-way traffic, stop, and others. The international symbol of access for disabled in wheelchairs should be used on direction and identification signs indicating special facilities.

Symbols should also be used consistently, their size relating to the character size of the alphabet. For a unified design effect, the designer should relate the pictorial style of the symbols to the style of the typefaces.

Arrows, too, should match the character of the typeface. Above all, they should clearly indicate direction—not something to be taken for granted, judging by the number of weak, illegible arrows seen on signs. The direction of the arrow is lost when the length of the shaft is out of proportion to the head.

The shapes and sizes of signs in a system are, of course, determined in accord with other elements. The designer studies and sometimes presents alternatives, testing the amount of information per sign category and how it fits at locations. Often the architecture is the key consideration: there might be beams across corridors, which would be perfect for long, rectangular signs, or there might be columns or furniture in open rooms that require other shapes. Often the amount of direction information needed at intersections eliminates the choice of long, narrow, horizontal signs and favors the choice of vertical or square signs, which can carry longer messages. Whatever the choice, the objective is to make distinctions among the major and minor signs, and possibly among direction, identification, and instructional signs.

"Predesigned" signs can be ordered from suppliers and catalogs, but one should first consider how they will fit with the architecture of the building. Unfortunately, few suppliers carry all the signs for all kinds of messages in one system—exterior, interior, in all categories. But whether signs are custom-made or bought from catalogs, different sizes and shapes should be determined by the functions of the signs—how they fit the locations and how they relate in modular, hierarchical form to each other. The sought-after pattern of recognition for information can be defeated by too many distracting sizes and shapes.

Color, used boldly and with enough repetition, can help to distinguish different places within the library. There are different ways of color coding areas or functions. Whatever the system, it works only when it is repeated clearly enough so that people notice that color is functional and not merely decorative. If different colors identify different major places in the library or different floors in the building, the colors should be used on every direction and identification sign to those major places or floors.

The name of the place, floor, or color itself should appear with the color so that people will associate the color directly with the place it represents. Color is really a supplementary visual aid. It adds emphasis and distinguishes among places or functions; the words primarily identify those places or functions.

Although there are psychological studies on the use of color and its impact on legibility and noticeability, there is relatively little information on the use of color coding. Studies suggest that people can distinguish and remember a relatively small number of categories by color: between 5 and 8 reliably, and 9–12 under optimal test conditions.[1] On those assumptions, color coding should be restricted to libraries that have no more than 5–8 major areas or floors.

The intensities of colors next to each other will create different effects; so will the degrees of contrast between different colors and their sign panel backgrounds. As signs are seen in all kinds of spaces, at different times of day, in different lighting conditions, with competition from other colors and from the things around them, the only sure way to know whether the colors are legible and attractive is to look at them in place, in their real context. When the same color is to appear in different materials, it is wise to compare samples of each material for a good color match.

Placement is another important design consideration. From the standard placement of signs, maps, and directories, people perceive, consciously or not, that a reliable pattern of information exists. People quickly learn to look for signs at reliably repeated heights. Unfortunately, most libraries were not built with space for integrated signage, and so exceptions to standards will occur. However, in general, the designer should try to find a series of typical heights for major and minor signs in direction, identification, and instruction categories, and for directories, maps, and wall graphics.

To communicate the differences among categories of information, the designer might arrive at something like this: all major direction and identification signs (to main reading room, catalog area, stack levels, reference room) are long bands hung from the ceiling over doorways and across corridors; all minor direction and identification signs (within each of those areas) are rectangular and wall-mounted; and instruction signs are rectangular and are either wall-mounted or freestanding on desks, tables, or countertops. All overhead long bands are placed eight feet from the floor, and all wall-mounted signs are five and a half feet from the floor (bottom edges in both cases).

At the end of the preliminary design stage, a presentation is usually submitted to illustrate the interrelationships of the signs and how each sign type will look in a general way. The presentation usually includes general cost estimates for alternative materials and methods of fabrication obtained by estimating the various sizes of signs and how they would be made. The preliminary designs include sketches and sometimes perspectives or study models to show signs placed at intersections, next to doorways, and at other typical locations. A few typical signs are lettered in to illustrate the appearance of the typeface and the layout of the type with symbols and arrows on various types of signs.

In the design development stage, the selected system is refined so that the artwork for the signs can be reproduced in final form. Letters, symbols, and arrows are reproduced precisely. Final, typical layouts are determined, with exact spacing and typographical relationships indicated. Sample signs are made, and maps are drawn in finished artwork form. This "mechanicals" stage is a precise, careful process that ensures good reproduction on sign faces and on other graphics. Samples are obtained for each material and color.

While the library is considering whether or not to buy signs, and whether to have them made outside or in house, or a combination of these, thought should also be given to how temporary signs will be made. If possible, temporary signs should repeat the same shapes and styles as the permanent signs, even if the materials differ because of cost and availability. As an example, if most directional signs are 12 inches square and wall-mounted, temporary direction signs also should be 12 inches square, wall-mounted, with the same typeface or a typeface that will be used for all temporary signs. Temporary signs are part of the system of communications and should be considered as serious components of it.

Documentation

The documentation stage consists of preparing working drawings and specifications to ensure that the signs are purchased or made to the design standards, and that future signs can be made the same way. The working drawings describe all dimensions and methods of construction in detail for all types of signs and other graphics, including the materials, layouts, typefaces, sizes, colors, placements, illumination, exceptional conditions and solutions, and how the signs are to be made. Specifications describe the scope of work, materials, colors, conditions for reviewing and accepting samples, and typical signs, maps, and directories, with manufacturing, purchasing, and delivery details, plus mounting data that must be described rather than illustrated (see Fig. 4-7). Lists of the copy for all signs are keyed to site and floor plans and included with the set of working drawings. If signs are purchased from catalogs rather than made especially for the library, the documents consist of detailed purchase orders. Bid documents describe bidding conditions and schedules. The library usually bids on or purchases the signs and other elements with the advice or assistance of the planner/designer, who checks samples and prototypes during purchasing and fabrication and at installation.

Sign Manuals

A sign manual is the single most important control for the continuing success of the sign system. Whereas the working drawings and specifications ensure that all signs are ordered, made, and installed correctly when the system is first implemented, the sign manual provides controls for the future, so the library staff, sign vendors and manufacturers can maintain the system as it was first installed.

The manual is a concise reference, giving definitive instructions about the principles of the system and each of its components. Customarily, it first describes the orientation and direction concepts—if there is color coding, and so on—and then describes each type of sign according to its use, placement, design, and any specifications that will be useful for reordering (see Fig. 4-8).

The *use* of the sign refers to its function. *Placement* refers to the height of the sign from the floor or ceiling, or distance from door frames, and the like. Each type of sign has a standard rule for placement. The shape of the sign is usually drawn as it is to be mounted on the wall, hung from the ceiling, or whatever, with dimensions clearly indicated. The *design* data includes the dimensions and shape of each type of sign, as well as layout, lettering, and colors. Layouts are drawn so that sign makers can see how the words are placed on signs of different sizes, with different lengths and numbers of lines

10E.04   SAMPLES OF MATERIALS

    A.   Submit samples of all materials in accordance with
         requirements of the GENERAL CONDITIONS and SUPPLEMENTARY
         GENERAL CONDITIONS and obtain approval from the Architect
         before ordering materials.

    B.   Materials to be submitted shall include the following
         in minimum size of 5" x 5", and of thickness as
         required by respective items:

         .020" aluminum laminated to 1/4" aluminum with specified
         finishes or 1/16" Micarta laminated to 3/4" resincore with
         specified colors.

    C.   After materials samples are approved submit letter style
         samples as shown on Drawings.

10E.05   DELIVERY AND HANDLING

    A.   All signs furnished under this Section shall be cleaned
         with non-abrasive cleaning agents without damage to sign
         surfaces prior to packaging and delivery.

    B.   All signs and items furnished under this Section shall
         be handled and delivered in a manner that will avoid
         damage.

    C.   Items which become damaged during delivery may be rejected,
         and such items shall be replaced by the sign fabricator
         without additional cost to the Owner.

10E.06   MATERIALS

    A.   Materials: of all signs shall be either "Metalphoto"
         or approved equal or "Graphic Blast Micarta" or approved
         equal as described herein.

    B.   Photo-Sensitized Anodized Aluminum: shall be .020"
         thick sheet of alloy 1100 series, H-14 (half-hard).
         Finish shall be satin finish with horizontal grain lines,
         clear anodized background, and black anodized graphics
         in sizes and styles indicated. "Metalphoto" or approved
         equal sheets shall be laminated to 1/4" thick non-
         corrosive aluminum plate of alloy 6061-T65 or approved
         equal, in sizes indicated. The "Metalphoto" or approved
         equal shall be laminated to the aluminum back up plates
         with "3M" #468 transfer adhesive or approved equal.
         The back up plates shall be blind tapped within 1/16"
         of the face to accept 10/24 stainless steel threaded pins 2"
         long, four (4) pins per sign, provided by manufacturer.
         Edges of laminated aluminum shall be flush, ground
         smooth, and finished with proper grit and radiused corners.

FIGURE 4-7 Sample specification document covers general and specific requirements of contract issued to bidders and vendors.

for each sign; how symbols and arrows appear with and without words; and what the letter size and spacing guidelines are for each category. *Specifications* list materials, mounting details, and special characteristics important to maintain, such as rounded or square panel edges.

The manual is in the form of a book or bound report so that it can be easily stored, retrieved, and reviewed. The illustrations are not as technical and architecturally drawn as the working drawings, and yet they are more specific than the design development drawings of the sign faces. Indeed, they are usually made especially for reproduction in the manual, to be understood by non-

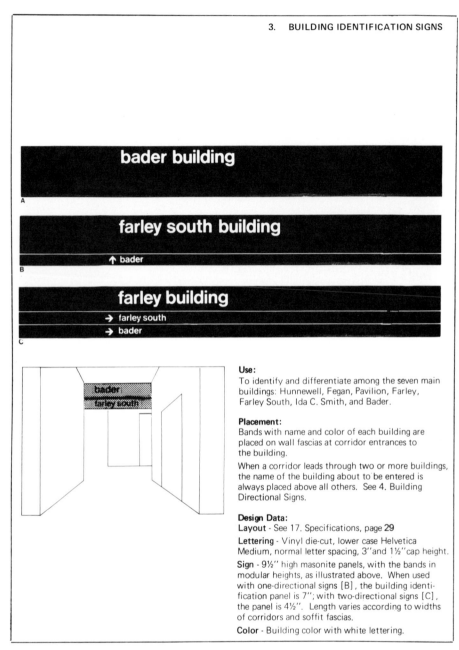

3. BUILDING IDENTIFICATION SIGNS

Use:
To identify and differentiate among the seven main buildings: Hunnewell, Fegan, Pavilion, Farley, Farley South, Ida C. Smith, and Bader.

Placement:
Bands with name and color of each building are placed on wall fascias at corridor entrances to the building.

When a corridor leads through two or more buildings, the name of the building about to be entered is always placed above all others. See 4. Building Directional Signs.

Design Data:
Layout - See 17. Specifications, page 29

Lettering - Vinyl die-cut, lower case Helvetica Medium, normal letter spacing, 3" and 1½" cap height.

Sign - 9½" high masonite panels, with the bands in modular heights, as illustrated above. When used with one-directional signs [B], the building identification panel is 7"; with two-directional signs [C], the panel is 4½". Length varies according to widths of corridors and soffit fascias.

Color - Building color with white lettering.

FIGURE 4-8 This page from a sign manual gives data on each type of sign in the system. (Page numbers and "see" directions in the text refer to other sections of the manual.)

technical people responsible for adding new signs to the system. The need for the manual should be understood and its cost budgeted at the beginning of the project. The manual's value will far exceed the cost of preparing it, for it consolidates in one place all practical information, instructions, and design guidelines to keep the system uniform.

The manual is not prepared until the signs have been ordered and all substitutions and alterations have occurred. Ordinarily, when signs are made to order from working drawings, the manufacturer submits shop drawings to the designer to show how the signs will be made. Since the drawings sometimes show improvements in technique or suggest acceptable alternatives, the designer waits to review shop drawings before producing the manual.

Supervision

Supervision should be planned for both fabrication and installation to ensure the final quality of the system. Many problems can occur during purchasing or bidding, fabrication, shipping, and installation, with numerous substitutions suggested. It is the responsibility of the designer to accept or reject the final products on behalf of the library.

Quality control ensures that small changes and graphic inconsistencies, which would weaken the system, do not occur. Final acceptance should not be given until all signs are correct and in place.

Even when all the processes of planning, designing, and implementing a signage system are undertaken in a logical and coordinated way, the entire system should be reevaluated after it is in use for some time. Since the various stages were evaluated and most of the decisions were tempered by the special conditions of the library, the hope is that the judgments were correct. Through the processes described in this chapter, librarians and designers attempt to create a feeling of reassurance and an appreciation for the signs put up in the public interest. However, no one can be sure of success until people actually walk through the library with a real sense of confidence and ease.

ACKNOWLEDGMENT

Research and illustrations by Madeleine Maxwell.

NOTE

1. Sidney L. Smith, "Color Coding and Visual Search," *Journal of Experimental Psychology* 64 (November 1962): 434.

The Role of the Design Consultant

JOHN KUPERSMITH

Planning a comprehensive sign system, particularly in a large library building where a variety of user needs and use patterns are involved, is very different from simply "putting up signs." Library administrators contemplating such a system should bear in mind that "by definition, a 'good' signage system provides correct information in the proper location, and . . . in a highly interesting and attractive form that is durable, changeable, and above all, readable."[1] The specialized expertise needed to plan graphics that communicate effectively and systematically can be obtained from several sources; in many cases, the most logical alternative is the use of a design consultant. The mere decision to employ a consultant does not, however, guarantee a successful result. To create a truly productive situation, the library administrator must realistically evaluate the expertise and potential uses of a consultant, take responsibility for a careful preplanning and selection process, and foster an open and collaborative relationship with the consultant.

Much useful literature on design consultants and their work is not specific to library situations; this includes articles by Follis, Smith, and others on the process of designing sign systems, and by Topalian on the general question of "design management."[2] The problem of integrating sign design into new construction is dealt with in Langmead and Beckman's account of a library situation and Follis's treatment of sign design in the context of interior planning.[3] The role of design consultants in library sign projects has been discussed by Pollet, and more recently by Kosterman.[4] Two useful treatments of library/consultant relationships, not specific to design consultants, are those by Lockwood and Blasingame.[5] There is a large body of literature regarding library building planning, but readers should note that the term "consultant" as used therein generally refers to a librarian acting as consultant; the discussions of librarian/architect relationships may prove more useful.[6] Finally, for those interested in seeing examples of the state of the art, the architecture and interior design literature includes numerous well-illustrated case studies describing sign systems and environmental graphics produced by noted designers.[7]

SOURCES OF EXPERTISE

Designing a sign system is a complex, multistep process during which the needs of library users must be adequately identified and defined, information must be organized in a hierarchy of importance to meet these needs, effective visual designs must be developed and translated into technical specifications, and fabrication and installation of the system's components must be carefully supervised. The many design decisions that are part of this process call for highly specialized expertise.

In presenting a generalized model for the use of consultants by libraries, James D. Lockwood identifies four possible sources of expertise: existing library staff; a specialist added to the staff; a short-term "critic" assisting the staff with a specific part of a project; or a consultant called in for an entire project.[8] In choosing among these alternatives, the library administrator should carefully consider the advantages and disadvantages of each.

Turning to one's own staff may seem appealing because of possible cost savings, but the large amounts of staff time needed to do the work properly must be taken into account. A more important question is whether the skills of the staff match the demands of the project. Some staff members may have an "art background"—studio art, art history, or perhaps design courses—but may nevertheless lack the practical knowledge and skills to perform the needed tasks. Of course, the staff's close knowledge of library use patterns and user needs will be essential in planning the system.

A second option is adding a graphics specialist to the library staff, thus providing the appropriate and needed expertise on an ongoing basis. However, this option will require a permanent budget line and involve substantial equipment costs.

A short-term critic can be useful in providing assistance with a particular aspect or phase of the project. For example, the library may have the staff available for graphic design, but require technical assistance with questions of structural design or sign materials. An important consideration here is that this option can be successful only when the overall project is properly handled and coordinated by library staff members. Otherwise, unreasonable demands may be placed on the critic, and a lack of unity—in the project and possibly in the finished product—may result. In other words, the short-term services of one or more critics are not a substitute for the comprehensive services a consultant can provide.

This chapter is concerned primarily with the fourth option—the use of a design consultant. Consultants who are trained and equipped to design and implement sign systems usually call themselves "graphic designers" or "environmental graphics designers," but the terminology may vary. They may work individually or as part of graphic design studios, architectural firms, or interior design or space-planning firms. Some sign companies, particularly those with a "systems" philosophy, may employ designers and provide design services as well as sign products.

The advantages of using a design consultant fall into two categories, which might be called technical and political. On the technical side, the authors of a design manual for sign systems advise that "the rational visual organization, precise skills and sensitivity for detail necessary to conceive and produce a successful scheme of any complexity require the services and advice of a professional designer."[9] A properly qualified design consultant can offer the specialized skills and state-of-the-art knowledge that are needed to design an effective system of graphics and to transfer that design into reality. A carefully selected consultant can also offer the library a background of experience in comparable situations, perhaps even in a similar size or type of library. Also, an external consultant, viewing the problem with fresh eyes, may be able to recognize large patterns that are often obscured by day-to-day familiarity.

The political advantages of using a design consultant are no less important. The design process is, in practice, a political process as much as an artistic or technical one. From initial planning to final implementation, such projects usually attract the participation and criticism of a large number of people. This is especially true in libraries, many of which rely on collegial, consultative, or participative management styles. An external consultant, not previously involved with the library staff, can offer an extremely valuable degree of objectivity. Equally desirable, and closely related to objectivity, is the aspect of authority—a design consultant with a good reputation, properly introduced to the staff, can lend form, continuity, and momentum to the design process. These political factors are so important to the success of any sign project that the designer's interpersonal style and skills should be taken into account in the selection stage.[10]

Naturally, there are some risks and potential problems associated with the use of a design consultant. Some consultants, although proficient as designers, may not be accustomed to libraries or aware of their special problems. Therefore, the librarian should select a consultant carefully and be equally careful about the quantity and quality of information he or she receives concerning the problem at hand. Another common difficulty—staff resistance—can arise in a situation in which "everyone fancies himself a sign expert because everyone has made or used signs at one time or another in order to communicate with others."[11] Staff members who are used to do-it-yourself methods may resist what they see as an intrusion by an expensive, jargon-spouting outsider. This problem can be lessened or prevented by making sure that the consultant and his or her role are properly introduced to the staff, and by maintaining open and meaningful communication once the project is under way.

A final problem is cost. A significant part of the total project costs can go for a consultant's services. The crucial fact is, of course, that proper design is not just desirable but essential if the finished product—the sign system—is to function effectively in daily use over a period of years. If the scope of the project is such that a consultant's services are needed, then it may be false economy indeed to avoid using one.

PREPROJECT PLANNING

The groundwork for a successful project is laid in the early stages of planning, when the staff members who will be involved are identified and a problem statement is formulated. Alan Topalian stresses the importance of planning: "When should a designer be introduced into a design project? There is only one sensible answer. The designer should be brought in *after* the client has thought through his problem, has defined his problem in some detail *in writing,* and has come to some decision as to how he will handle the project."[12]

The library's first step in preproject planning should be to create a planning committee that will function throughout the project.[13] This committee—including the library director or a representative, the heads of relevant departments such as reference and circulation, and the building manager—should decide in advance how it will operate and who has the decision-making authority. One of the members—if possible, a volunteer—should be designated to function as liaison with the consultant.

The next step, still preceding the selection of a designer, is to formulate a concise statement delineating the objectives of the desired system by defining the problems—common directional mistakes by users, lack of coordinated signs, incorrect or outdated information on signs—that the project aims at solving. If there are special constraints or conditions, such as an absolute budget limit, a need for vandal-proof signs, or special considerations for the handicapped, these should also be included.

Formulating a problem statement deserves some care on the part of the planning committee. A vaguely worded statement will only create confusion; on the other hand, an overly specific statement, particularly one that goes too far in anticipating solutions to the problem, will be a restriction rather than an aid to the designer. A successful problem statement clearly defines the project and at the same time leaves room for innovative solutions. Then it becomes a useful tool in selecting a consultant as well as in communicating the scope and proposed effects of the project to the rest of the library staff.

If the scope of the project, as shown by the problem statement, indicates that a design consultant is warranted, the planning committee should discuss the specific services needed, the characteristics sought in such a person, and the structure, timetable, and possible fee arrangements of the consulting engagement. These considerations will be important in selecting a consultant and in the subsequent negotiations. Once the groundwork is laid in this way, the selection process can begin.

SELECTING A CONSULTANT

There are several possible sources for locating a design consultant, and it is sensible first to explore those closest at hand. A library that is part of a larger organization, such as a college or university, may well find a consultant within the parent organization, either in a graphics office, publications office, facilities office, physical plant department, or sign shop. In fact, the parent organization's signage policy (if there is one) may require or strongly encourage the use of these in-house services. Academic librarians may also find faculty members in architecture or graphic design departments who can act as consultants or provide referrals.

If no such resources are available, many librarians will solicit word-of-mouth referrals from colleagues who have been involved in similar projects. This method can be very effective if substantive, evaluative comments are sought; whenever possible, the libraries in question should be visited to determine their relevance to the project at hand. Another possibility is to begin one's search by surveying successful sign systems in other types of institutions such as hospitals or airports.

Librarians may contact the professional associations to which designers belong—such as the American Institute of Architects, American Institute of Graphic Arts, Industrial Designers Society of America, Society of Environmental Graphics Designers, or, in some of the large cities, art directors' clubs. Although such organizations may have reservations about recommending one member over another, some offices will provide referrals and assistance. As for published directories, probably the best for use by American libraries is the Yellow Pages of the telephone directory under "Designers," "Graphic Designers," and "Signs."

The next step is to contact the most promising potential consultants to obtain several kinds of information: a list of past projects and clients from the designer's brochure or résumé; an indication of graphic style from the designer's portfolio of photographs or drawings; a sense of work environment and methods from a visit to the designer's office; and valuable information on working style, interpersonal skills, and general ability to "make things happen" from conversations with the designer's past clients, perhaps supplemented by on-site visits. At the same time, the library representative who contacts the designer should be prepared to discuss the intended project and to supply a copy of the problem statement. Interested candidates can then visit the library, discuss the situation in more detail, and submit brief proposals confirming their understanding of the problem, outlining tentative solutions, and giving fee estimates.[14]

The actual selection of a consultant, whether the decision is made by the planning committee or by one individual, should take into account the following factors: the consultant's past experience, including the scope and relevance of problems handled and the aesthetic and practical qualities of solutions reached; the likelihood of a productive working relationship between the consultant and the library staff; and the consultant's grasp of the library's needs, as shown by an expressed understanding of the problem statement or by appropriate suggestions for changes in the definition of, and approach to, the problem.

The hiring of any consultant should be considered final only after the terms of the consulting engagement have been negotiated. Whether expressed in a formal contract or in an exchange of letters of intent, these terms should include scope of the project and problems to be solved, services to be provided by the consultant and any subcontractors, supportive services and information to be provided by the library staff, phase structure of the project, and timetable and fee arrangements for each phase.[15] Fees may be charged on a flat-rate basis for the entire project, a flat rate for each phase, a percentage (which may be 20–40 percent[16]) of fabrication and installation costs, or perhaps a per diem or hourly basis. Design fees should always be considered in relation to the value of the specific services expected; an extremely low bid that includes only partial services is no bargain.

CLIENT AND CONSULTANT ROLES

No design project of any magnitude should be approached as a "one-man job." As Topalian points out, both the client and the consultant have significant responsibilities:

> Ultimate responsibility for the success or failure of design projects always lies with the client. This is true even though the designer has a professional responsibility towards his client. . . . The client contributes to a successful outcome by diagnosing his . . . problem correctly, and by formulating a clear and effective design brief. He contributes by selecting the right designer for the project; by ensuring that the designer gets the necessary co-operation within his organisation—principally, appropriate information and timely decisions—to carry out the work; by preparing his organisation for the implementation of the solution; and by extending the experience gained through the project into other areas of his organisation. In turn, the designer contributes by organising himself to create an effective solution, by formulating an effective solution, by efficiently managing any necessary production, and by helping to create the environment that will accept the proposed design solution.[17]

Each of Topalian's points is relevant to sign projects. During each phase of such a project, the library staff and the consultant interact to produce specific outcomes. Although in each phase the final report is produced by the consultant, the work cannot succeed without the active help and support of the library staff. This collaborative relationship will on occasion require the client to act as the consultant's consultant, providing information and advice.

Besides being hard work, this reversal of roles—or, more correctly, flexible shifting and trading of roles—can cause difficulties in communication if either party resists the process. In a study of architect/client relationships, F. I. Steele cites "blocking of alternatives, narrowing of standards and norms, over-evaluation or too early evaluation (both of ideas and people)," and "defensiveness" as possible hazards. Although some such problems are likely to occur in the course of any project, Steele points out that they can be lessened by a "free flow of communication . . . whether [of] ideas or feelings," by the development of mutual trust, and most fundamentally by both parties displaying "a willingness to take risks" in confronting difficulties and expressing ideas.[18] A shared sense of humor might also be mentioned as a significant element in successful communication.

These interpersonal factors will operate most frequently between the consultant and the library's liaison person, but they will also affect the planning committee and other staff members. As the collaboration between the library and the design consultant moves through the successive phases of the project, the care taken in preproject planning and in the initial meetings will begin to pay significant dividends in terms of well-understood roles, clear objectives, and well-defined information needs.

STRUCTURE OF A SIGN PROJECT

Sign projects can be organized in a number of ways, depending on the manner in which phases are defined.[19] For those considering such a project, the following display presents an appropriate model for libraries, indicating the responsibilities of client and consultant and the desired product of each phase. The project described here involves a relatively full range of services by the consultant and supporting activities by the client; details could be modified to suit individual situations.

Preproject Planning

Client   Identify staff to work on project: planning committee, decision-making authority, liaison person. Prepare problem statement and distribute to library staff. Select and engage a design consultant.

Consultant   Submit proposal indicating understanding of problem and suggesting tentative solutions.

Product   Documents, including proposal and contract or letters of intent, establishing "ground rules" for project.

Phase 1: Research and Problem Analysis

Client   Familiarize consultant with library through tour, meetings with staff, existing user studies. Provide detailed information including correct names of library resources (rooms, collections, departments), location of materials, building plans. Brief consultant on projected changes. Assist consultant in clarifying and organizing this information.

Consultant   Gather additional data as needed, through studies of user behavior and traffic flow, directional problem-solving exercises, photographic inventory of building, and possibly consultation with a behavioral psychologist or other communications specialist. Determine architectural and building code requirements affecting project. Organize information to be presented into a hierarchy of importance.

Product   Consultant's report defining and interpreting problems in detail, describing proposed system in terms of component parts and information to be presented. Sketches and typographical specimens will be helpful at this stage in communicating designer's intentions to library staff.

Review   Planning committee should organize staff review of Phase 1 report, prepare a substantive response defining any problem areas, and discuss this response with consultant.

Phase 2: Schematic Design

Client Re-edit and refine information listed under Phase 1 as necessary, making decisions to eliminate vagueness, ambiguity, or duplication in resource terminology and room numbering. React to rough design concepts as presented by consultant.

Consultant Develop schematic design for all elements of system: signs, graphics, maps, printed materials. Specify visual vocabulary (typography, colors, layout, and other graphic devices) and verbal vocabulary (terminology, syntax, and abbreviations to be used on signs). Discuss rough design concepts with library staff as needed.

Product Consultant's report including: sketches of typical components; photo-montages or drawings showing components in context; full-size mock-ups of some components for testing in the building; preliminary sign schedule (list of signs keyed to locations in the building); resource lists (building directory, location of materials) in final form; indications of sign materials, structures, maintenance needs, and costs.

Review Planning committee should see that Phase 2 report is properly presented to staff, organize staff review, prepare a response, and work out any unresolved design problems with consultant.

Phase 3: Design Development

Client Functions chiefly to review and approve completed designs, specifications, and maintenance manual, the latter with a view to usability by library staff.

Consultant Translate schematic designs into working drawings, specifications, and sign schedule for construction. Produce or arrange for production of floor plans or other artwork. Obtain cost estimates for all parts of system. Prepare maintenance manual.

Product Specification documents suitable for use by sign fabricators and installers. Maintenance manual for future use of library staff in producing elements in house or ordering new or replacement elements from suppliers; should specify graphic standards, structural requirements, and sources of supply.

Review Planning committee should organize a very careful review of these documents.

Phase 4: Fabrication and Installation

Client Determine whether system is to be installed all at once or in phases. Determine method of awarding contract: competitive bidding or negotiated proposals. Work closely with consultant, sharing supervision and giving approval as needed.

Consultant Identify and contact suppliers and contractors, acting as client's representative in negotiations. Supervise fabrication and installation to see that specifications are met by contractors.

Product Sign system installed in library building.

Review Client and consultant should work together in final inspection and approval.

Postproject Evaluation and Maintenance

Client   Conduct studies as desired to determine effectiveness of system and need for modifications. Delegate responsibility to staff members for maintaining system and ensuring that standards are observed.

Consultant Make follow-up visits as needed. Assist library staff in resolving any maintenance problems.

In this design process, the consultant—aided in significant measure by the library staff—functions as a problem solver in three areas: informational, ensuring that the information presented is correct and consistent; visual, ensuring that the signs and other graphics function as a coherent system; and structural, ensuring that the physical elements of the system are adapted to current needs and projected changes. The degree of care and sophistication with which the library staff and the consultant address these problems, and the quality of their collaborative relationship, will determine the eventual success of the sign system in communicating information to library users.

NOTES

1. John Follis, "Vital Signs: Guidelines for Developing a Workable Signing System," *Interiors* 135 (June 1976): 75.

2. Ibid.; Charles N. Smith, "Sign Systems," *Interior Design* 46 (October 1975): 148–153; ISD (Interior Space Designers) Inc., "Campus Graphics: Designing a Campus Signage System," *College and University Business* 47 (November 1969): 79–84; Wayne Kosterman, "Early Involvement of Signage Designer Makes Graphics More Understandable," *Contract* 19 (August 1977): 73–75; and the following five articles by Alan Topalian: "The Why and How of Design Decisions," *Design* 335 (November 1976): 43–45; "First Catch Your Hare . . .," *Design* 341 (May 1977): 36–39; "Design Projects Are Difficult to Manage Because . . .," *Design* 345 (September 1977): 29; "Don't Just Hire the Nice Guy," *Design* 347 (November 1977): 50–51; and "Not Paid to Be Nice Guys," *Design* 348 (December 1977): 44–45.

3. Stephen Langmead and Margaret Beckman, *New Library Design: Guide Lines to Planning Academic Library Buildings* (Toronto: John Wiley and Sons Canada, 1970), especially pp. 66–68, 80–81, 118ff.; Follis, "Vital Signs."

4. Dorothy Pollet, "You Can Get There from Here: New Directions in Library Signage," *Wilson Library Bulletin* 50 (February 1976): 456–462; Wayne Kosterman, "A Guide to Library Environmental Graphics," *Library Technology Reports* 14 (May-June 1978): 287.

5. James D. Lockwood, "Involving Consultants in Library Change," *College & Research Libraries* 38 (November 1977): 498–508; Ralph Blasingame, Jr., "Introduction," in *Directory of Library Consultants,* ed. by John N. Berry III (New York: Bowker, 1969), pp. [ix]–[xiv].

6. See, for example, Dorothy D. Corrigan and Hoyt R. Galvin, "Library Building Consulting: Problems and Ethics," *ALA Bulletin* 62 (May 1968): 505–510; Keyes D. Metcalf, *Planning Academic and Research Library Buildings* (New York: McGraw-Hill, 1965), especially pp. 36–38, 239–258, 313–315; Ernest R. DeProspo, Jr., ed., *The Library Building Consultant: Role and Responsibility* (New Brunswick, N.J.: Rutgers University Press, 1969); and "The Role of the Building-Planning Team," in *Library Buildings: In-*

novation for Changing Needs, Proceedings of the Library Buildings Institute, June 22–24, 1967 (Chicago: American Library Association, 1972), pp. 160–175.

7. James Gutman, "How Campuses Use Signage to Improve Communications," *College and University Business* 47 (November 1969): 85–90; "Sign Program for a University," *Architectural and Engineering News* 10 (June 1968) 58–59; Wayne Hunt and Dave Hammer, "JF&A [John Follis & Associates] for Sea World of Florida," *Industrial Design* 22 (May-June 1975): 60–63; C. Ray Smith, "A Graphic Renovation Earns Dividends," *Industrial Design* 24 (July-August 1977): 44–47; Edward K. Carpenter, "What Goes On Here: Messages in the Environment," *Print* 30 (March-April 1976): 37–49; "This Way In . . . You Are Here . . . This Way Out," *Industrial Design* 19 (May 1972): 68–77.

8. Lockwood, "Involving Consultants in Library Change," p. 500.

9. Crosby/Fletcher/Forbes, *A Sign Systems Manual* (London: Studio Vista, 1970), p. 5.

10. A relevant discussion appears in Topalian, "Don't Just Hire the Nice Guy."

11. Karen E. Claus and R. James Claus, *Signage: Planning Environmental Visual Communication* (Palo Alto, Calif.: Institute of Signage Research, 1976), p. 4.

12. Topalian, "Not Paid to Be Nice Guys," p. 45.

13. Lockwood, "Involving Consultants in Library Change," p. 499. Lockwood's discussion of the planning and selection process has been an extremely useful resource in preparing this section and the following section.

14. Useful discussions of proposals, and consultant selection in general, occur in Lockwood, "Involving Consultants in Library Change," pp. 505–507, and Topalian, "Not Paid to Be Nice Guys," p. 45.

15. For Lockwood's treatment of these "topics of mutual obligation and agreement," see "Involving Consultants in Library Change," pp. 503–505.

16. Follis, "Vital Signs," p. 75; compare Kosterman, "A Guide to Library Environmental Graphics," p. 287.

17. Topalian, "The Why and How of Design Decisions," pp. 44–45. The term "design brief" is equivalent to "problem statement."

18. F. I. Steele, "Interpersonal Aspects of the Architect-Client Relationship," *Progressive Architecture* 49 (March 1968): 132–133.

19. Much of the structure and terminology used in this section is derived from reports and documents prepared by Joel Katz, designer, for the Van Pelt Library, University of Pennsylvania, 1976–1978. For similar materials in the published literature, see: Follis, "Vital Signs"; Smith, "Sign Systems"; ISD Inc., "Campus Graphics," pp. 81–84; Hunt and Hammer, "JF&A for Sea World of Florida," p. 63.

Sign Materials and Methods

WAYNE KOSTERMAN

"I don't care how it's constructed—what will it look like?" The designer's response to this typical question about sign fabrication is that materials and construction methods will often influence the appearance, and always the cost. But materials and methods also affect many other factors, including size, style, color, and changeability of the message; replacement needs (replacements or new units may cost more and take longer to get than the initial quantity order); quality or sharpness of the image; needs of the visually handicapped; and susceptibility to vandalism and weather deterioration (e.g., fading in exposed interior signs caused by the sun's ultraviolet rays). An additional factor to be considered is the in-house fabrication requirements: sometimes library personnel initially will want to order signs from an outside source, then later assemble new or replacement units themselves to match or blend with the outside order.

While the number of methods and materials available to fabricate signs can be very large, the options are usually restricted by cost, availability, or aesthetic considerations.

MATERIALS AND METHODS

Following is an overview of the common material options, their respective advantages and disadvantages, and a summary of the criteria used to narrow the field of choice, based on what the signs are to accomplish. (This chapter is excerpted with permission from "A Guide to Library Environmental Graphics," by Wayne Kosterman, *Library Technology Reports* [May/June 1978].)

Adhesive Film Die-Cut Letters

These extremely thin vinyl or plastic films with adhesive backings are supplied either individually (see Fig. 6-1) or as preassembled words on peel-off carrier tapes ready for application either to a background panel or a wall surface (see Fig. 6-2). The advantage of this type of sign is that it is relatively inexpensive. It is also easy to manufacture and has good crisp images in virtually unlimited color combinations. It can be applied directly to a wall surface, thereby eliminating the cost of an extra panel surface. Reflective and metallic message can be utilized. The letters (or words) should always be tested on the background before placing large orders, since some surfaces, such as vinyl wall coverings, will not accept the adhesive used. They can be ordered with either permanent or less expensive temporary (removable up to one year) adhesive. They can be supplied in a wide variety of standard colors or, for an added fee, in virtually any opaque color supplied as a sample for matching.

Depending on the alphabet selected, letter sizes and symbols can range from $3/8$ inch up to 12 inches, cut from either thermal or steel rule dies. Some alphabets are available from reverse cut dies, which allows mounting to the back side of a transparent surface to reduce vandalism (library hours placed on the inside of a glass door, for example). Some companies will supply die-cutting machines that can be used for in-house production where the library decides that the quantity justifies their use and that the time delay in obtaining them from outside sources is undesirable.

Transfer Letters

These letters are printed in vinyl inks, usually white or black, on the back of a carrier sheet. The letters are then optically spaced one at a time and rubbed on

FIGURE 6-1 Art supply stores and some sign companies carry individual adhesive film die-cut letters like these, which can be stocked in-house. Part of the backing is removed to allow the letter to be slid into position and partially adhered before removing the remainder of the backing. By ordering a small supply of standard-size matte acrylic sign panels, a library can apply letters as needed for relatively inexpensive signs on short notice. Courtesy of Chartpak, Inc.

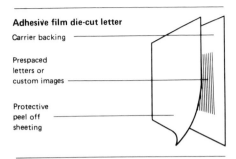

Adhesive film die-cut letter

Carrier backing

Prespaced
letters or
custom images

Protective
peel off
sheeting

Flat letters on 1st surface

Panel surface

Silk screen, vinyl, or
mask and spray
letterform

FIGURE 6-2   Adhesive film die-cut letter.

by burnishing. If used on an exposed surface, they are highly subject to vandalism, and so should be used under a protective cover, or where vandalism is not a factor.

Photographic Film

With the use of a copy camera and a film processor, crisp, photographic-quality letterforms and symbols in either film or paper, and in either positive (black image on clear or white background) or negative (clear or white image against black) form can be produced, either in-house or outside. Some suppliers have plastic carrier frames with snap-in plastic covers in which photographic images can be held (see Fig. 6-3). The paper images (or photostats) can also be dry-mounted to a background panel for temporary signs.

Photographic film inserts can also be used in changeable strip, internally illuminated directories.

Plaque signs can be fabricated using a subsurface photographic matte (no glare) clear image laminated to an acrylic background panel for a high quality, vandal-resistant sign. Silk-screen images produced from photographic film are used to produce flat letters on first, or front, surface when multiple applications of the same image are desirable (see Fig. 6-4).

FIGURE 6-3   Photographic film image, subsurface.
Courtesy of Environmental Graphic Systems, Inc.

FIGURE 6-4 Photographic silk-screened letters allow for excellent image size and color flexibility. The message is generally applied to the underside of cast clear acrylic sheet or to clear vinyl, or it is applied to the outer surface and sprayed with a protective clear epoxy. These methods provide vandalism resistance. Courtesy of Cooper Architectural Signs.

Plastic

Available in a variety of forms, plastic is probably the most widely used sign material. For interior use, acrylic and laminated plastic are the most common. Plexiglas acrylic is available in a variety of colors, including transparent and translucent colors. For in-house use, acrylic panels can be ordered precut with finished edges to provide a standing inventory for the later application of vinyl messages. They can be ordered either matte or gloss, and can be used in their standard colors or sprayed with acrylic paints to match virtually any color. Their advantage over wood is the minimal amount of expensive labor required to finish edges and surfaces. Individual letters can also be either cast or cut out of acrylic for application to walls or acrylic panels.

To increase vandal resistance, the image and message can be applied (by adhesive die cuts or silk screen, for example) to the reverse side of clear

FIGURE 6-5 In hot stamping, the letter colors are fused to satin matte finished acrylic plastic and will not fade or be damaged under ordinary maintenance procedures. Stamping can be used outdoors without fading or being damaged by the elements, but should not be used where subject to surface abrasion. Courtesy of Cooper Architectural Signs.

Foil letter applied
by heat and pressure

Panel
Material

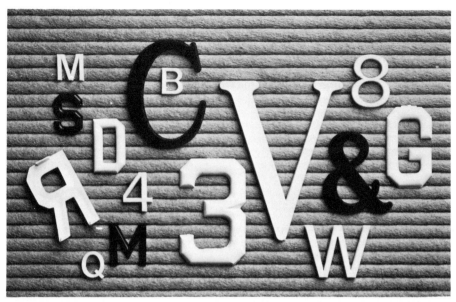

FIGURE 6-6 Cast plastic letters. This is the standard method used for changeable-letter directories, using cast plastic letters in slotted felt. Some suppliers also use slotted rubber or molded plastic backgrounds. These signs are usually housed behind glass to prevent vandalism. Courtesy A. C. Davenport & Sons Co.

acrylic, followed by the background color, making the image subsurface. The brilliance of the image suffers slightly, depending on the thickness of acrylic used. For a more finished look, an acrylic panel can also be mounted within a variety of metal or plastic retainer frames in matching or contrasting colors.

Another method, hot stamping, uses heated brass type, pressure, and colored transfer foil to imprint acrylic plastic. Several alphabets and many colors, including gold and silver, are available as stock items. Stock alphabet sizes normally range from $1/4$ inch to 1 inch (see Fig. 6-5).

Although plastics can be fabricated in other ways, the only other methods applicable for signs are casting, used to produce small letters in mass quantities, primarily for changeable-letter bulletin boards (see Fig. 6-6), or forming, used for interior display letters. Several suppliers now produce a Helvetica-style letter that is more contemporary than the traditional Gothic styles.

Two-color laminated plastic is widely used for engraving. Contrasting colors are laminated together, then the image is engraved through the face to

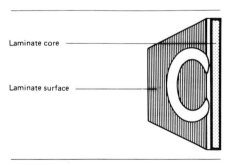

Laminate core

Laminate surface

FIGURE 6-7 Machine engraving uses revolving cutter blades to skim the outer color off a phenolic plastic sandwich, exposing the inside contrasting color. Less scratch-resistant acrylic or any of the sign metals can also be engraved, then filled with white or black enamel.

FIGURE 6-8 Although seldom used, wood is still available for signs such as this. The graphics have been engraved and then painted.

expose the core color. Engraved plaques are relatively vandal resistant and are available in many color combinations. Engraving machines are available for in-house fabrication, using plaque blanks in standard sizes. Engraved messages usually have radius (rounded) corners, a characteristic produced by the revolving cutter blade in single-stroke engraving. Multistroke engraving using small diameter blades can achieve finer details (see Fig. 6-7).

Photographic-quality engraved images can also be produced by a sandblasting technique referred to as "Graphic Blast" (Best Manufacturing Co.).

Wood

Wood is historically one of the oldest and most common sign materials. Plastic and metal, however, are replacing wood for the bulk of interior applications, with the exception of some large custom signs, like donor plaques, where the richness of wood is desired as a surface for engraved, routed, sandblasted, or applied dimensional graphics (see Fig. 6-8).

Metal

Here is an extremely versatile material for sign fabrication. Aluminum is widely used for its nonrusting qualities in exterior signs, and appears in interior use as fabricated boxes or background panels. It can be painted in virtually any color with baked-on enamels, hard-anodized (usually as medium bronze, dark bronze, or black), clad in adhesive films, or finished in its natural white metal color in either satin or polished finish.

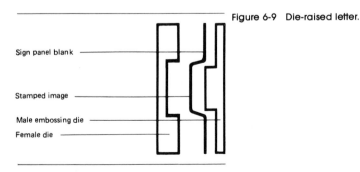

Figure 6-9 Die-raised letter.

Sign panel blank

Stamped image

Male embossing die

Female die

FIGURE 6-10 Clear acrylic strips.

FIGURE 6-11 Movable Inserts.

Bronze and brass are heavier, harder, and more expensive than aluminum and are used for high-quality signs. They can be cast as plaques or sawed from sheets. Yellow brass can also be chrome plated. Messages are cast from molds, engraved, or photoetched. Photoetching gives the truest reproduction, casting the least. Casting is used for sculptured, bas-relief forms. In the areas where metal is removed from the face, whether etched, engraved, or cast, color enamels are often used to fill in letter forms for greater contrast.

Where photographic halftones or other very fine, detailed images must be faithfully reproduced as well as durable, they can be photoetched onto thin aluminum plates and hard coated for virtually indestructible images.

Die-raised letters are produced by pressure stamping sheet metal between a male and a female die of the letterform, leaving the partially sheared letterform raised above the surface. The image produced is quite durable, and can be used for exterior as well as interior applications (see Fig. 6-9).

Another method of producing durable images is silk screening copy on steel panels, then effectively making it subsurface with a porcelain enamel finish.

Changeable signs can be made of various materials. They can be used as inserts which are slid in and out behind clear acrylic strips (see Fig. 6-10), or as movable metal or plastic inserts which can be interchanged without being removed from the frame (see Fig. 6-11). The most common changeable-letter signs are those utilizing cast plastic letters in slotted felt as shown in Fig. 6-6.

FIGURE 6-12 Freestanding, internally illuminated directory displays floor plans and an alphabetized list of destinations. When the button is pushed next to a destination listing, the position of the destination lights up on the map. Courtesy of Brodart.

Special Techniques

Photographic blowups can be used as a display device to generate interest in a specific department or subject area. Color photographs, computer-scanned and reproduced in large scale on many kinds of surfaces by 3M's Architectural Painting technique, might appear as long-term-use visuals for an area. Neon, historically an unlikely candidate, could be used for a striking yet tasteful interior application. Flag nylon or cotton and wool nylon might form colorful banners. Visuals might appear in hand-carved wood, granite, marble, glass, mirror acrylic, or fiberglass. Sound could be combined with visual elements and structures to promote certain departments or equipment, possibly in a push-button, question-and-answer format used in exhibits. Printed communications might be prepared to complement signs, such as smaller, hand-out reproductions of the you-are-here directory map with departments labeled. The free-standing directories can also be internally wired to have alphabetized destinations light up in position on a floor map at the push of a button (see Fig. 6-12).

Image/Method	Material/Surface	Durability	Vandalism resistance	Image detail/quality	Small messages (3/8''–2'')	Large messages (2½''–)	Suitability for low unit run per message (under 5)	Suitability for high unit run per message	Suitability for in-house fabrication	Suitability for in-house assembly	Bright colors	Muted colors	Metallic colors	Suitability for visually handicapped	Relative cost range
1 Adhesive film die cut letter	1st (front) surface acrylic, glass	2	4	2	2	2	1	3	2	1	1	1	1	4	Low
2 Adhesive film die cut letter	Subsurface	1	1	3	2	2	1	3	3	2	1	1	1	5	Low
3 Transfer (rub down) lettering	Any smooth surface	4	5	2	1	4	1	5	1	1	2	5	5	5	Low
4 Transfer (rub down) lettering	Subsurface	2	1	3	1	4	1	5	2	2	2	5	5	5	Low
5 Photographic film image	Subsurface	1	1	1	1	2	3	1	5	5	3	2	5	5	High
6 Photographic silk screened letter	1st surface	2	2	1	1	1	4	1	4	3	1	1	2	5	Low-high
7 Photographic silk screened letter	Subsurface	1	1	2	2	1	4	1	4	3	1	1	2	5	Med.-high
8 Cut plastic dimensional letter	1st surface acrylic or wall	2	4	3	3	2	2	4	4	2	1	2	4	2	Med.
9 Cast plastic letter	1st surface acrylic or wall	2	4	3	2	4	2	3	5	2	1	2	3	1	Low
10 Foil hot stamped letter	Acrylic	2	3	3	2	5	2	3	5	5	3	3	1	4	Low-med.
11 Formed plastic letter	Wall surface	2	3	2	4	1	1	2	5	2	1	1	4	2	Med.
12 Photo-mask sand blasted letter	Phenolic plastic sandwich	1	1	1	2	1	3	2	5	5	2	3	3	3	High
13 Cut metal letter	1st surface metal or wall	1	3	2	2	1	2	4	4	2	3	3	1	2	High
14 Cast metal letter	1st surface metal or wall	2	2	2	4	1	2	3	5	4	3	3	1	1	High
15 Machine engraved message	Phenolic plastic sandwich	1	2	4	2	5	1	3	2	2	1	2	5	4	Low-med.
16 Machine engraved message	Bronze, brass	1	1	3	2	5	2	3	4	4	4	3	1	5	High
17 Photo engraved message	Aluminum	1	2	1	1	3	4	2	5	5	4	3	1	4	High
18 Die raised letter	Aluminum	1	2	3	4	2	2	3	5	5	1	1	1	3	Med.
19 Photo screened letter	Porcelain enameled steel	1	3	2	2	2	3	2	5	5	1	1	2	5	High

1 Excellent
2 Good
3 Average
4 Below average
5 Not recommended

FIGURE 6-13   Method Selection Chart. To use the chart first determine the considerations (shown vertically) that are most appropriate to the project needs; then refer to the horizontal row for fabrication methods with the most favorable rating.

Fiber optics can create silently changing, illuminated color images to attract visitors to specific subjects such as biography or the physical sciences.

Some libraries, whether due to size, available budgets, or other reasons, will never need to implement components beyond the simplest hardware presented earlier for their needs. For others who are able to do more, the environmental graphics concepts listed above provide at least a partial picture of the methods available (see also Fig. 6-13) to make a facility more usable and interesting to its audiences.

The Language of Signs

BARBARA S. MARKS

When Humpty Dumpty told Alice that a word "means just what I choose it to mean," he was not as cavalier as he sounded. He expected Alice to understand him. For words are units of language that function as carriers of meaning, and meaning must be interpreted. Only then does communication take place.

Library signs are a form of communication. They help those unfamiliar with libraries or with the resources and architectural idiosyncrasies of a particular library, and they help the staff by reducing the number of repetitious informational questions.

In speech we address people whom we know or about whom we know enough to make ourselves intelligible, for even strangers offer clues that enable us to communicate with them. Instinctively a speaker attunes language to the audience, varying the vocabulary in accordance with assumptions about levels of knowledge, simplifying it when talking to young children or to those whose grasp of English is limited.

Speech has the advantage of being interactive, providing the opportunity of finding out if the words chosen carry the intended meaning. The hearers' reactions indicate if they understand, and both to be sure and to reassure themselves, speakers pepper speech with "you know what I mean?" and "in other words," and "what I am trying to say."

Audiences for letters, reports, term papers, minutes, or professional publications are also known—people with whom the writer is acquainted or who have similar interests, who speak the same language. In writing, as in speech, one can repeat and summarize. But signs permit no such luxuries.

SIGNS AS COMMUNICATION

As conveyors of quick information, signs must be economical of time and space. They must communicate to an audience of whom nothing is known except that it is very likely composed of all ages, backgrounds, and educational levels.

In spite of such problems, libraries have always had signs even if limited to those that said QUIET. As library collections grow in size and complexity and shrinking staffs cope with ever-changing and often larger user populations, more signs and more sophisticated signs become increasingly essential.

Signs give visibility to names or designations (REFERENCE ROOM) or to concepts (OPEN MONDAY THROUGH SATURDAY). Signs may inform (PUBLIC TELEPHONES DOWNSTAIRS), direct (TURN LEFT), warn (EMERGENCY EXIT ONLY), or set limits (EATING IS NOT PERMITTED). They answer unspoken questions (LIBRARY OFFICE—SECOND FLOOR), thus supplying an information need, or they may provide unsolicited information that users did not know they would need or want (LECTURE SERIES BEGINS NOVEMBER 15).

How and why words function as instruments of communication is not fully known, and finding the right words is a combination of testing and luck. I discovered the magic of the precise word when teaching an eighth-grade class how to take notes. After sternly warning them that copying is plagiarism, I said, "Read a paragraph and write down the ideas in it." Blank faces greeted me. With a sudden inspiration I added, "Make a *list* of the ideas." There was a stir of comprehension, a flash as though lights had been turned on behind two dozen pairs of eyes. They got the message.

Copywriters are advised to write to the sixth-grade level because simple language is not resented by educated people and is the only kind most people understand. The library staff will know quickly if the signs are not effective (assuming them to be well-printed, well-placed, and not too numerous), for people will continue to ask the same questions that the signs were designed to answer, and will ask them just as often. They will even ask to have the signs explained.

It is unwise to commit oneself to a permanent format until sure of the wording. Expensive signs are not replaced quickly even when they are unclear or have errors. I wince each time I see a handsomely engraved plaque in my library that says A GIFT BY THE SOCIETY FOR THE LIBRARIES. I had convinced the society's board that it should be replaced using THE GIFT OF or GIVEN BY until we discovered that a new sign would cost $100. The solecism will remain.

Sign making has not been included in library school curricula, so without knowledge or experience, how does the novice go about formulating signs that will get the necessary messages across to an unknown audience? Copywriters may be born with the ability to write pithy, effective messages. Experience sharpens their skills, and, besides, they work at it full time. Those of us whose talents lie elsewhere and who are pressed for time without sign making have something of a problem.

One can, however, benefit from experience as a sign user by reading what the copywriters have written; watching the commercials on television; reading ads, especially on billboards, and newspaper headlines; looking closely at signs on the street, in shops, and in public buildings; and taking a new look at what is already in the library. By analyzing the signs that work to determine what makes them work and thinking about those that do not, one can avoid the same pitfalls. In addition, one should allow sufficient time to write out the sign in several different ways and return to it the next day or, better yet, a few days later. The best one or two should be shown to others—not just other librarians—for their opinions. When a decision has been made, the sign may be put before the public, preferably in temporary format, even if it is still messy and amateurish.

SIGNS AS PUBLIC RELATIONS

Signs are a form of public relations. Librarians are selling libraries, library resources, and services as surely as General Foods is selling Jello. If what must be said is said well, a good selling job is done. Consumers who are displeased with one brand of soap will try another. Disaffected library users are not likely to have that option.

Helping people to be self-directed is good public relations, since few are sufficiently self-assured that the need to ask questions causes no twinges. Most people dislike revealing ignorance and may even resent the necessity of doing so. By installing signs, librarians spare people this discomfort, but may reinforce their insecurity if the signs fail to inform or direct. Unless the readers are pathologically humble, they will rightly blame the library staff, not themselves, for the failure to communicate. Some may even be irritated at the staff for putting them at a disadvantage. Puzzling signs are unfriendly and so are signs with insufficient information, such as REST ROOMS ON FLOOR B. Which is Floor B? How does one get there? In a sense such a sign compounds the problem, for if there were no sign at all, one could more easily just ask for the rest room.

What words and combinations of words will convey to library users the messages that need visibility? There are rules, of course. Successful messages have clarity, simplicity, brevity, and specificity. The literature of advertising endorses these rules, and research in advertising, psychology, and linguistics has confirmed them. The greater the informational clarity, the greater the obtained compliance. The level of difficulty of the message has a significant impact on its ability to convey meaning. People tend not to read long messages. And, finally, specific directions (PLEASE PUT TRASH IN THIS BASKET) are followed better than those that are vague (PLEASE DO NOT LITTER).

IS THE MESSAGE CLEAR?

Presumably, habitual sign-users should have no trouble composing their own signs, but the ability to use signs evidently does not automatically carry with it the ability to create clear messages. The world is full of confusing, inadvertently amusing, and sometimes downright incomprehensible signs. Many are memorable only because of their absolute failure to achieve their intent, and some of these are in libraries.

I am indebted to *The Times* (London) for some choice specimens, which no doubt were models of clarity to those who conceived them, but have subsequently caused some confusion.*

WAITING LIMITED TO 60 MINS IN ANY HOUR
HOT MEALS DELIVERED OR TAKEN AWAY
PARKING ALLOWED ONLY ON BOTH SIDES OF THIS ROAD

As an example of utter incoherence, we have

CATTLE AND CALVES
←—TURN RIGHT
PIGS STRAIGHT ON

(Of this last one, *The Times* commented that it was a pity to confuse the sense of direction of cattle who had bothered to learn to read.)

Lest anyone think that confusing messages are limited to the United Kingdom, here are two from very respectable East Coast libraries. One may be apochryphal, but I have been told on good authority of a student in a large university library who went to the front door of the building after seeing a card in the catalog that read "See Main Entry." The other I saw myself as I entered an urban public library, where on top of a catalog cabinet I saw NEW CLASS BOOKS. Momentarily I was completely mystified. New *class* books? Textbooks? In a public library? Oh! a new classification system! My four companions were equally bewildered. If five experienced librarians were confused, what must have been the effect of these words on library patrons? What should that sign have said? I have toyed with that one ever since, and it is one of the problems that makes me envy the copywriter who merely has a furniture sale to worry about. (OUR NEW BOOKS HAVE A NEW NUMBERING SYSTEM or NEW BOOKS WITH A NEW NUMBERING SYSTEM IN THIS CATALOG or DEWEY IS OUT—LIBRARY OF CONGRESS IS IN or NEW BOOKS = NEW NUMBERS?)

Under any circumstances, clear, concise English is not easy to write, but somehow library messages are especially difficult. For example, if book trucks are put near the stacks to encourage library users to put the books on the trucks rather than back on the shelves, what do you say so they will comply? PLEASE RETURN BOOKS TO TRUCKS. PLEASE DO NOT RESHELVE BOOKS—PUT THEM HERE. PLEASE PUT BOOKS HERE WHEN YOU HAVE FINISHED USING THEM. None of these is good, but what would be satisfactory? (How often should "please" be used? It becomes meaningless after a while, and sometimes seems to be used for self-gratification to make sure that everyone knows we have nice manners.)

Words are the instruments used to convey meaning, but many words have several definitions. *Will* is power, desire, and a legal declaration. *Game* may be an amusement or wild animals. *Class* and *entry* also have more than one mean-

*From 1972 through 1976, the weekday column "Diary" published snapshots, contributed by readers of *The Times*, of absurd signs. Nearly all were reproduced without comment.

ing. Communication is not the delivery by one person to another of a substance called "meaning," but a relationship between or among people. When different meanings are imputed to identical words by the sender and the recipient of a message, misunderstandings occur.

Usually we depend on the context to provide the particular meaning intended, but sometimes even the context fails. Words also have connotations and imply meanings beyond their dictionary definitions.

A colleague once brought me a large sign stating that the library would be open during the Christmas recess, but that VISITORS WILL NOT BE SERVICED. I rejected it on the spot. My colleague was astonished until I explained delicately that my experience with farm animals made the verb unacceptable. The double entendre had never occurred to him. In a Colorado library the directions for using a fire extinguisher were provocative: TO PLAY TURN BOTTOM UP. Back in the days when certain books were locked in the office, one library's catalog had a card saying, "Sex—see librarian." Sometimes the context itself causes the problem: LIVERPOOL MATERNITY HOSPITAL (NONACCIDENT). Obviously words relate to each other and meaning can be affected by juxtaposition, with unforeseen results: BEWARE—EXTREME DANGER—CHURCH ENTRANCE AHEAD, and DANGER—SCHOOL CHILDREN ROUND THE BEND. These examples contributed by readers of *The Times* should convince us, like the drivers to whom they were addressed, to go slowly.

NEW CLASS BOOKS and MAIN ENTRY are library jargon. The difficulty with much library language is not that it is loaded with arcane terms, but that it uses familiar words in a special way. A library clerk reported that on her first day on the job she was asked to fetch a truck. She was baffled. A *truck*? Inside the building? On the second floor? It had never occurred to her supervisor to call it a book truck. Although Webster does admit the use of the word for "any of various wheeled devices used for moving loads," the average person reserves the term for large motor vehicles found on streets and highways.

Webster's first meaning for *catalog* is the library's use of the word, but for the general public its most common meaning is the publication of a mail-order house. The publications of academic institutions which describe course offerings are also called catalogs. In one library, staff who assist people at the desk next to the card catalog, known as the catalog desk, are quite accustomed to getting telephone requests from those who want a copy of the catalog of one or another of the university's schools. Most people know what a library catalog is, but it cannot be assumed that everyone does.

REFERENCE and RESERVE are frequently confused. Can it be because both words begin with the same two letters? Is it because reference books are always "on reserve" and cannot be borrowed? CHARGE OUT, the innocuous sign found in many libraries, brings forth visions of leaving the building on a prancing steed, complete with lance and flying pennants. CIRCULATION may have anatomical connotations.

Once a decision on a term is made, that term should be used consistently. Librarians tend to use words interchangeably. Books are not only charged out and circulated, they are also checked out, lent, and borrowed. Publications are serials, periodicals, magazines, or journals. The catalog is also the card catalog, the public catalog, and sometimes the union catalog. Some terms are ill-defined and vary from library to library. "Public services," for example, is a catchall term that may or may not include circulation, interlibrary loan, and reserve. But the profession's fuzziness should not stop individual librarians from making terminological decisions. If a staff member says "periodicals" and the sign says "journals," the patron may be thoroughly confused. In truth, if someone says "washrooms," the directional sign says "rest rooms," the signs on the doors say "women" and "men," people will probably not notice and will get there just the same. But librarians should be consistent with library language.

Multisyllabic words can cause confusion in signage. Connecticut's highways are well supplied with signs stating: CROSSING MEDIAN DIVIDER PROHIBITED. A high school teacher in that state reports that her students were surprised to learn that all that verbiage means nothing more than NO U TURN. On a family swimming expedition as a child, I raced ahead of my parents only to return with the statement that we could not use that beach. "A large sign," I declared, "says PRESBYTERIANS ONLY—VEGETARIANS NOT ALLOWED." My somewhat startled elders found upon inspection that it actually said PEDESTRIANS ONLY—VEHICLES NOT ALLOWED. Why not NO CARS? For the very young and for those whose schooling has been limited, Latinate words are either not understood at all or, as in my case, so confused with others that the meaning is thoroughly distorted. I was told of a sign in the Ritz Carlton Hotel in Boston that reads THIS IS NOT AN EGRESS. The Ritz has forgotten that P. T. Barnum counted on people's *not* knowing that word so that he could move crowds out.

In my own library a proposal for a sign to be posted on the desk near the card catalog to say INFORMATION—DIRECTIONAL AND CARD CATALOG was revised in the nick of time. What is now in place reads simply LIBRARY INFORMATION. Not long ago I was stopped in my tracks by a new sign on top of a catalog adjacent to the rest of the catalog. This cabinet has always held author cards for dissertations, arranged by year. What I beheld was:

RECENT ARABIC BOOKS
AUTHOR/TITLE CATALOG ONLY
SEE MAIN CATALOG FOR FULLY CATALOGED MATERIALS
ALSO NYU DISSERTATIONS

What *I* understood at first was not much. What must have been the effect on library users? I am happy to say that this gibberish (which referred to PL480 books and cards) was removed forthwith.

Obviously no perpetrator of ridiculous signs is malevolent, nor are there culprits. Such horrors happen out of haste, ignorance, or lack of forethought. A good solution is to give one person responsibility for all library signs, thereby reducing the risk of semantic inconsistencies. With experience comes awareness of potential meaning—or the lack of it.

A colleague once apologized for the length of his letter, explaining in a postscript that he did not have time to make it shorter. Length is easier. Compression requires time and effort, but they are well worth it. The longer the sign, the more it costs, but more important is the fact that the human span of attention is limited. In any case, few people have the time—or are willing to take the time—to read more than a few words. Most signs should be capable of being absorbed in passing. Standing in front of a sign to study its message is a public confession of ignorance, acceptable perhaps in a hospital or an office building, but somehow less so in a library. A subtle psychological factor operates here. It is all right to admit unfamiliarity with most public buildings. One is not expected to know where surgery is or on what floor to find the insurance company's office. These are somehow respectable gaps in one's fund of information. But many people hesitate to admit ignorance about libraries, as though they should have been born knowing where to find the science books. Reference librarians are familiar with this diffidence: "I've never used *this* library before" and "I'm sorry to bother you." Some of this could be ascribed to the awesome image of libraries and librarians, which library personnel have been trying to overcome in recent decades. Some of it, however, stems from the feeling that to confess ignorance in a library is to confess a kind of socially unacceptable illiteracy.

Thus, brevity has significance, not only as a time-saver but also as a face-saver. Let librarians be kind and helpful and provide signs that can be read at a glance, leaving out unnecessary parts of speech. Signs do not have to contain complete sentences. MUSIC—SECOND FLOOR is quite sufficient. The words "is on the" are implied. That one is fairly obvious, but how much detail is needed? And at what point? Should it be MUSIC AND MICROFILM—SECOND FLOOR or MUSIC SECOND FLOOR EAST—MICROFILM SECOND FLOOR WEST? Perhaps it is better to use the shorter sign on the main floor and post one on the second floor that reads

MUSIC EAST ⟶
⟵ MICROFILM WEST

Since it is not known exactly how much people can absorb in a short time, the aim should be not to overload.

Traffic signs are masterpieces of brevity—sometimes overdone. PED X ING is brief, but when the driver finally realizes what that means, it may be too late. GO SLO has been defended as attention-getting. (In Texas one effort reads SPEED LIMIT 29 MPH. Why 29? Because 30 is ignored.) Very near my home is a sign under yellow lights that fills me with indignation each time I pass it: YOU ARE SPEEDING WHEN FLASHING. I am invariably moved to respond, "I am *not* flashing!" In all fairness, however, I have been unable to think of a five- or even six-word replacement. Grammatical and orthographical perfection can be sacrificed for speed, but I doubt if libraries, as educational institutions, will wish to promote linguistic sacrilege.

Even short messages convey tone. Signs should be in character not only with the weight and nature of the message, but with the atmosphere of the library. Signs should be as inviting as greeting people with a smile, and should accentuate the positive. SMOKING ONLY IN LOUNGE is preferable to NO SMOKING EXCEPT IN LOUNGE. Especially attractive are the signs in Washington Square Park inviting New Yorkers to:

WALK RUN PLAY
PICNIC ON THE GRASS
PLAY MUSICAL INSTRUMENTS UNTIL 10 PM
RIDE BIKES IN THE CENTRAL PLAZA
PLEASE KEEP YOUR DOG ON A LEASH

Restrictions have been listed below these attractions and are restrained, merely requesting that dogs and wheeled vehicles be kept off the grass, that alcohol not be used, and that loud amplified sound be avoided. How nice it would be to have a library sign saying:

READ BROWSE RELAX
LISTEN TO MUSIC
WATCH FILMS
BORROW BOOKS

Of course, there is such a thing as being too restrained. In Boston and Cambridge many years ago, the lawns had small, low signs that said just PLEASE. They were so polite and inconspicuous that they were for the most part ignored.

How formal or informal signs are depends on the atmosphere of the library, the character of the message, its location, and the permanence of the sign. Colloquialisms that would be quite out of place in a stately structure might be entirely appropriate in a neighborhood branch library. What is posted in the young adult room can be different from what is at the main entrance. On the whole, humor and breeziness should be reserved for temporary signs, for the informal situations to which they are suited, or for exhibits or notices of forthcoming events. The note of folksiness will pall and even irritate after awhile.

Negatives should be saved for situations that require them, such as NO STROLLERS ON ESCALATORS or DANGER—MACHINERY. Certainly a threatening tone should be shunned no matter what depravities one is trying to stop. Stern warnings will not deter the determined vandal. It is better to say PLEASE USE PHOTO-COPYING MACHINES—ONLY 5¢ PER PAGE and hope that the appeal to the pocketbook will do the trick. It takes very little ingenuity to rip the pages from a book out of the sight of the library staff, so threats are futile. They may even make you look foolish. The toll booths in the New York City area are decorated with signs that are a good example of the empty threat: COUNTERFEIT MONEY WILL BE CONFISCATED. That probably means you will not get change for a phony bill, but it still prompts a smile. And this raises another point. Dire warnings addressed to the law-abiding are an affront to them.

Finally, wording should be sure, not tentative or equivocal. In New York State, road signs say FALLING ROCKS, so drivers make a hasty exit to avoid being bashed. Nearby in Pennsylvania, the risky areas are marked FALLEN ROCKS, so drivers slow down to pick their way carefully. It hardly seems possible to ascribe the difference to a variation in geological conditions. The moral is that sign makers must know in advance how they want people to act after reading the messages. If they are uncertain, the signs will surely confuse their readers.

The arrangement of the words has great importance. To begin at the beginning is hard enough when writing a report, an essay, or even a formal letter. The difficulty is even greater when it comes to signs. With only a few words there is less flexibility, so determining the best order might be thought easier. But what is the beginning in a simple message, such as that the library will be closed on July 4? There are three elements: the library, the closing, and the date. Presumably the most important of these should come first, as an eyecatcher. Which is the most important: the library? the closing? the date? If the sign is in the library, one would consider that the least important, but if the library adjoins the police or fire department, as some do, then the word "library" would have significance. Should one say CLOSED JULY 4 or JULY 4—CLOSED or NOT OPEN JULY 4?

The order in which words are set down does affect the meaning. Reported to *The Times* was a sign in Pakistan: PLEASE SLOW BUMPY ROAD UNDER CONSTRUCTION. And from Africa: RHINOS PLEASE REMAIN IN YOUR VEHICLES. The only way to get around either one is to rearrange the words: BUMPY—PLEASE SLOW—ROAD UNDER CONSTRUCTION, and PLEASE REMAIN IN YOUR VEHICLES—RHINOS. A local emporium advertises: HAVE A CUP OF COFFEE AND ROLL DOWNSTAIRS. From Canada there is EAT HERE GET GAS, and, from the *New York Times* as seen in the Hayden Planetarium: TO SOLAR SYSTEM AND REST ROOMS. There seems to be no way to rearrange that one. Two signs are needed to avoid combining the sublime and the ridiculous.

More than one sign may be preferable for another reason. Two or more may prevent the overload that might occur when too much information is squeezed into one. By separating dissimilar or incompatible messages, the chances of having the second (or third) receive attention are improved.

Small warning: the words (and the size of the lettering) must fit the space available, lest the sign resemble that in a university library regarding the availability of temporary storage facilities for coats, but installed in a frame slightly too small. The message therefore reads HECKROOM ON THIS FLOO.

A check should be made from time to time to make sure of continuing accuracy. Has something been changed? Moved? And do the signs still say what they did when they were originally installed? One posted over *Psychological Abstracts* to advertise the availability of on-line service had said: MORE MONEY THAN TIME? ASK ABOUT OUR COMPUTER SEARCH SERVICE. Somewhere along the line the question mark disappeared. The sign now reads: MORE MONEY THAN TIME ASK ABOUT OUR COMPUTER SEARCH SERVICE. Quite another kettle of fish.

So much for caveats. Although knowing what to watch for and what to watch out for can help, there is no easy way, no magic formula. Wording should be brief, clear, simple, and specific. The sign makers should take their time, test, and try again. Practice may not make perfect, but it helps. Semiology is the science or art of signs. Anyone who has struggled to put the right words together in the right sequence, who has suffered to make words work, knows that there is precious little science. Like the art of librarianship, signs require a happy blend of interest, intuition, and common sense.

Signs for the Handicapped Patron

HYLDA KAMISAR

Any design for a library guidance system should consider the needs of handicapped patrons. Until recently, designers of libraries and other public service institutions have demonstrated little awareness of the difficulties that handicapped people encounter when they try to use facilities and services that were set up—as is usually the case—to answer only the needs of the average person.

Integrating disabled citizens into the mainstream of society has been a long held but largely unrealized goal. Handicapped people make up perhaps the last minority group to demand redress for past actions and omissions that amount to outright discrimination. The passage of some federal laws, chiefly in the areas of education and vocational rehabilitation, has supported these demands for an end to discriminatory practices. Most significant for libraries was the 1977 regulation pursuant to Section 504 of the Rehabilitation Act of 1973. Section 504 states that "no otherwise qualified handicapped individual in the United States, shall, solely by reason of his handicap, be excluded from the participation in, be denied the benefits of, or be subjected to discrimination under any program or activity receiving Federal financial assistance."[1] This regulation extends to all units of state or local governments and any activity or program those governments support financially.

Given the scope of the federal presence in library services, hardly any program or facility would fall outside the sweep of this regulation. One immediate consequence is a widespread concern for eliminating architectural barriers. The literature on this subject is approaching flood tide; however, little of it reflects the significance of signage as an extension of architectural design. Serious research on signage as it affects the handicapped is clearly lacking.

Two basic sources of information on standards and specifications for environmental modifications are published by the American National Standards Institute[2] (sponsored by the Department of Housing and Urban Development) and the General Services Administration.[3] (A revision of the Institute's standards is underway.) While neither publication deals extensively with signage per se, they do establish general guidance principles. In the absence of a single national standard for building modification, several state bodies have published their own guidelines; Illinois[4] and New York[5] are good examples.

When one designs a signage system to suit handicapped patrons, three major groups must be kept in mind: (1) the visually handicapped, ranging from those with some sight impairment to the totally blind, (2) the hearing impaired, and (3) persons in wheelchairs and those with other serious mobility limitations.[6] Since hearing impaired and physically handicapped persons have little problem reading conventional signs, most modifications in library guidance systems will be for the benefit of the visually handicapped.

A DESIGN CHECKLIST

Following is a checklist of major design elements to be considered when developing a total guidance system. It may not be practical or necessary to adopt every element or to implement them simultaneously.

1 Sign placement to provide maximum visual exposure, particularly along routes of travel

2 Large size, sans serif typefaces

3 High color contrast between characters and background

4 Glare-free sign surfaces

5 Consistent pattern in shape, size, and placement of signs

6 No sharp edges or exposed fasteners on signs

7 No signs that present hazards, e.g., those that project into space or are placed on the floor

8 Clear, brief room identification signs, using raised letters or numerals in combination with tactile markings

9 Audible signals in elevators to indicate direction of movement

10 Floor designations in elevators in raised numerals (use of braille should be limited to a few letters or numerals to identify facilities such as rest rooms and elevators; in this context, braille characters should appear in combination with large print or raised letters or numerals[7])

11 Alarm systems that combine visual and audible signals

FIGURE 8-1   Symbol of Access.

12 A general brochure in large print, braille, and on tape, introducing patrons to library facilities

13 A tactile orientation map of public service areas

14 Tactile cues on walking surfaces to indicate approaches to stairs and ramps or to designate the locations of special features, and such aids as knurled door knobs or handles to indicate entrances to areas not open to the public

15 Telephone intercom systems on all floors to minimize travel from one service area to another

16 Colored signs or stripes on all-glass doors

17 Handrails on both sides of stairways and in long corridors

18 Display of the International Symbol of Access in libraries that provide accessible entrances, elevators, rest rooms, water fountains, and telephones, even though some areas, such as book stacks, may not be accessible (Fig. 8-1).[8]

Existing guidelines are not in complete agreement on precise specifications and measurements in designing signage for the handicapped. The most widely cited recommendations are: (1) white lettering on a black background, (2) Helvetica typeface, (3) raised letters and numerals at least 1 inch high and extending $1/32$ inch from their background, (4) wall signs mounted 54 inches to 66 inches from the floor, and (5) tactile cues on walking surfaces at least 2 feet wide and consisting of strips or grooves $1/8$ inch in height or depth, spaced 1 inch apart.

The Chicago Public Library's branch for the blind and physically handicapped displays an innovative application of tactile cues. The circulation counter consists of a series of dips and curves, each change in contour signaling the location of a service area and a library staff member. An indentation in the lower part of the counter enables a person in a wheelchair to move out of the line of traffic (Fig. 8-2).

Considering the special needs of handicapped patrons will quite probably result in good design for the general population also. For example, large-size lettering, high color contrast, and consistency in shape and placement of signs

FIGURE 8-2   Interior view of the Illinois Regional Library for the Blind and Physically Handicapped,
Chicago, shows the circulation counter and 165-foot window, which echoes the counter's curves.

are features to be incorporated into any effective guidance system.[9] Extra
costs can be held to a minimum by combining special design features for the
handicapped with those of the basic system. Participation in the planning
stage by handicapped individuals and groups in the community can help librarians focus on the most important problems and achieve practical, economical solutions that will benefit all users.

NOTES

1. PL 93-112. U.S., Congress, House, *Rehabilitation Act of 1973*, 93rd Cong., H.R.
8070, September 26, 1973.

2. American National Standards Institute (ANSI), *American Standard Specifications for
Making Buildings and Facilities Accessible to, and Usable by the Physically Handicapped* (New York: ANSI, 1961).

3. U.S. General Services Administration, Public Buildings Service, *Design Criteria: New
Public Building Accessibility* (Washington, D.C.: 1977).

4. Illinois, Capital Development Board, *Accessibility Standards Illustrated* (Springfield:
1978).

5. New York, State University Construction Fund, *Architectural Accessibility for the Disabled of College Campuses* (Albany: 1976).

6. No accurate data exist on the number of handicapped persons in the United States. Five percent of the total population is a conservative estimate. The visually handicapped number approximately two million.

7. Only 10–15 percent of the blind population reads braille.

8. In several states, legislation has been passed regarding use of the symbol in buildings constructed with public funds, and laws generally specify criteria for accessibility. Details on the required design, size, and placement of the symbol itself can be found in the booklet *People Are Asking About . . . Displaying the Symbol of Access*, available from the President's Committee on Employment of the Handicapped, Washington, D.C. 20210.

9. The possible need for compromise among the special requirements of user groups is mentioned in Chapter 4, pp. 55–56 [Eds.].

Symbol Signs for Libraries

LAWRENCE J. M. WILT   JANE MAIENSCHEIN

Nonverbal signs, when used properly, offer advantages over verbal signs. They convey their messages more effectively and efficiently and can introduce a simplicity that is aesthetically more pleasing than words alone.[1] When used improperly, however, symbols are confusing and, at worst, can suggest the wrong messages. Therefore, the problem for librarians who wish to incorporate symbols into sign systems is to determine when they are appropriate and to coordinate efforts that will ensure an effective standardized system.

The appropriateness of symbols in library signage depends on the needs of each particular library. For a very small facility, such as a shopping mall minilibrary, symbols may not offer any advantage since the library probably needs few signs. But a large departmentalized university library frequented by foreigners could obviously benefit from an effective symbol system. Librarians must not accept pat solutions for signage problems, but must apply general principles of effective signage to their own circumstances, taking into account the nature of their libraries, patron needs, size, layout, and other factors.

SYMBOLS AND THEIR USE

Symbol signs are potentially useful in any situation for which signs are needed. such as for direction, identification, and instruction. (See Chapter 4 for a detailed discussion of these categories.) When they are easily recognized, symbol signs present their intended messages clearly and effectively without words. When symbols are less easily recognized, they should be used with explanatory words. Studies have shown that words should be placed either below or at the right of the symbol.[2]

Direction Symbols

Direction signs include those pointing the way to the library building. Although many libraries do not now have exterior signs, these signs may be worth setting up for some libraries. In such cases, a standard symbol for a library might be combined with the word "library."

The main use for direction signs occurs in the library interior. These signs direct people toward such facilities as rest rooms and lounges or toward service areas and library materials such as the circulation desk or the periodicals room.

For many of the more easily identified facilities, symbol signs have already been developed and put into wide use. Although variations do exist, efforts are underway to standardize some of these symbol signs.[3] The adoption of standard symbols for libraries can improve the ease with which patrons locate various facilities. Of course, such words as "rest room," "telephone," or "lockers" convey the same messages as their symbols do, but such common symbols are recognized universally, even by those who cannot read or understand the words. Pictorial symbols tend to be recognized more quickly than words. Therefore, the patron can glance briefly at the symbol, absorb the message, and move on confidently rather than having to slow down to read a sign. Symbols reinforce words and are more easily remembered; hence, they normally are more efficient.[4] In short, most symbols present messages more effectively than do words alone.

Airports and the Olympic Games offer exemplary sign systems, although the functions of these institutions obviously differ from those of libraries. The primary purpose of signs in an airport, for example, is to enable large numbers of people to move through the area quickly and efficiently, minimizing false turns, confusion, and congestion. Presumably the pace is slower in most libraries, yet libraries also should strive to ease frustration, and not force patrons to ask questions or to read complicated verbal signs when a simpler, more direct way of presenting the same information is available through symbol signs.

Aside from their functional role, symbols could also be visually more attractive than longer verbal messages and could "decorate" verbal signs in a way that is both artistic and functional. For many purposes libraries may find that the combination of verbal messages with symbols, as used in the airport, makes the best direction signs. Generally, direction signs to facilities should be of this combined type (see Fig. 9-1).

Direction signs to service areas and library materials present greater difficulties. They often involve relatively abstract and complex concepts, which are

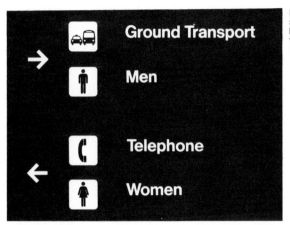

FIGURE 9-1 Combined word-symbol signs. From the hand-book prepared by AIGA for the U.S. DOT, *Symbol Signs*, section 5.

FIGURE 9-2 These symbols all indicate ticket purchasing. From AIGA for U.S. DOT, *Symbol Signs*, sections 3 and 6.

not easy to present in symbols.[5] Airports have had problems in portraying such service areas as the ticket counter (see Fig. 9-2). When there is no universally recognized object identified with an area, the development of a symbol becomes so difficult that it may not be useful at all. So far, there are no recognized symbols for even such vital library service areas and locations as the circulation desk, reference area, stacks, or periodicals room. If properly explained, however, perhaps in an introductory guide to the library or on a master sign at the entrance, symbol signs might prove useful even for service areas. Some pictorial messages, although not immediately comprehensible, might be learned, especially if the symbols occur with words.[6]

Arrows, as indicators of direction, may not seem ambiguous in intent, yet they are often used ambiguously. Specifically, there is a problem when arrows are used pointing downward or upward to indicate "straight ahead," because they could also be interpreted as pointing to something directly below or above the sign, or even to a change of level. To standardize usage and eliminate ambiguity, the Department of Transportation suggests that movement straight ahead be represented by a downward arrow, with straight horizontal arrows to indicate sideways movement. Changes of level (by stairs or escalators) call for diagonal arrows.

↓	↑	⇆	↗
downward	upward	horizontal	diagonal

If possible, any sign with arrows should be placed at the point where the change of direction occurs so that the direction indicated is completely clear. Studies show that arrows should be placed to the left of other symbols, which are, in turn, placed to the left of the words on the sign (as shown in Fig. 9-1).[7]

FIGURE 9-3   These symbols for mail, men's rest room, and elevator
illustrate conceptual and design problems. *Left:* mail symbol uses
thin lines that are difficult to see clearly. *Middle:* rest room sign is
ambiguous. *Right:* elevator sign is too abstract. From AIGA for U.S.
DOT, *Symbol Signs*, section 3.

Identification Symbols

Symbol signs are useful for identifying locations quickly and directly. Generally, symbols for identifying things or places should not appear for the first time at
the entrance to or inside an area, but should repeat the symbols used for directions to get there. Rest rooms, the circulation desk, or stacks, therefore, would
have the same symbols as those used in their direction signs, although perhaps in a different size, and these symbols could appear without words if the
messages were clear.

Instruction Symbols

Instructional messages include regulatory signs, such as PARKING or NO SMOK-
ING, and instructions for how to do something. Regulations can be effectively
presented in symbol signs without accompanying words. In contrast, how-to
instructions are often difficult to present, although for such tasks as using a
microfilm reader, a movie projector, or other machine, the pictorial diagram
often seems to work better than a verbal description. In addition, elevators,
lockers, and vending machines often have their own nonverbal instructions.
For such tasks as using photocopying machines or telephones, however, verbal or combined messages probably work better.

EFFECTIVE SYMBOLIZING

It is difficult to determine the effectiveness of particular symbol signs before
they have been tested in normal use. As a result, designers have produced too
many ineffective and inappropriate symbols, as well as too many competing
systems. The resulting confusion renders each distinct system less effective.
Although there is room for experimentation with symbol signs, librarians should
avoid the temptation to strike out entirely on their own. They should strive,
whenever possible, to be consistent with comparable symbol systems being
developed in other areas such as recreation and transportation.

　　Many symbols fail because of conceptual problems. They present an incomprehensible picture, suggest conflicting or ambiguous meanings, or rely
on complicated or highly abstracted messages. Others fail because of design
problems—a poor choice of style, shape, color, or background (see Fig. 9-3).

　　To combat this problem, one expert has advised that prospective designs
be tested by mixed groups of professionals in the field and by people from
outside fields. Rudolf Modley has also suggested abandoning efforts to sym-

bolize concepts that are too complex or difficult, arguing that some messages cannot be effectively represented by symbols and that efforts to force them into symbols only produce poor results.[8]

In designing and adopting symbols, librarians should remember that the purpose of symbols, as of signs, is to present messages directly and efficiently. If a symbol is too complex, it may be harder to interpret than words. It may even prove incomprehensible. The following principles should be applied to create effective symbols:

1 Each symbol must be direct and not ambiguous conceptually; simple and efficient; stylized, but not too abstract; easily and widely identifiable; timeless, not subject to changes in style; easy to learn and remember; noncontroversial; and unique in meaning.

2 The entire symbol system should be coordinated so that styles, colors, shapes, sizes, and backgrounds remain consistent.

3 The number of symbols used should remain as small as possible, with no more than one symbol for each message.

4 Symbols should be placed on signs consistently with respect to words. Locating symbols to the left of words seems preferable, with arrows to the left of both symbols and words.

SUGGESTED LIBRARY SYMBOLS

A study group of librarians and professional designers should be formed to ascertain when symbols are useful for libraries. This group would develop symbols, test them in a variety of settings, and recommend a system of standard symbols for general library application. Librarians need a widely accepted set of symbols to avoid the confusion that is likely to result if they independently design their own systems. As patrons move from other public places to libraries and from one library to another, they should be able to expect and perceive some consistency, not a mélange of creative but confusing, and therefore dysfunctional, symbol signs.

As a starting point for generating a standard set of symbol signs which can be applied in libraries according to need, the following examples have been selected (see Figs. 9-4 to 9-6). They include both symbols already widely used in the United States and suggestions for new ones. Even standard symbols, such as those for rest rooms, may need further revision and refinement as they achieve more universal testing and acceptance. Therefore, librarians must be alert to changes in order to keep their symbols consistent with currently accepted usage.

Recommended Symbols

These symbols have achieved wide recognition in the United States and conform to the general principles outlined above. Consequently, they may be recommended for use with or without words as appropriate.[9] Figure 9-4 shows a group of symbols prepared by the American Institute of Graphic Arts (AIGA) for the Department of Transportation (DOT). Note that the circles with slashes

Telephone

Restaurant

Snack Bar,
Coffee Shop

Information

Lost and
Found

Lockers

Elevator

Toilet,
Men

Toilet,
Women

Toilets

Smoking

No Smoking

Parking

No Parking

No Entry

FIGURE 9-4   Recommended symbols. From AIGA for U.S. DOT, *Symbol Signs*, section 6, entitled "Transportation Related Symbols."

FIGURE 9-5   Symbols for handicapped and bicycles. From Modley with Myers, *Handbook of Pictorial Symbols*, pages 87 and 89 respectively.

(usually red in color) indicate prohibitions and that all of the symbols are uniform in style and scale.

Figure 9-5 shows symbols used by the National Park Service that have been widely adopted in the United States. They may be used alone or they may be combined with words or other symbols, such as those for parking or rest room.

Proposed Symbols

Figures 9-6 and 9-7 show symbols that may prove useful for libraries, such as those for coat rack, fire extinguisher, auditorium, periodicals. Note the different symbols for circulation, reading room, and stacks or books. Some of these symbols need revision; for example, they must be standardized with respect to shape, size, and choice of color.

FACILITIES

Change   Fire   Fire Hose   Coat Rack   Vending
                Extinguisher

COMMAND   SERVICES

No Food or Drink   Circulation

FIGURE 9-6   Proposed symbols. From AIGA for U.S. DOT, *Symbol Signs*; Modley with Myers, *Handbook of Pictorial Symbols* (fire extinguisher, fire hose, and vending pictografics, © 1978, Paul Arthur, VisuCom Ltd., Toronto); and Lawrence J. M. Wilt and Jane Maienschein (symbol for "no food or drink" and the first circulation symbol).

INTERIOR LOCATIONS

Periodicals   Stacks or Books

Children's   Reading Room   Auditorium
Collections

EXTERIOR LOCATIONS

Library

FIGURE 9-7   Proposed symbols. From *Symbol Signs: Handbook of Pictorial Symbols* (children's collections and first reading room pictografics, © 1978, Paul Arthur, VisuCom Ltd., Toronto); and Wilt and Maienschein (exterior locations symbols).

NOTES

1. Wolf von Eckardt's well-written article "This Way Out—From Our Mad Jumble of Signs" (*Smithsonian* 8 [December 1977]: 108–117) contains a convincing call for developing effective symbol signs. "Most of the rest of the civilized world has long since discovered," he writes, "that graphic symbols, pictorial devices, pictographs, pictograms—call them what you will—are far more effective in getting a message across than a lot of verbiage" (p. 11). The general use of symbols and visual presentation has been discussed by Rudolf Arnheim, *Visual Thinking* (Berkeley: University of California Press, 1969).

2. Some symbols not yet recognized will achieve general acceptance; they can be made useful now by presenting them in combination with words. But it is important to avoid "oversigning" by using words when none are needed or by using too many words. Ralph Norman Haber has argued, in "How We Remember What We See" (*Scientific American* 222, no. 5 [May 1970]: 104–112), that the combined use of words with visual images can dramatically facilitate recall of messages. See examples for symbol placement in the handbook prepared by the American Institute of Graphic Arts (AIGA) for the U.S. Department of Transportation (DOT), *Symbol Signs* (Washington, D.C.: 1974).

3. Collations of symbols can be found in Henry Dreyfuss, *Symbol Sourcebook: An Authoritative Guide to International Graphic Symbols* (New York: McGraw-Hill, 1972); AIGA for the U.S. DOT, *Symbol Signs*; Rudolf Modley with ·William R. Myers, *Handbook of Pictorial Symbols* (New York: Dover, 1976). *Handbook on the Design of Symbols Signs* (mimeographed), prepared by the U.S. General Services Administration (Washington, D.C.: n.d.), offers examples and discussion of principles. Rudolf Modley and Margaret Mead tried unsuccessfully, through their newsletter *Glyphs*, to establish a central archives for symbols. The International Council of Graphic Design Associates (ICOGRADA) has also attempted to generate standard symbols, but theirs have not been generally accepted either; see *Print* (November–December 1969) for the special ICOGRADA issue. In their second newsletter (December 1977), the Society of Environmental Graphics Designers (SEGD) endorsed the DOT study. These are all preliminary attempts to standardize symbol signs, which will hopefully result in a centralized and eventually internationalized effort.

4. Haber, "How We Remember What We See," especially pp. 104–105.

5. Modley and Mead consider limitations in a number of *Glyphs* issues. Modley discusses specific problems in "World Language Without Words," *Journal of Communication* 24 (Autumn 1974): 59–66, especially on pp. 62–64: "Let's not expect others to follow complex mental processes to guess what is meant by a pictographical symbol."

6. Haber, "How We Remember What We See," p. 105, argues that learning improves when words and symbols are combined. See also Modley, "World Language Without Words," pp. 62–63. Clearly, words become less important as the symbols gain wider recognition.

7. Arrows are discussed in *City Signs and Lights: A Policy Study, Prepared for the Boston Redevelopment Authority and U.S. Department of Housing and Urban Development by Signs/Lights/Boston*, a project of Ashley, Ayer, and Smith (Cambridge, Mass.: MIT Press, 1973), especially pp. 165–166; and Herbert Spencer and Linda Reynolds, *Directional Signing and Labelling in Libraries and Museums: A Review of Current Theory and Practice* (London: Readability of Print Research Unit, Royal College of Art, 1977), sections 6.1–6.5.

8. Modley, in his *Handbook*, in "World Language Without Words," and in *Glyphs*, calls for testing designs and abandoning concepts that seem too complex.

9. We need an international system, as Margaret Mead pointed out ("Anthropology and Glyphs," *Print* 23 [November–December 1969]: 50–55), but "such a system should not be frozen too soon." Other discussions in the same issue of *Print* and elsewhere support Mead's position.

Evaluating Signage Systems in Libraries

JOHN LUBANS, JR.   GARY KUSHNER

Evaluating or testing sign effectiveness can go a long way toward avoiding signs that mislead because they are poorly conceived and designed. The sign program at the Pompidou Centre in Paris (which includes a library) is considered by some to be misleading. "Some of the [building's] hostility and some of the confusion [among users] undoubtedly stems from the graphics design programme"[1] and contributes to the finding that people are "simply travelling up and down the moving staircases on the outside of the building without coming to grips with the interior at all."[2]

Most readers can no doubt cite their own examples of user confusion in libraries. Consider the double meaning of the commonly used phrase "main entry," and how a librarian's wording often contributes to user uncertainty and exasperation. Evaluation can make one sensitive to the general tendency to *label* rather than to *guide*. Does wording such as "Reference Desk" or "Bibliographic Information Center," for example, achieve the same purpose as "Ask for help here"?

Instructional program evaluation has potential benefit for a graphics design program, especially as it relates to user orientation. Within libraries, signs, although part of the architectural program, can also be legitimately viewed as part of the orientation/instruction package, i.e., those elements that facilitate a new user's finding and using a library's services and resources.

Librarians who teach the public about information seeking and use have been actively concerned with evaluating the success or failure of their efforts. Several good discussions of library instruction evaluation are available and should be helpful to anyone considering evaluation.[3]

At the same time, some aspects of library signage evaluation can be viewed as part of "availability" or "document delivery" studies. This research tries to analyze the delays that users encounter in finding information, especially when they *know* what it is they want. Book or shelf arrangement, card catalog use, circulation data, and numbers of copies available are all considered in how easily a library's holdings may be used. Lancaster suggests that the "ease of use" of a collection includes "physical accessibility (e.g., where the library is located) and intellectual accessibility (e.g., how well a collection is cataloged or indexed, how easy the catalog is to use, how clearly the shelves are signposted)."[4] These may be the subjective measures of service that Lyle implies when he states: "Libraries which are distinguished for the quality of their instructional signs, guides, and exhibits also give outstanding service."[5]

Marketing analysis may well provide some insights of value to library sign programs. One article on marketing research as applied to libraries does briefly consider "wall graphics" as part of the marketing analysis, especially as the "atmospheric" component of "communication."[6] Although it is quite possible to borrow some ideas from evaluation techniques and methods developed to test other types of signage, such as that in airports or supermarkets, a library tends to be a more complex system. The basic complexity of any library is often further complicated by the building of addition upon annex, floor upon wing, resulting in many libraries' becoming difficult-to-use, mazelike structures. Apart from the implied confusion of the "information explosion" and the development and growth of a variety of new and traditional services, libraries may be unique in that their users frequently do not have a definite purpose, or have at best an ill-defined one, in visiting the library. Contrast this with a person seeking an airport parking lot or a can of tomatoes in the supermarket, and one should perceive some differences in the sophistication needed for designing and evaluating library sign systems.

DEFINING EVALUATION

Evaluation is *not* finding a scapegoat for a poorly received sign design, or the opportunity for uncovering long-held but best-buried axes. Rather, evaluation, if properly used, can channel information into a design program before the final stage of the sign program, providing essential feedback on the needs of staff and users.

Evaluation methods have been described as having a wide and varied spectrum: "At the one end . . . evaluative methodology is dominated by the attempt to obtain objective, scientific data through carefully structured research; at the other is a preference for a subjective, humanistic interpretation and a relatively unstructured approach to data collection."[7]

The first step in any type of evaluation—especially of instructional programs—is setting goals and objectives. Without this statement of expected results, there is no standard, other than personal likes or dislikes, against which to evaluate a projected or completed design. Evaluation, then, best begins at the first discussion of "new signs" for the library. The reason for spending this effort and money should be clear to all involved in the planning process. Simply put, a goal is where one wants to be in relationship to where one is. Perhaps where one is, is obvious, but the value of knowing that fact cannot be overstressed in the planning process. All the major pluses and minuses of the present signage program should be examined along with the needs of users. It is not enough to consider only what the staff wants; after all, the user is the audience and the hopeful beneficiary of an effective sign system. Users are the ones who get lost; staff normally do not.

It is at this goal-setting stage that limitations need to be discussed. They are usually restrictive, such as a finite budget. Building codes and federal or local regulations may also prohibit or require signs in certain locations.

Within this framework, objectives are fitted into place. The overall goal may be to publicize all resources/services of the library, but an objective (which is always subordinate to a goal) may be stated as in the following: a freshman user will be able easily to find the areas in which necessary services/resources for completion of a library research project are located.

EVALUATION METHODS

Here are some suggested evaluation guidelines, with illustrations from the University of Colorado Libraries signage program, as designed by Communication Arts, Inc., and fabricated by Sign Associates, Inc., of Denver.

The nature of designing a new signage program or of modifying an existing one suggests the use of what is known as "formative evaluation," which takes place during the planning, constructing, or modifying stages. This would include the design of "walk-through" models, e.g., photographs with superimposed signs (see Fig. 10-1) for staff and user reaction. From this feedback, constructive changes can be made in a program while the design is in the forming stage. As one designer states: define your goals, then test them; design a solution, then test that; put the solution into practice, then test again.[8]

"Summative evaluation" occurs after the full sign system has been installed. Because of the formative evaluation in the evolving design, this stage should produce no surprises about how the system works. If it were used alone—to "sum up"—it could be a rude awakening to the proponents of the "design for design's sake" school. Also, when a summative evaluation follows an implemented program that is suspected of having some design flaws, its report of findings, including suggestions for improvements, can be costly.[9]

The same methods that are of value in formative evaluation can also be used to summarize a program. There are various commonsense approaches, both quantitative and subjective, for evaluating the effectiveness of a signage system. The question at this point is whether the signs will direct or guide people as they are meant to do. (For a more detailed discussion on methods, especially user surveys, see Line's work.[10]) Some suggestions for evaluating a signage system are:

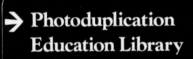

FIGURE 10-1 Walk-through photographic model. The "Photoduplication/Education Library" sign corresponds to the inked-in placement in the foreground. These signs are seen from the second floor landing. One is centered above a door; the other hangs from a relatively low ceiling.

➔ Photoduplication
Education Library

↑ College Undergraduate Library
Audio Visual/Reserve

1.   A panel whose members represent most segments in the library should provide guidance for the subtle decisions: style of typeface (Fig. 10-2), color, sign format (e.g., horizontal vs. vertical, and legibility), wording, and what symbols or pictographs, if any, are to be used or developed. The panel does not constitute collective decision making, but is rather a means to provide

Library

HELVETICA MEDIUM

FIGURE 10-2   Considerable discussion by the University of Colorado Library Sign Committee centered on the "best" typeface. Two of the top contenders were Helvetica Medium, widely used for direction and information signs where quick readability is desired, and Goudy Extra Bold, which has an appealing traditional quality instead of a slick, contemporary look. Less readable than Helvetica Medium, Goudy Extra Bold suits the subdued library atmosphere where fast and frantic readability is not considered a necessity.

Library

GOUDY EXTRA BOLD

the designer and the librarian(s) in charge with adequate criticism on which to base informed decisions.

2.   Photographs of the "before" and "after" systems may be used to illustrate changes graphically (see Figs. 10-3 and 10-4). For example, are the new signs an improvement in appearance over the old printed or "wild" hand-lettered ones?

3.   What comments came from the "question/answer book" or the "suggestion box" about signs or sign-related problems; what were the comments after the new signs appeared? Relevant suggestions may demand improvements in the library environment, frequently implying regulatory signs such as "No Talking" or "No Smoking." If the signs have had an impact on the annoyances that users encounter, there should be some evident correlation in the types of complaints received before and after the new sign program.

4.   Those libraries that keep categorized statistics on user queries should pay close attention to what appears to be an inordinate number of users who need direction and regulation.[11] If it is realistic to expect a drop in such questions after a new sign program, does this, in fact, happen? And with the increased national attention paid to standardizing the way in which user questions are counted, it would be of interest to see if the new signs that are judged effective in assisting wayfinding actually *promote* the asking of questions. Are the questions different or previously unasked (which might indicate a new level of service)? For example, user diffidence is often cited as one reason for the failure to ask questions. Can certain graphics "open up" or make some services more inviting to users? Implied in the use of statistics in evaluation is the need for some norms against which a library can measure itself. Apart from the uniqueness of each library's physical area, can a ratio be established between types of questions that could be used as a yardstick of good or bad signage? For example, could one say that for every research-level question, X number of direction questions will be asked? Without national levels, it is nearly impossible to judge the performance of one library against that of another.

5.   Questionnaires that were given to users to ascertain the general view of the library can be scrutinized again for comments on direction problems. A follow-up questionnaire may reveal changes in user attitudes and behavior. The questionnaire (or structured interview) specifically tailored to the sign pro-

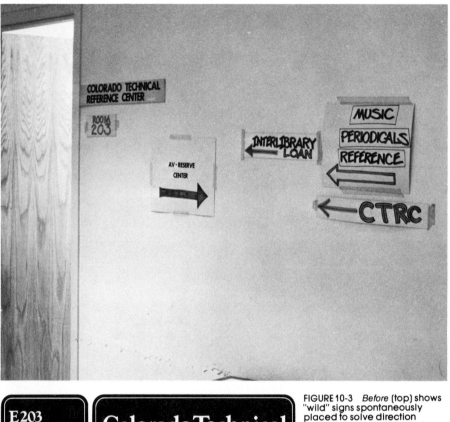

FIGURE 10-3 *Before* (top) shows "wild" signs spontaneously placed to solve direction problems. *After* (left) illustrates the improvement when signs are replaced in other parts of the program and only the Reference Center is signed according to the standards developed for the new system.

gram is an effective device for collecting data on which to base judgments. The anonymity of a questionnaire often encourages expression of true feelings for or against a style or system of signs, but a more direct approach may prove even more revealing. An interview table can be set up in some area in which staff can talk with users about signs. This informality, and many people's preference for talking rather than writing, is likely to produce insights not to be gained from a formal questionnaire. This technique usually requires two staff people—one to take notes on user comments while the other asks conversational questions.

6.   Observation can be of value in finding out how users get lost. A new system can be tested by the "obtrusive" method (not methodologically pure, but helpful), which means that you ask patrons if you can follow them around the library as they pursue their missions. A variation would be to pay new users to take part in an experiment, for example, present them with a directional problem and have them describe to the investigator how they solved it.[12]

7.   Charting the paths that users take in a library is one method that may be easily adapted from work flow analysis, a technique most frequently used to

FIGURE 10-4   *Before* (top) shows the usual mélange of signs at key information points. *After* (left) shows the improvement when most of the signs are incorporated into the overall program standards. "Interlibrary Loan" is retained to denote its immediate location both in lettering and in braille. (The braille illustrated is representational only.)

study office procedures.[13] Two approaches may be used, a procedures analysis work sheet or a "bump" diagram. Both summarize—the first in narrative, the other graphically—the steps users take by recording their detours, stops, backtracking, and start and finish. A record of the time it takes for users to get from point A to point B also can be made. Improved signs should provide a smoother, less "bumpy" trip for users, as illustrated in the "before" and "after" diagrams in Fig. 10-5.

There are, of course, more evaluation techniques than those discussed here, for example, those utilizing the tools of time and motion measurement—tachistoscopes, stopwatches, tape measures, clipboards, numerical counters. Data collected by these methods may show, for example, that people have difficulty in reading vertically lettered signs. However, simple observation with

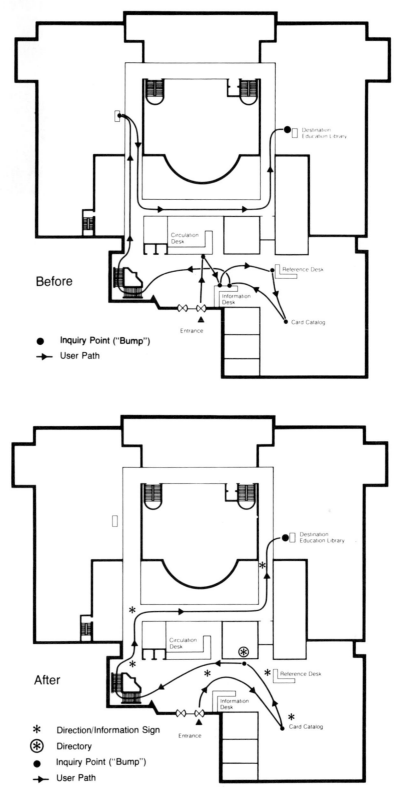

Before

- ● Inquiry Point ("Bump")
- ➤ User Path

After

- ✳ Direction/Information Sign
- ⊛ Directory
- ● Inquiry Point ("Bump")
- ➤ User Path

FIGURE 10-5 "Bump" diagrams illustrating the confusing complexity of reaching a destination (the Education Library in this case) *before* the design program and the less labyrinthine route *after* the program.

no technological assistance will very likely provide the same information since people tilt their heads to one side to put vertical letters into horizontal perspective. In conclusion, then, an evaluation technique similar to the one used in evaluating library instruction programs seems to be a useful approach. Many evaluation methods exist, but common sense, well-thought-out purposes in the collection of data, and formative evaluation in the design of sign systems should enable one to make a realistic judgment on the outcome and continuing effectiveness of a sign program.

NOTES

1. Alastair Best, "Why the People Stay Away from a People's Culture Center," *Design* (London), no. 354 (June 1978): 52.

2. Ibid., p. 51. (Much of this issue of *Design* is devoted to design evaluation.)

3. J. G. Brewer and P. J. Hills, "Evaluation of Reader Instruction," *Libri* 26 (1976): 55–65; Colin Harris, "Illuminative Evaluation of User Education Programmes," *Aslib Proceedings* 29 (October 1977): 348–362; Jacquelyn M. Morris and Donald F. Webster, *Developing Objectives for Library Instruction* (n.p.: New York Library Instruction Clearinghouse, 1976).

4. F. W. Lancaster, *The Measurement and Evaluation of Library Services* (Washington, D.C.: Information Resources Press, 1977), p. 312.

5. Guy R. Lyle, *The Administration of the College Library*, 4th ed. (New York: H. W. Wilson, 1974), p. 274.

6. Trudi Bellardo and Thomas J. Waldhart, "Marketing Products and Services in Academic Libraries," *Libri* 27 (1977): 191.

7. Brewer and Hills, "Evaluation of Reader Instruction," p. 60.

8. Ann Ferebee, "How a Brand New Metro Lost Its Way," *Design* (London), no. 354 (June 1978): 49.

9. Ibid., p. 47.

10. Maurice B. Line, *Library Surveys: An Introduction to Their Use, Planning, Procedure and Presentation,* rev. ed. (London: Clive Bingley, 1969).

11. John Lubans, Jr., comp., *Reference Statistics, 1975–76: An Analysis and Recommendations* (Boulder: University of Colorado Libraries, 1977) (ERIC ED139 408).

12. Richard W. Seaton, *Testing UBC Signage*, photocopied (Vancouver: University of British Columbia, June 1972), p. 8.

13. W. Lyle Wallace, ed. "Work Simplification," in *Reader in Library Systems Analysis* ed. by John Lubans, Jr., and Edward A. Chapman (Englewood, Colo.: Microcard Editions, 1975), pp. 235–248 (examples of work flow diagrams are on pp. 241, 245, and 246).

Part
3

Practical Library Solutions

11

Signs and the School Media Center

EVELYN H. DANIEL

Today's children face school library media centers of incredible complexity. Wayfinding in this maze of materials, equipment, activities, and services can be a daunting prospect. Yet, it is possible to make the modern media center inviting, appealing, and comprehensible to the puzzled student. A system of signs can be the answer.

To solve the problem of graphics in the school media center, we must explore the changing context of the center, various kinds of signs and their potential applications, and the practical difficulties encountered in developing an appropriate signage system.

Topsy's plaintive statement that she "just grew" might apply to school media centers as well. Relatively unplanned and unassimilated into their environment, such centers have not been the central concern of those in charge. Still, they have grown—in physical size, in staffing, and in kind and number of collections. These are quantitative changes. More profound are the qualitative changes that have accompanied the physical expansion. The incorporation of nonprint media into the small, print-oriented school libraries of the 1950s was a significant transformation.

The enormity of such changes and the impact that the media center's increased complexity has on student and teacher users are only now being realized. For example, the range of types and kinds of nonprint media now included in the media center means that these small centers may have as many different collections as does the large university library—filmstrips, slides, audiotapes, recordings, videotapes, 8mm films, film loops, 16mm films, study prints, photographs, kits that combine two or more media, and often many others. Each of these formats may have a different acquisition system, require different access procedures, be organized and stored differently, and need a different piece of equipment for use. This creates more than a trivial problem in organization. Yet, all of these different items should be integrated in some way so that a subject approach to the center will yield all the pertinent material. Intershelving is one possibility; interfiling of catalog card surrogates is another. In either case, it is necessary to inform users through a visual guidance system about the wealth and variety of material that exists for them in the media center.

The physical facility itself is changing. Currently there is tremendous variety in these facilities. In many places, the small reconverted classroom is still in use as a media center, but more and more frequently the center can be characterized in one of two ways. First, and most common, is the warren of rooms not always physically close to each other, but within which the media specialist has the responsibility of situating collections and user space and somehow making a coherent organization for the user to understand. Second, and in some ways an equally difficult problem, is the huge, empty rectangular space that has to be made comprehensive and partitioned with stacks and tables into some kind of effective (and defensible) working area. All too often the growing collections no longer fit the alcove or area allotted, and the logic of the sequence must willy-nilly be interrupted because of space considerations, which can create tremendous frustrations for the user unless there is an adequate system of signs.

The media center program also has undergone considerable change. In fact, the very idea of a program of services and activities is relatively new. Where the school library was a passive agency that concentrated on circulation and reference work on demand, the new media center has a proactive posture of instruction, consultation, production, and community resource liaison. The depth and variety of the services offered are not always clear to the users. It is not a simple matter of responding to questions about these new services, but rather of raising the level of understanding so that the questions address the new areas. A sign system reinforced by lists of media services posted in classrooms would no doubt have considerable impact on the problem.

SIGNS AND THEIR USE

Signs in the school media center may accomplish six functional purposes:

1 direction and guidance
2 orientation for new students and teachers

3 identification of specific materials, collections, and services

4 instruction and information on scope of services

5 information on rules and regulations

6 demonstration of a hospitable, inviting atmosphere

Within each category, the signs should be uniform in appearance, although the messages will differ. A brief examination of these areas may help in specifying the nature and number of signs to employ.

Direction and Guidance

Direction finding starts at the front door of the school. The trend in recent years has been to build larger and larger schools, to add on new wings and otherwise redesign old structures, so it is often a challenge for the new student or teacher to locate the library media center. A simple sign that says LIBRARY, with an arrow indicating direction, posted at eye level and at frequent intervals, will help to solve this problem. LIBRARY is probably the preferred term since it is the more familiar; MEDIA CENTER should be reserved for a slightly larger sign placed above or on the door of the center. Remember that eye levels vary. In elementary and middle schools, signs should be placed lower than those in high schools.

Signs for the library should be placed at every possible decision point—where corridors intersect, dead-end, or angle off. Each sign should be uniform in color, size, kind of arrow, and type of lettering. Although the media center may have a logo or some other symbol that is used for individualization inside, it may be best to keep signs outside the library free and simple.

The sign on the center itself might be in colors that contrast with the colors used on other library signs, as well as slightly larger. If the center has a distinct name, for example, the John F. Kennedy Library Media Center, the name might appear above the library designation and in smaller letters, such as:

John F. Kennedy
LIBRARY MEDIA CENTER

Orientation

Once users have been directed to the center, a second set of signs must orient them to the major functional areas. A large part of the library instruction program focuses on the similarity of one library to another, so that learning to use the school library media center can make it possible to use other libraries.

Orienting signs should focus on similarities. Every library has a circulation/distribution area, a catalog area or other index to the collections, a ready reference area where fact books, bibliographies, and indexes are located, study spaces, one or more major collections of material, and a librarian's office, desk, or work station. In addition, there may be a production area, a television studio, a teacher's workroom with lounge, preview rooms for audiovisual material, conference rooms, a student lounge, closed stack areas, a receiving and processing work station, staff specialist offices (for example, special reading and math teachers), classrooms, and so on. As an added complication, the facility may be located on several floors or in a series of nonadjacent rooms.

It is important to keep orienting signs simple and to provide *only* the information that is necessary and that the user is learning to expect. Too much information at the entry point is unnecessarily confusing. It is best to identify only the main areas for orientation purposes, leaving other important but less common areas to the next level of signs—identification signs. This method demonstrates an information hierarchy leading from the general to the specific, an important principle to teach students, as it extends beyond the library classification of knowledge into almost every other field of endeavor. Hierarchies, as scientists are finding, are innate and natural mechanisms that all living systems use to organize information.

The main orientation signs should be the largest and the simplest within the center. The relationship between general information and simple form is another principle that can be demonstrated here. Thus, each of the six or so signs should consist of one or two common words, and no more. The following might be appropriate choices.

1 *Circulation.*   There may be a separate distribution area for equipment, another circulation desk for certain kinds of audiovisual material, and yet another for reserves, but all that is unnecessary information at the orientation level. Direct the user to the main area, and then the user can be led to the more detailed and specialized areas by means of an identification sign at the main circulation point.

2 *Catalog.*   This word may soon become an anachronism as libraries switch to terminals, book catalogs, and microfilm or microfiche indexes, but it is still the most familiar term today and should, therefore, be used until a substitute gains general acceptance. At every point in the system, instruction as well as information should be conveyed covertly as well as overtly. Instruction at the orientation level involves the recognition and expectation of familiar areas and the principle of using general, simple organizers to lead to more specific information levels.

3 *Reference Books.*   Some librarians use the term "information" to refer to this area, thereby including the reference librarian. They argue that "reference" is professional jargon. Although the argument has merit for some libraries, it probably does not apply to the school media center. First, the staff is not usually large enough to have a person at the reference desk all the time to provide information. Second, and more important, the center's primary purpose is to teach students to become independent gatherers and users of information. Reference tools are an important type of material with which students should become familiar from their earliest school experiences. It is an essential part of education to learn reference book use.

4 *Study Area.*   Since a major service to students is providing space to study, this orientation sign will not only point out what may seem obvious, but also emphasize the service being provided. As with circulation, there may be several study areas; however, there is usually one main area and a logical point at which the user may find an additional identification sign pointing to alternative study areas, such as group study, overflow space, conference rooms.

5 *Collections.*   This area is one of the more difficult to specify ahead of time, and, actually, "collections" is not a good word to use. The most useful term here depends on the center and how it is arranged. If all material is intershelved in one collection of stacks, the sign might say BOOKS AND MEDIA. If divided into two distinct areas (an unfortunately common occurrence), the one sign might become two. Similarly, the collection may be divided between FICTION and NONFICTION. Frequently, materials designated for the primary grades are separated from upper-level material in the elementary

school. In this case, a sign indicating EASY BOOKS (where books may be a generic term for all types of media) would be useful. If, as is often the case, the collection is placed along the outer circumference of the room, a sign may not be necessary.

6 *Librarian or Library Media Specialist.*   The first term is probably preferable because it is simpler, although the aim may also be to educate users to the second term. This is the only sign that refers to a person. Since people move about, the sign and the person often may not be in the same place at the same time. However, it will probably be useful to emphasize through the orientation sign system that the librarian is a necessary and central element of any library. Also, it is a good idea to have all the staff in the media center wear tags indicating name and position as another educational and informational aid.

All these major signs should be similar in size, style, and color. An alternative to a uniform color might be a different color for each major sign, with the same color recurring in the next level of signs that further identify and provide more detail. For example, CIRCULATION might be green, and the additional sign(s) identifying the reserve area, the equipment distribution area, the audiovisual materials area, and others would be green also, but with smaller lettering.

Orientation signs should be placed in eye-catching positions. For most large open media centers, they might best be reversible and suspended from the ceiling. Ideally, upon entering, the user will be able to see all orientation signs from a point just inside the center.

In addition to the signs, large centers should identify major areas on an outline map at the entrance to the media center. These maps are often duplicated and made available to students and faculty during orientation tours or reprinted in student handbooks.

Identification

Signs for identification will be the most complex and the most numerous. This level may consist of several little sign hierarchies leading from general information to specific location data. Identification signs are virtually all locational. Each library media center will have unique requirements, but some general categories can be discussed.

There are several kinds of identification signs, including those giving more detail about other staff specialists, additional study spaces, other functional areas, collection types, and organizing principles. The first identification signs must be placed at one or more of the major orientation sites and lead from those to the specific areas.

The kind and location of other specialists (such as television specialist or educational communications director) should be identified at the CIRCULATION and LIBRARIAN orientation points. Identify only those specialists with whom the students might be working. Specialists for faculty and other staff can be named in some other way. Communications research shows that nonrelevant information can frequently interfere with the comprehension of relevant information; it is best to provide only the information that has meaning for students. Other identification signs at the actual stations of the specialists will, of course, be necessary.

Additional study spaces also must be identified at the orientation sign for STUDY AREA. Whether these study spaces need identification at the point of use depends on their extensiveness.

Functional areas such as the production area, television studio, and preview rooms must be identified. A sign should lead to their control places from the CIRCULATION orientation point. The areas themselves must be identified at the point of location. If they are physically separate from the rest of the media center—for example, in another room or with clearly marked boundaries—the direction-orientation-identification signage model may be useful to follow on a smaller scale.

Identification signs are necessary to specify the types of materials in the collection, and, at a still finer level of detail, the physical organizing principle used. If most book and nonprint materials are intershelved, small signs may be all that is necessary in addition to the BOOKS AND MEDIA orientation sign. Inclusive classification numbers should be posted at eye level on the ends of stack ranges, and guide word signs placed on the front-facing edges of the shelves identifying major subject areas, for example, "Zoology" in the high school and "Animal Life" in the elementary school. These guide words must be suitable to the level of student.

If there is a variety of materials with a variety of arrangements scattered all over the media center, a more detailed sign or set of signs will be required. One possibility is to create a semipermanent sign to be posted beside the outline map at the entrance to the center detailing the kind and location of the various collections. In addition, if students do not have direct access to some materials, this should be indicated on the sign with directions for access.

Signs are necessary on or adjacent to each special collection, indicating its nature and organizing method: "Newspapers—Arranged alphabetically," "Filmstrips—Arranged by number in order of receipt," or "Vertical File—Pictures and Pamphlets—Arranged alphabetically by broad subject categories." Guide signs further subdividing the main arrangement will be necessary if the collection exceeds fifty items.

In listing the different types of material and their locations, the media specialist may decide to integrate (at least partially) and simplify the arrangements. In this case, the sign system will have served a useful organizing function.

Scope of Services

The next set of signs includes those that provide information. Within the media center, there are three areas where information is frequently supplied by visual means—the production area, the card catalog, and the reference collection. Outside the media center, one might consider creating a sign for each classroom listing the important services of the media center as a public relations/educational activity.

Information on how to use a particular piece of equipment, on how to read a catalog card, and on how to use the *Readers' Guide* or other reference tool is most often given on posters mounted at the point of use.

If the center has production space for a permanent setup of certain kinds of equipment, such as copy cameras, duplicating and audio-recording machines, transparency production, and the like, simple diagrammatic signs are not only a useful courtesy; they also pay off in a lower incidence of equipment breakage and malfunctioning. If permanent space is not available, the media center may set up temporary spaces for one special kind of production activity and then rotate it with others on some regularly scheduled basis. Along with the temporary setup, the appropriate diagrammatic sign also should be provided.

A sign (or signs) mounted on top of the card catalog showing the important elements of the catalog card and indicating types of cards, color codes (if used), or other special aspects of the catalog is necessary. An alternative is mounting the sign on an easel beside the catalog. If reference tools contain good instructions on their use, it may be sufficient to post a sign calling attention to the page or other designated place where this information may be found. Some centers use short audiotapes for instruction on use of practical reference tools.

One of the most useful information signs may be designed and created for permanent display in the classrooms. It should be a simple reminder of support services offered by the media center. It may be necessary to obtain the principal's permission to post such signs, and to get this, it will be helpful to develop a model. The classroom sign should be placed high enough in each classroom so that it is inaccessible to certain "creative attempts" of students. The lettering should be large enough to be read easily from any point in the room. The colors should be eye-catching without being garish.

Rules and Regulations

Every media center has rules about things that are not allowed ("No Eating," "No Talking"), circulation ("Overdue Fine—5¢ a Day"), limitations on use ("Only Four Students at a Table," "Reference Books to Be Checked Out Overnight Only," "Two Periodicals Only May Be Checked Out at a Time"), and the like. Media specialists should use discretion about these signs, for their general effect is often negative and such information may be best conveyed in a student handbook or by word of mouth. If some admonitory or rule-oriented signs seem necessary, use a style, size, or color different from that used for information signs.

Atmosphere

The type of sign most frequently found in library media centers today is the welcoming kind. These signs are intended to be an invitation to enter, to browse, to explore. Bulletin boards and other similar kinds of temporary display carry this message. They underline, point out special aspects, suggest interesting material for use with a special day or special event. Variety is the key here, but not so much or in such overwhelming amounts that basic orientation and location signs must compete for the user's attention. If the sign systems are simple and well designed, they will serve to create the hospitable atmosphere that the center wants to convey.

DEVELOPING A SIGN SYSTEM

Analysis and planning of a sign system should be part of the larger analysis of the facilities, traffic patterns, and use of the center. A systematic plan must be developed in draft form on paper before looking for ways and means. Following the analysis, the first step is to identify the several sets of signs that are necessary, and then to specify for each the actual wording, letter size, color, material, and location. The plan can then be presented to potential funders, such as the Parent-Teachers Association, local community agency, or school administration. If the sign system proposal, with tentative cost estimates, is carefully thought out, its adoption, at least in some modified form, will be more likely.

One thing is certain for any sign system: money will be needed. In addition to the initial outlay, maintenance money is necessary each year. Although the initial funds may come from a gift, annual maintenance costs must be built into the regular budget. This may seem like a large expense for a nonmaterial item, but it will be money well spent. To spend money for media center materials without making them accessible is certainly wasteful. It is necessary to make these materials intellectually available through card catalogs, classification systems, and indexes. We must also invest in making them physically accessible. A sign system is an investment that will more than pay off in terms of enhanced use, positive attitudes, and basic education.

First, one should develop a master plan, enlisting teachers and students on a committee to study the problem and make recommendations. The tentative plan should have details of type, cost, and location of materials for signs. More than one alternative may be developed for presentation. While the search for ways and means goes on, temporary signs may be used to pilot some ideas and test specific wordings and placements, but these must not, for want of a plan, become the permanent ones. It may be useful to divide the total plan into a series of phases, remembering that the first step is the most crucial one.

The following points should be kept in mind when developing a sign system for the school media center:

1 The sign system should be dynamic. As the program changes, the signs should change. Some signs will be relatively permanent; others will be temporary. The system of signs itself should be ongoing. This necessitates keeping some kind of control manual, or at least a folder, with the initial proposal, the enacted plan, and the changes that are being made.

2 All signs should be coordinated. The entire set of signs should have some common unifying treatment, perhaps relating to the architecture and interior design of the center. It may be that only the style of lettering will be similar, even though several different sizes will be used. Each subset of signs should be similar and coordinated with the main sign system.

3 There will be major signs and minor signs. The need for a hierarchy of signs from the most general (the fewest and the simplest) to the most specific (the greatest number, which also convey the greatest amount of information) should be stressed.

4 Signs should communicate simply. This is an important principle. More is not necessarily better; in fact, it is frequently worse. Each sign should tell only what is necessary at that particular point. As the user's need for information increases, more information should be provided at the point where it is needed.

5 Signs should be fresh and clear, and replaced at the first indication of wear. There is nothing more defeating than discolored, tattered, torn, or tacky signs. Signs can create a negative, as well as a positive, impression of the entire media center.

6 Any surface that seems appropriate can be used. Floors, walls, ceilings, and easels are all possibilities. Many centers use footprints or color lines on the floor to lead users to a place that may be difficult to explain in words or through the use of arrows. Other centers use the ceiling imaginatively, not just to mount hanging signs but to carry messages. For example, one media center had the students create a "great, green, greasy swamp monster" by adding new scales with the names of books read and the child reading them onto a long body that led from the middle of the center on the ceiling, out the door, and down the hall until it stretched to the door of the children's classroom. This type of imaginative sign demonstrates hospitality and creates interest in the center as a lively place.

7 A good sign may not always be a necessary one. Space limitations may preclude some useful signs, since the result could be visual clutter. Some unique spaces and items probably will be omitted in any sign system. However, directions and information for use can be presented through audiocassettes. In some cases, as in user instruction for complicated reference books, audio information may be preferable to visual information. In other cases, where the facility, collections, and services are extremely complex, an audiotape orientation tour with numbered stations throughout the center is a good solution. If so, or if it is used as a supplement to a visual sign system, the same principle of general to specific, simple to complex, should be applied. The audio tour might begin with an overview and then go into detail on each part. It becomes especially important to provide verbal organizing cues when no picture is available.

A visual guidance system in the school media center will enhance the everyday flow of operations within the facility by introducing additional communications mechanisms and greater organization. A sign has great potential power, as demonstrated by the following story.

A motorist was driving along a country road when he saw a big sign— BEWARE OF THE DOG. Farther down the road was another sign, BEWARE OF THE DOG. Quite leery by now, he arrived at a farmhouse where he saw a small poodle standing on the lawn. "Do you mean to say," asked the motorist, "that this little dog keeps strangers away?" "No," replied the farmer, "but the signs do!"

An Approach to Public Library Signage

MILTON S. BYAM

The public library has special signage problems. Because it serves all age groups and educational levels, it must communicate clearly in a language that all will understand. Its services extend beyond the book format and the Dewey classifications to include slides, tapes, recordings, films, maps, and pamphlets. The public library is a public institution, and as such its architecture and outside signage are usually conservative.

A factor not usually considered in designing public library buildings—particularly central libraries—is that in addition to providing library service, the public library functions as an office building, a factory, and an auditorium. In central libraries payrolls are prepared, books are processed, and lectures and concerts are given. Public librarians generally feel that part of their responsibility is to draw people into the library, even for nonlibrary purposes. Therefore, the library is designed so that anyone who has business there, except perhaps delivery people, enters the library proper to complete his or her transactions. If someone wants to sell typewriters or services to the library, he or she sees the purchasing agent only after walking through the main library.

Someone seeking employment walks through the library. And if a book is desired, one may be shunted from information desk to catalog to subject division to librarian to shelf.

No public library has completely solved the problem of effective entry. Most buildings have easily recognizable entryways, and people are forced, by one device or other, to move in prescribed directions. Some buildings use turnstiles. Office buildings have elevators; department stores have aisles. In a library, however, one usually enters a large room that leads everywhere with no visible route to what is sought, such as the book collection. Consequently, in public libraries one either questions the person at the charge desk and is then referred to a centrally placed information desk, or one goes to the information desk only to be referred to the charge desk. Signs have not helped anyone up to this point; a small INFORMATION sign placed on a desk can be counted only as a feeble attempt.

Because the characteristics of a collection often determine its location, the library building usually does not provide a logical progression inward. For example, the Social Sciences Division, with its Dewey 300 numbers, is generally the busiest spot in public libraries, and it must be placed away from entrances so as not to create a bottleneck. Also, larger collections must have more floor space so that a minimum number of books are consigned to the stacks. The result is that there is no natural progression of Dewey classification. Subject divisions are scattered pell-mell throughout the building without regard to the overall library organization of material among format divisions (such as the film division), service divisions (special groups such as the blind), age group divisions (children, young adults), and library office space.

Good signage may not erase the problem, but it can go a long way toward making some sensible order from the illogical arrangement in public libraries. And some attempts do work. The Detroit Public Library, for instance, uses lighted directories or maps that show users where they are, with lights showing them how to get where they want to go. Numbers on the directory correspond to the huge three-dimensional numbers that are set in front of each division as a guide.

BUILDING A SIGN SYSTEM

To set up a logical library sign system, three points must be followed:

1 Locate signs and instructions for public use in the proper places.

2 Use terms that most people will understand clearly.

3 Avoid ad hoc signs that solve immediate problems without considering the whole.

As one approaches the average public library building from the street, it is apparent that the library would benefit from a tasteful sign on or near the roof simply stating the library name and indicating that it is free; for example, MIDDLETOWN FREE PUBLIC LIBRARY. The sign should be visible from all sides of the building, and a similar sign should be located at street level at the front of the library.

In the entry there should be a visible directory listing the many services of the library. Particularly in central libraries, it should inform citizens of the numerous functions performed by the large staff. The directory should be single-sided, should face the entrance, and should also list subject, form, and special divisions, as well as the technical processing department and the purchasing agent's location. Locations might also be indicated at this point by simply saying "This Floor, North Wing," "Lower Level, South Wing," or by giving room designations.

Signs might simply direct the user who enters the main hall to the point where one returns books or registers for cards. There are three common arrangements of public library charge/discharge (or circulation) desks and each has a unique problem with regard to signage. First is the center island desk, which may be freestanding or against the back wall of a room (Fig. 12-1). With this type, signs are often placed below the counter lip, indicating charge, discharge, and registration. Usually they are barely visible to the patron and would be better placed at eye level on the wall behind the desk or on a three- or four-sided structure hanging from the ceiling. Again, language must be carefully chosen and symbols clearly marked so that users know what is expected of them.

The second type of charge/discharge operation, frequently found in larger libraries, uses two separate, often L-shaped, desks (Fig. 12-2). Here, there is sometimes no alternative but to make the information available to the patron after he or she has passed the desks. The signs should generally be in a large typeface for easy readability and to attract the user's attention. The signs are placed over the desks. They can be attached in one of two ways. These signs, indicating the functions of the desks, can be suspended from the ceiling. They may also be attached to the rear wall. Either way, they are readily seen by the entering patron.

The third type of desk avoids direct-eye confrontation between clerk and patron, so obvious in the island type, by placing the desk to the left or right of the library entrance (Fig. 12-3). This "side" charge/discharge desk presents the most difficult signage problems. For even with a large suspended or wall sign indicating the desk's function, something else is needed to tell the user to

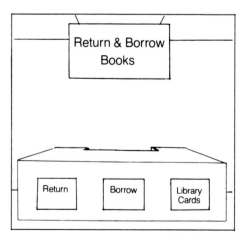

FIGURE 12-1   Center island desk arrangement.

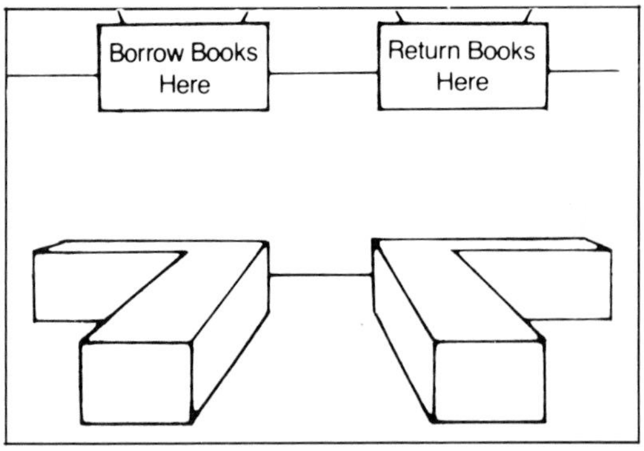

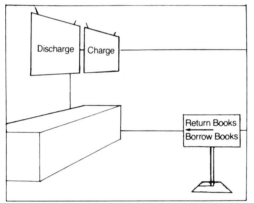

FIGURE 12-2 Separate desk arrangement

FIGURE 12-3 Side charge/discharge desk arrangement.

look for the sign. This might be accomplished by a standing or pendent sign just inside the entry. Its short message and arrow directs the user to the side desk.

As one enters the main hall from the lobby, there should also be another general sign, preferably suspended from the ceiling, which provides follow-up information. It should be four-sided and, therefore, visible from any angle. An example of two sides of the general sign directly opposite each other is shown in Fig. 12-4.

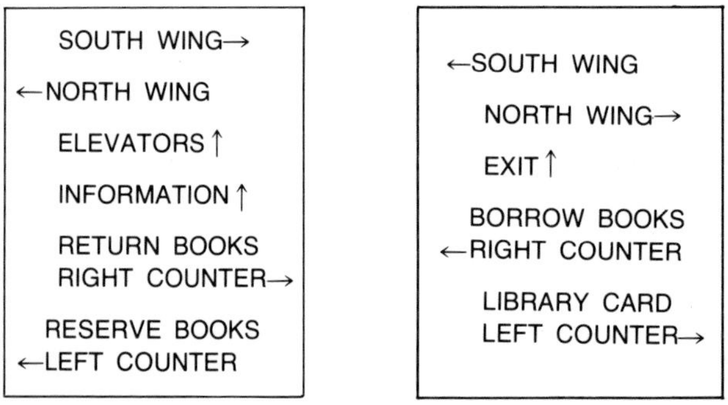

FIGURE 12-4 General Information sign for main hall.

```
   SOUTH WING→

←NORTH WING

   ELEVATORS↑

   INFORMATION↑

   RETURN BOOKS
   RIGHT COUNTER→

   RESERVE BOOKS
←LEFT COUNTER
```

```
←SOUTH WING

   NORTH WING→

   EXIT↑

   BORROW BOOKS
←RIGHT COUNTER

   LIBRARY CARD
   LEFT COUNTER→
```

Proceeding inward, users take an elevator, stairs, or escalator to the desired floor and wing. Reaching the correct floor, they should see ahead another directory that indicates the floor and lists the specific services to be found there, such as:

SECOND FLOOR

FILM DIVISION   ROOM 207

SECURITY   ROOM 200

Along the walls, hotel-type signs would be useful, such as:

ROOMS 200–249→

←ROOMS 250–274

Although each of the office doors might show simply the room number and the name of the office, e.g., Room 200, Security, all divisions should be clearly designated, e.g., Science and Technology Division.

Somewhere near the division entrance, the Dewey description of its contents should be included with what is peculiar to that library's collections:

APPLIED SCIENCES

Medicine
Engineering
Agriculture
Domestic Arts and Sciences
Managerial Services
Chemical and Related Technologies

After entering a specific division, the patron sees the librarian and is told to go to a given stack or to the catalog. Finding one's way through library stacks is not easy, and labeling them coherently and intelligently has proved extremely difficult. Some libraries have alphabetic or numeric symbols on the end panels to refer to specific locations. Others, such as the Bibliothéque Publique d'Information at the Centre Georges Pompidou in Paris, have color coded the stacks to aid the user. Stack end panels have also been colored and labeled with call numbers and subjects. Shelf labels indicate specific areas of interest. None of these methods, however, has been fully successful. One device is to remove shelves in the top section of each beginning stack section and to place there posters, signs, or letters in large print, together with the beginning Dewey numbers of that section. Then, if librarians *must* point to something, they are pointing to something specific. Another idea is to use 12-inch square decorated boxes with plastic faces affixed in the same location to indicate by general subject the information included in the stacks, e.g., Medicine.

Form, special service, and age divisions are treated differently from subject divisions. Special exhibits or displays might be mounted at the entrance to the specific division. In this way, a patron should be able to see the functions of these units at a quick glance.

A form division, such as the periodicals room or the audiovisual department, cannot simply be labeled by that title, since it may not be clear to the public. A display or even a specially designed poster might show at a glance that records, films, slides, and framed paintings are all located in the audiovisual department. The directory at the entry might list "Films, 16mm; Paintings for Home Use; Videotapes; *see* Audiovisual Department." The listing under Audiovisual Department would read, "Lower Level, South Wing."

Special service divisions take various forms and, therefore, present different problems. Services for the blind and physically handicapped can be identified by special reading equipment placed in a display near or in the entry, as in the District of Columbia Public Library. Braille signs, of course, should be strategically located near the buttons for the elevator and, as a guide for the blind to follow, braille strips could be placed on the walls.

Divisions such as the Adult Education Division should boast large display areas and officelike decor to assure both actual privacy and the sense of privacy. The bulletin board area might contain notices of free classes and other instruction, available jobs, or news about students who succeeded by studying on their own. A sign on the wall or door might simply say:

> Study On Your Own?
> High School Diplomas
> College Degrees
> Graduate Study
> ASK HERE

As with the audiovisual division, the directory at the library entry would bear the information:

> High School Study *see* Adult Education
> College Degrees *see* Adult Education

Under Adult Education, one would find "Third Floor, Room 306."

A sign to the children's room needs only the simple words "Children's Room" or "Children's Library" somewhere near its entrance. Children's rooms in many public libraries are not self-descriptive, and therefore an exhibit or display can make clear the room's purpose. The objective is not only to steer away those who do not wish to enter the children's room, but, more importantly, to motivate children to go inside. Many libraries have special entrances for children. In this case, a directory for the children's library should be provided just before the entrance to inform the child and/or interested adult of the many things available—records, cassettes, toys, games, fairy tales, mystery collections, and so on. This is not a location directory, but simply an information source.

Of course, in any public library there is always a need for ad hoc signs—to point out special programs, special materials, new information. If possible, these signs should be in type compatible in style with the overall sign system. Ad hoc signs might be placed on easels so they can be easily removed. Signage is also required for special collections such as government documents, mysteries, pay collections, maps, or foreign-language materials. These signs can be more permanent, but, again, consistency should be the aim so that the whole effect is not a clash of colors, sizes, and shapes.

ADAPTING A SIGN SYSTEM

The principles discussed above apply to any public library, whatever the size, but their specific application will differ. In many small libraries, the architect has designed much of the permanent signage and provided a list of other needed signs. But buildings—like the services in them—are not static; they change constantly. So there is a continuing need for signage to reflect new, revised, or discontinued services. When only one building is involved, this can be taken care of quite easily. However, in a library system that includes branches or individual libraries, adapting signage can become a headache of major proportions.

Each branch or individual unit of a system has probably been designed by a different architect with a different approach reflected in the graphics and colors inside the building. When most of the signs and posters are supplied by a centralized public relations office, it becomes difficult to make them consistent in color, size, and shape in each of the facilities. One remedy might be to ask the branch librarian or head of the library to note the revisions in services and request signage to correct them. However, since libraries do not select administrators on the basis of graphic sense, the need is often not perceived. If it is, the branch librarian is generally restricted to centrally provided wording, boards, and colors, and would be at a loss to describe needed lettering styles in any case.

A second alternative might be to have the signs made in the library itself. However, not all library staffs are prepared to make signs in a professional manner. Moreover, they often seem guided by the assumption that signs correct evils, so more emphasis is placed on signs that tell people what they cannot do than on signs that guide patrons in the use of the library. Therefore, a profusion of signs springs up about eating, smoking, and drinking in the library, but there is no sign indicating where to go for a library card. Signs on locked doors announce that something is "private," but there are no signs pointing out the location of the public children's room.

A third alternative would be to send a public relations representative to the scene if the problem is recognized. In a small system this might be possible, but in a system of more than 20 units it becomes a burden. Assuming the public relations director can recognize and remedy the directional problems involved, typefaces as well as sign backing and print colors would have to be specially and expensively acquired for a branch building with, for instance, cerise, yellow, or blue walls.

One other solution might be to promote some type of standardized coloring for the walls of branch libraries. This would permit a far-removed public relations department to prepare appropriate, attractive signs and posters for branch libraries without being on the location. Signs could be produced with some awareness that colors at least will blend in, although typefaces and artistic work are another matter.

CONCLUSION

The problem of sign systems for the public library involves creating logic out of an exceedingly illogical plan. It can easily result in overdoing, although it has more often been underdone. There is usually insufficiently clear visual guidance. The challenge is to remedy the confusion this causes the patron.

Floor plans alone should not be used to attack the problem. They are not patron sized, and therefore errors may be made in scale that become obvious in the actual setting. The building first should be walked through. The needed directions to get to different points should be plotted and then reexamined to make certain of their consistency and clarity. The use of unclear or little-known library terms should be avoided. These words may help the library staff, but they leave the patron uninformed. There are already too many barriers between the library user and the materials. The sign system in any public library should be uniform, eye-catching, and attractive, but, above all, it must be simple, clear, and helpful.

13

Signs in Special Libraries

The matter of signs in special libraries (as in all other matters affecting that particular grouping of institutions, it seems) depends on each individual library. It is not possible to apply general principles to what are often unique, and in any case highly individual, organizations. The varied approaches taken by special libraries are interesting, sometimes inspiring, and even humorous. Signage problems are often solved with imagination and a certain flair that is not usually found in public library systems and state-supported educational libraries.

Most libraries go out of their way to make passersby aware of their existence. In contrast, The Boston Athenaeum never had its name on its building on Beacon Street until it was designated a national historical monument in 1965. That act required that the designation be advertised, and a restrained bronze tablet affixed to the right of the front door now announces the fact. Until then, the only sign to be found was the number 10^1/$_2$ painted on the leather door.

The prevailing philosophy of designing signs to provide directions or information also varies. In a museum library such as Lyman Library in the Museum of Science, Boston, the library signs are just as carefully executed as those in the exhibit cases. In fact, most museum libraries would receive high grades for their signage systems since they are usually extensions of the museums' own professionally designed system and are maintained by museum staff. In museums, signs are regarded as important and are thought to be of considerable educational value. This philosophy carries over to signs in museum libraries as well, especially if they are open to the public. The plants that are part of the decor of Lyman Library are labeled with both their common and their botanical names, as one would expect. However, one museum library in Boston has signs deliberately lettered so that they will *not* be easy to read. By obscuring the signs, it is hoped that those who wish only to view the object itself will not be distracted by an obtrusive sign—still, the sign is there for those who wish to know more.

The corporate identity image, a concept eagerly embraced by many American companies, enables all of a company's products and departments to be identified with the company itself through the use of a particular typeface, logo, slogan, or other device. When companies move to new quarters or refurbish old ones, a professional designer is often asked to fashion a graphics design program that projects the corporate identity image to all parts of the firm. Sometimes, however, there is no allowance for providing compatible new signs that surely will be required as departments shift and activities change. At Houghton Mifflin Company, in Boston, the library signs (a variation of the graphics design program for the entire company) were designed in Helvetica Medium white letters on bright blue plastic laminate. The library staff now uses transfer letters in the same typeface and color on bright blue Bainbridge board, and therefore can cope with changes in card catalog drawers and pamphlet file headings, as well as other kinds of changes that are normal in a busy library, without violating the signage system as originally designed. Many company librarians are fortunate to have access to an in-house graphics or art department that can design or make signs as needed.

Special academic libraries usually have images of their own, each one quite different in tone and style from others in the same university. This pleasant diversity in the increasing standardization of a mass-produced world is due in part to the different times and fashions when the libraries were built and the generosity of the donors. The marbled magnificence of Widener is not at all like vivid Monroe C. Gutman Library, nor is the newer John F. Kennedy Library like either of them, and yet they are all at Harvard along with many more. Gutman's uncluttered interior is essentially a design in color, and brilliant color at that— green, purple, orange, red, blue, and black. The signs are designed with subdued black serif letters on clear plastic. The staff keeps up with new bulletin boards, displays, and directional signs by using an Embossograph sign machine. Gutman purchased a compatible, although not identical, type font and so can turn out professional-looking signs in short order.

Small special libraries in nonacademic parts of the nonprofit sector often do not have access to graphics design programs, nor do they attract wealthy donors to provide them with their surroundings. Their signs and their images must depend on the ingenuity and the interest of the librarian. The most common solution is still to resort to the typewriter and colored marking pencil. The result is usually far from professional, but it *is* cheap and instant. Action for Children's Television, Inc. (ACT) is an activist, grass-roots organization with fewer than 20 employees, housed in a small white frame building in Newton, Massachusetts. Its tiny library is located in one of the six rooms it occupies. The librarian, who is also the chief researcher, writes and edits information about ACT and speaks to groups in different parts of the country about its programs. The librarian stated that she had no signs except for a few typed ones on file drawers and Magic Marker labels on legal-sized folders. In a very small organization where no one uses the library except with the assistance of the librarian or clerk, and where the physical arrangement is confined, it seems no more necessary to have a formal sign system than to wear a button that says "Hello! My name is Mother (or Father)" at home. The ACT logo, however, would lend itself to attractive variation if the library should ever require a more formal arrangement of its contents (Fig. 13-1).

The Boston Athenaeum, a "special" special library and one of the oldest private libraries in the country, owes nothing to professional designers, graphic artists, or signage experts as far as its beautiful and unusual signs and other graphic elements are concerned. They are rather a reflection of the great care, patience, imagination, and skill exercised by the staff. Signs in The Boston Athenaeum are elegantly executed, unobtrusive, and considered as much a reflection of the spirit of this institution as its books, artworks, and traditions.

David McCord, in *About Boston* (Boston, Mass: Little, Brown and Company, 1973), described The Boston Athenaeum as combining "the best elements of the Bodleian, Monticello, the frigate *Constitution*, a greenhouse, and an old New England sitting room." It is one of about fifteen private libraries in the United States and depends on endowment income, gifts and bequests, and the generosity of its Proprietors. Originally, The Boston Athenaeum was an art gallery, and one enters the present building to find oneself in a sculpture hall. The interior of the library is filled with fine furniture, Oriental rugs, palace vases, busts, portraits, and other works of art. These are considered part of the house furnishings and are in use by the staff as well as the readers, so a cataloger works at an eighteenth-century desk with a marble Venus on the right and a Renaissance bronze on the left. The staff moves objects about the building to display them better or to improve a room, and this further adds to difficulties in labeling or adding signs.

The worst exit sign I have ever seen is in a public library in Massachusetts. It is made from a stencil available at hardware stores and spray-painted directly on a painted brick wall. An arrow, askew, has been stenciled beneath. The irregularities in the surface of the brick wall have caused the red paint to

Action for
Children's
Television

46 Austin Street
Newtonville, Ma. 02160
617·527·7870

FIGURE 13-1 ACT logo.

run at the edges; the whole effect is dreadful. In contrast, the exit signs at The Boston Athenaeum conform to the Boston building code; they are the proper height and width, and are displayed as they necessarily must be. Yet they are elegant examples of the printer's art. They are set off by being covered with glass and put into gold frames. The lesson here for everyone is that a care for detail can make a tremendous difference in the kinds of signs used in libraries. Although a small matter by themselves, signs—which are meant, after all, to be noticed—help to convey and complete the impression of accuracy, care, imagination, and taste that is intended for the entire library.

14

A Signage System for a
University Library

MARVIN E. WIGGINS   MCRAY MAGLEBY

Over many years, without design or plan, hundreds of ineffective and unread signs had accumulated in the Harold B. Lee Library at Brigham Young University in Provo, Utah. In October 1973, a survey of what was then a 200,000-square-foot library assessed the number and kinds of signs in use. The results were startling—a 20-page list of 656 different signs for a total of 1,032 signs in all! The signs were primarily on matboard (heavy cardboard), but some were on metal, plastic, glass, or paper. Lettering processes included printing, painting, engraving, handwriting, typing, stick-on letters, rub-off letters, Magic Markers, and photocopying. Black on white was the most frequent color combination (438 signs), but other combinations included black on yellow, black on orange, black on brown, black on red or pink, black on green, black on gray, black on blue, brown and yellow, blue and green, red and white, and red and green.

THE SIGN COMMITTEE

The Public Services Committee, consisting of all public service librarians, formed a sign committee chaired by Marvin E. Wiggins, who represented the General Reference Department. Membership included subject specialists from each of the other four floors as well as the head of the Learning Resource Center in the library.

In April 1974, preliminary planning was begun for the construction of a major library addition. Fortunately, function was the overriding consideration in the floor plan for the new library. The task of developing a signage system was simplified because the old and new addition floor plans formed an "H." Reference areas were in the same location, the center connectors of the "H," on all five levels.

The sign committee decided to make all signs uniform with white-on-black coloring, and to eliminate signs produced by photocopying, typing, and Magic Marker lettering. An Embossograph process, with letters embedded into matboard, was temporarily adopted. The committee concluded that as many signs as possible should be eliminated, although no definite plans were offered by the librarians. However, two assistant directors did suggest that the committee burn everything and start over.

The committee toured several libraries and office buildings in Salt Lake City, photographed the various kinds of signs utilized, and collected catalogs of sign-making equipment and high-quality signs produced by commercial companies. They listed the advantages and disadvantages of each kind of material, process, and color combination, arriving at the following conclusions:

1 Direction pillars (Fig. 14-1) would provide an overview as patrons enter the library, as well as an orientation to each floor.

2 Hanging signs would help the patron to quickly locate the major services on each floor.

3 All signs would be silk screened on dark Plexiglas, a high-quality material, for a clean, crisp image.

4 All signs would be printed in the Helvetica typeface.

5 A large felt wall directory, using plastic changeable letters behind glass doors, would display call numbers and collection locations in the library.

Work on the signage policy continued from November 1974 through April 1976. The subject librarians on the sign committee were asked to produce the actual wording of the signs needed on opening day. With a committee in charge, decision making was slow and laborious, but once conclusions were reached, the committee became a powerful instrument to convince the other subject librarians to agree. This helped bring about consistency and uniformity. Compromise had watered down the goals slightly until the committee was influenced by an article on signage that appeared in the February 1976 *Wilson Library Bulletin*.[1] The committee was very impressed with the article's philosophy of "you can get there from here," and the committee members felt that they had laid sufficient groundwork to implement this philosophy.

The next step was to obtain bids from professional silk screeners in Salt Lake City and on the Brigham Young University campus. (Although the library has its own in-house display and graphics department, the committee felt that

FIGURE 14-1   Direction pillars. Librarywide directory on main floor pillar (*top left*), direction panel on history/religion pillar (*top right*), floor map on humanities pillar (*bottom left*), subject directory on science pillar (*bottom right*).

FIGURE 14-2 Hanging signs for major services.

the personnel and facilities were insufficient for such a major project. However, it is feasible for future additions to the signage system to be handled by this department.) Professional advice was solicited in design and layout as well as in implementing the library's signage philosophy. Since the graphics department of the Brigham Young University Press submitted the lowest bid and had a reputation for quality work as recognized by many national awards, it was given the contract.

THE SIGNS

The Graphics Department suggested that a standardized size, layout, and color be used for individual signs. The largest signs would give broad information for the entire library and individual floors. The next-sized signs would be placed in major service areas so that all such services for the entire floor could be seen from one vantage point. Once users located the general area desired, they would find smaller signs for the services and tools available within that area. The smallest signs would be placed next to individual rooms, including rest rooms. A single color, typeface, and layout would be selected for all signs.

FIGURE 14-3 Stairwell signs indicate floor numbers and directions for services.

The largest signs are four-paneled 7' by 2' direction pillars. These are placed on each floor by each of the two stairwells. The first thing students see as they enter the library is a pillar containing a librarywide directory listing floor and wing locations for subjects. The panel facing the students as they leave each stairwell instructs them where to go for the services on that floor. An additional panel contains a map of the floor showing the location of collections and call numbers. The fourth panel lists major call numbers in the library, both Dewey and Library of Congress. See Fig. 14-1.

The next-sized sign is 16″ by 48″ and hangs from the ceiling (Fig. 14-2). These signs are limited in number and are used only for the major service areas on each floor, such as circulation, current periodicals, general reference and information, catalog assistance, and reserve library. A student is able to see at once all the major service areas on a floor. Two other-sized signs serve the same function. Two 24″ by 24″ signs are placed in the stairwells to indicate the number of the floor and the direction in which a patron should go to obtain the various services (Fig. 14-3). A 12″ by 24″ sign is used for secondary levels of service such as the photocopy center and interlibrary loan (Fig. 14-4).

FIGURE 14-4   Secondary service sign.

FIGURE 14-5   Direction signs for specific departments.

FIGURE 14-6   Desk or shelf top direction signs.

After patrons are directed into specific parts of the library, two types of signs help them identify the resources in those areas: a 12″ by 12″ direction sign and a 12″ by 16″ desk top sign with the bottom four inches folded under so that the sign sits on a desk or on top of a reference shelf (Figs. 14-5 and 14-6). The smallest signs, 6″ by 6″, label group study rooms, typing rooms, and rest rooms (Fig. 14-7).

Decisions of layout and color involved the designer, the assistant director for public services and coordinator of the new building, the sign committee, the public service librarians, and the Lee Library display artist. The designer convinced most of the staff that blank space and few words effectively focused the viewer's attention on a sign. He suggested that all lettering be flush with the left-hand margin, giving a clutter-free, uniform effect throughout the library. This eliminated a great deal of expense, since silk screeners did not have to center information or justify right-hand margins.

Color was another area of standardization. The library is furnished in gold and dark brown. The designer advised a dark brown, opaque, quarter-inch Plexiglas. Many librarians wanted blue for higher contrast. The discussion centered on whether 294 signs in "BYU Blue" would be too much contrast with the decor, resulting in a cluttered appearance. There was strong support for each side. In the end, the majority shifted to the dark brown, deciding that a white silk-screen letter would be adequate contrast and that the signage itself would complement and harmonize with the library as a whole. Full-scale, comprehensive layouts of glossy black backgrounds were prepared, resembling dark brown Plexiglas, with white lettering, which enabled the committee to visualize what the finished signs would look like when mounted in the library.

The committee was aware that silk screening is an expensive process. However, it was the least expensive of the professional processes examined.

FIGURE 14-7   Small signs for study room, typing rooms, rest rooms, and so on.

Lettering was crisp and clean for multiple-copy signs, and 4' by 8' sheets of Plexiglas could be cut into the specified dimensions without waste. Also, library display personnel could later produce additional copies as needed at slightly lower than the original cost.

There was an additional need for temporary signs and signs communicating detailed information either made by silk screening or using rub-off letters on matboard. A piece of Masonite was mounted on the wall with screws, and the matboard sign was placed behind clear Plexiglas, which was then screwed to the Masonite. The Plexiglas could be removed and the signs changed as needed. These signs were made for the tops of reference desks, ends of index tables, group study room areas, typing rooms, and for conveying information near the interlibrary loan office (Figs. 14-8 and 14-9).

The Graphics Department of Brigham Young University Press was to produce all but the changeable signs needed for the library. Between August 1976 and March 2, 1977 (the dedication date of the Lee Library addition), one-half of the signs were completed and mounted.

Not wishing to drill holes through the faces of permanent signs, the sign makers hung the large signs from the ceiling by drilling a small hole into the top quarter-inch edge of the Plexiglas and embedded with epoxy 150-pound test model aircraft wire designed to resist twisting and breaking. The wall sign Masonite backings were cut one-eighth inch smaller than the signs and then screwed into the wall. The signs were attached to the Masonite with double-stick foam tape. The tape held so firmly that the only way it could be removed was to twist the sign with great effort or to cut the tape between the sign and the Masonite with a sharp knife. The library purchased a sign bender, or a heat rod, for bending the desk top signs to make a four-inch freestanding base.

All individual signs were completed by August 1977. The direction pillars

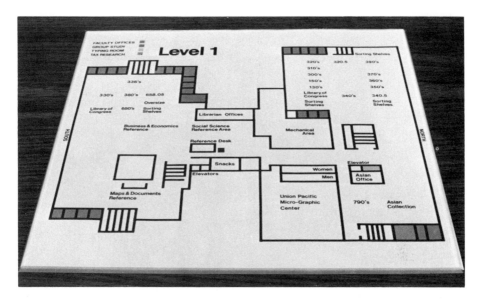

FIGURE 14-8   Matboard signs covered by clear Plexiglas. *Top:* Reference desk sign. *Bottom:* Index table sign.

FIGURE 14-9   Matboard signs covered by clear Plexiglas. *Left:* Sign for group study area. *Right:* Information sign.

were finished in October, and the information and temporary signs were completed by July 1978. The pillars were the most expensive part of the system.
Each one cost $700 to construct, plus $100 to screen each unduplicated
panel. The sign budget covered only the silk screening. The pillars themselves
were conceived by the architect and were part of the new building budget. The
sign committee felt that the direction pillars added considerably to the cost of
the signage system, but were a basic element in it, and the library staff was
generally pleased with the end product.

However, the pillars did pose one serious problem: silk-screen ink etches
the Plexiglas and leaves a ghost image when erased by a solvent. Yet floor
maps and direction information are subject to revision. Attempts to solve this
problem on the map portion of the pillars included using dry transfer-type letters, which have a film backing and do not etch the plastic as badly. These dry
letters can be scratched by a fingernail and require repair every three months.
Otherwise they would have been used more extensively. If the pillars are ever
rebuilt, the library staff might consider using changeable pieces of matboard
slid between two panels of Plexiglas, making revisions more feasible.

In addition to the direction pillars, the total number of different signs came
to 152. Twenty-two of them were made in multiple copies, totaling 142 additional signs, for a total of 294 signs. For a 430,000-square-foot library, 294 signs,
as opposed to 1,032 signs previously used in a 200,000-square-foot library,
demonstrates one result of a high-quality signage system. If the 1,032 signs

were produced with rub-off letters on matboard by in-house labor, the cost (including overhead) would amount to about $4,000, or $3.88 per sign. The cost for the Plexiglas and the silk screening of 294 signs came to $4,790, or $16.28 per sign. The new signage produced an effective and less-cluttered system at little more cost than the cluttered and ineffective old system. The committee found that purchasing a more expensive, high-quality sign caused them to be more conservative in the number of signs ordered. This will be particularly true in future years when the money for new signs will have to come from supply funds rather than capital expenditure funds. There was also a savings in the silk-screening process when producing multiple copies of signs.

THE WORKING SYSTEM

Good signage must be considered as only a part of an adequate library information system. Functional library architecture is helpful, and pamphlets, handouts, bibliographies, and library use instruction round out the program. The Brigham Young University Harold B. Lee Library has produced an effective library guide, listing the major collections, services, and floor plans of each level. The library is producing more detailed guides for each of its major services. A self-paced library use instruction package has been developed for English Composition students. The program includes a taped cassette tour for each year's 5,500 freshmen students. Sophomore students take programmed instruction in the use of the card catalog, periodical indexes, and book and newspaper indexes. A fourth unit on the *Monthly Catalog* is being added. All programs are self-instructional and include required posttests in which students actually use the card catalog and indexes studied. These programs have been statistically validated to guarantee high levels of learning.[2] Additional instruction in the form of workshops, miniclasses, bibliographies, and the like is being considered for upper-division and graduate-level curricula.

The Lee Library has yet to conduct a formal evaluation of its signage system. However, when faculty members were surveyed about the services of the library, they expressed a favorable attitude toward the signs, their design, and the overall concept.

The experience of the Lee Library has shown that the combination of a good communications and signage system will do much to aid students, staff, and faculty in helping themselves and obtaining specific assistance as quickly and as efficiently as possible.

NOTES

1. Dorothy Pollet, "New Directions in Library Signage: You Can Get There from Here," *Wilson Library Bulletin* 50 (February 1976): 456–462.

2. Details of these programs are available in the following articles: Marvin E. Wiggins, "An Effective Approach to the Development of Library Use Instructional Programs," *College and Research Libraries* 33 (November 1972): 473–479; and "Evaluation in the Instructional Psychology Model," in Richard J. Beeler, *Evaluating Library Use Instruction* (Ann Arbor, Mich.: Pierian Press, 1975), pp. 89–97.

Low-Budget Guidance Ideas

WILLIAM HAMBY

Inflation, along with budget cutbacks, can severely restrict and sometimes completely prevent the development of a sound and effective library locational graphics system. Many libraries, unable to afford a professional graphics layout, may either use a makeshift "sign-by-sign" approach or else conclude that it is better to have no graphics at all than an unprofessional product. Despite this apparent absence of acceptable alternatives to professional sign manufacture, there are a number of graphic design and fabrication procedures that can be easily applied by library staff to create a low-budget graphic system both functional and compatible with the library environment.

Simplicity of design, consistency of format, and patience in execution are all necessary to produce such an in-house locational graphics system. By reducing the number of steps and adopting a simple geometric typeface, the layperson can learn, with practice, to produce professional-looking signs quickly and efficiently.

Two graphic systems in the Reference Department of Olin Library, Cornell University's main research facility, Ithaca, New York, are examples of how graphic models can be produced almost completely in-house to solve different interior guidance problems. One procedure solved the problem of guiding patrons through a corridor to the Interlibrary Lending and Borrowing Office. The second demonstrated one method of making a reference collection accessible through a simple, easily constructed graphic system.

The solutions to these two problems are potentially applicable to other libraries seeking low-cost methods of creating effective guidance systems. Through the use of locally available materials and easily learned procedures, the virtually zero-budget graphic systems used at Olin Library increase the efficiency and attractiveness of large spaces without the cost of sophisticated materials and workmanship.

A review of the methods used to develop a program of visual guidance information will show that such systems can be created and maintained by library staff members themselves.

CORRIDOR GRAPHICS

When the Reference Department expanded, the Interlibrary Lending and Borrowing Office was moved downstairs from the main reference area and placed at the end of a complex of offices and storage rooms. The basic design problem was to guide patrons through the corridors and identify each entrance until they reached the office. Here, continuous graphics in the corridor, requiring a minimum amount of material, succeeded in guiding patrons to the office and created an attractive environment out of empty corridor space.

After a scale version of the proposed graphic system was drawn and transferred to the corridor walls, horizontal and vertical bands of inexpensive decorator tape were applied to the pencil layout (Fig. 15-1). The graphic pattern also incorporated certain rectangular sections, which were set aside for the application of solid colors. (The contact paper used to produce these colors was put in place before the tape was applied to insure that the banding would conceal all seams.)

Blue was selected as the background color for written information, such as directions and office door identification, and white vinyl die-cut letters were placed on the blue fields to provide the necessary contrast for legibility. Placement of this type of manufactured lettering on vinyl backgrounds enabled the staff to make changes in the messages without replacing or disturbing the background color fields. It permitted signs for office identification to be personalized more economically. The continuous interweave of bright, compatible color patches and written signals produced an open, light, and pleasant effect easily understood by the patron.

GRAPHICS FOR THE OPEN
REFERENCE AREA

The special nature and function of reference areas require unique solutions when designing a graphic system for staff and patrons. Priorities include giving the staff open and rapid access to all parts of the collection, visual access to the complete collection layout so that staff can guide patrons with a minimum

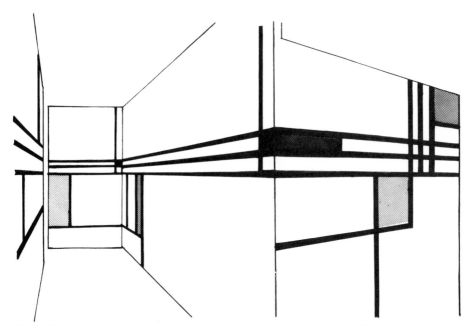

FIGURE 15-1   The interweave of vertical and horizontal banding produces a unified wall treatment, which joins all corridor surfaces. The occasional placement of primary color patches brightens the corridor environment and provides the necessary contrasting background fields for written messages.

FIGURE 15-2   The large single- or double-letter signs placed on stack range ends enable staff and patrons to identify all areas of the collection at a glance.

number of steps, and easy and economical replacement and alteration of graphic elements.

The staff of the Reference Department decided to dismantle the reference collection and reassemble it along the perimeter of a large, central consultation space. The collection was divided into three sections by stack placement. Each of these sections could be viewed from virtually anywhere in the room.

Locational graphics were used to emphasize the geographic placement of the area's collections. Primary color plates were cut from low-cost construction board and affixed to stack range ends with small tabs of double-stick masking tape. High visibility and clear legibility from the farthest distance in the space were the determining factors for both color and size selection of the background fields and their corresponding written messages. Color fields 16″ by 20″, with 10″ by 14″ single or double letters representing the first Library of Congress designation for each section of material in the collection, enabled both staff and patrons to locate their desired area at a glance (Fig. 15-2). Olin Library's reference collection graphics were divided into three color areas, further emphasizing the hierarchy of the collection's classification scheme.

The materials used to produce this graphic system were chosen for economy and ease of application. Rather than being drawn with pens or markers, the large-format letters were cut from black construction paper and affixed to the background by wax adhesive for easy removal and replacement. By using block letters, a single template could be cut to trace the outline of most desired letters (Fig. 15-3). After the letter is traced on paper, a mat knife and steel ruler are used to produce clean edges on the cut-out letters. Errors are easily trimmed from the large-format design without seriously altering the proportions of the letters or requiring their reproduction.

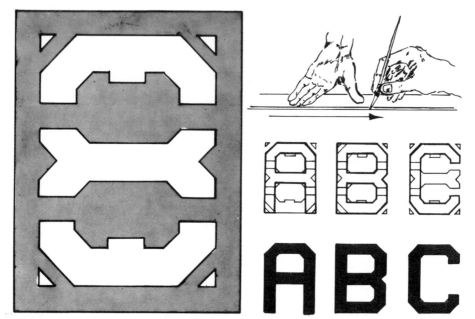

FIGURE 15-3   The simple shapes of the letters shown can be cut from construction paper with a straightedge and applied to the appropriate background fields with wax adhesive.

Smaller-scale signs with word messages can be made in-house by inking with standard letter stencils. The stenciled image of the letter is traced with a fairly dry felt-tipped stylus and then filled in with an opaque marker. By tipping the pen off a straightedge, the illustrator can connect the stencil breaks to produce a clean, professional-looking letter at virtually no cost other than time.

These projects are examples of ways in which library staff, unable to afford professionally commissioned graphic layouts, can pool free time to improve their environments through the innovative combination of soundly tested, basic graphic ideas and extremely low-cost materials. None of the procedures requires more than one or two hours of practical instruction. In-house execution of low-cost graphics allows for flexibility and continuous maintenance. The key to good graphic models is simplicity in both design and execution, which enhances rather than precludes function and beauty.

Wayfinding in Research Libraries: A User's View

CLAIRE RICHTER SHERMAN

The point of view expressed in this chapter represents the experiences of a scholar in medieval studies who has worked in both large and small research libraries in the United States and Europe. These experiences pointed up some basic problems in using research libraries for the first time. Discussions with other scholars about mutual experiences revealed that reactions to the success or frustration of one's mission involves strong responses to the library as a total environment. Indeed, this examination of the wayfinding process in the library clearly indicates that the physical character of the library—including the responsiveness of the staff—significantly influences the ability of researchers to use available resources effectively.

Since this book focuses on total systems of signage, including supporting printed materials and personal communications, as ways of improving how libraries work for readers, let us consider the main problems of wayfinding in the library environment and possible solutions in two main areas— the library as a public space and personal environment, and the library as a setting for intellectual and research work. Obviously this arbitrary division involves some overlapping subjects. The

THE RESEARCH LIBRARY

Designed by McKim and White.
Opened March 11, 1895. Registered National
Historic Place, May 8, 1973.

In-depth collections, historical and current, for
use within the Library. Specialized subject
reference departments.

Books, periodicals, and other materials serviced
by staff.

Library Hours:
Monday — Friday 9:00 a.m.-9:00 p.m.
Saturday 9:00 a.m.-6:00 p.m.
Sunday (October — May) 2:00 p.m.-6:00 p.m.
Closed on all legal holidays.

Materials, Services, Facilities and Location

Administrative Offices (RL only)	2
Book Delivery Desk	2
Catalog Information	2
Change (Sales Room)	1
Copying Machines	1, 2 & 3
Elevators	
Front (Main corridor of each floor)	1, 2 & 3
Rear (Across courtyard)	1 & 3
Fine Arts	3
General Library Passages	1 & 2
Government Documents	1
Humanities	2
Interlibrary Loan (At Catalog Information)	2
Lavatories (In General Library)	GLC
Microtext	1
Music	3
Newspapers (Entrance across Courtyard)	1
Prints (Wiggin Gallery and Balcony)	3
Rare Books and Manuscripts	3
Sales Room (In GL / RL passage)	1
Science	2
Social Sciences	2
Telephones	1

Some Points of Interest

Abbey Paintings	2
Bates Hall	2
Chavannes Paintings	2
Cushman Room	3
Dioramas	3
Elliott Paintings	2
Koussevitsky Room	3
Sargent Paintings	3
Wiggin Gallery	3

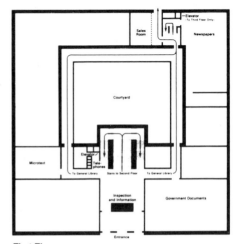

First Floor

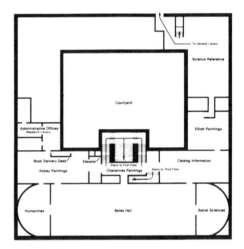

Second Floor

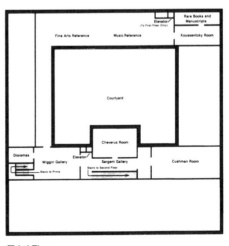

Third Floor

first part of this chapter stresses the library as a total environment to which the researcher must adapt and respond on a human level. This physical aspect will also affect the scholar's ability to accomplish intellectual tasks. The second part addresses more directly processes of locating and using library materials.

THE LIBRARY—PUBLIC SPACE AND PERSONAL ENVIRONMENT

Many great research libraries are nineteenth- and early twentieth-century buildings of monumental architecture. Designed in Renaissance or neo-classical styles, these buildings convey a sense of the majesty and dignity of knowledge embodied and encapsulated in books and artifacts. The magnificent Renaissance structure of the Boston Public Library, for instance, is most impressive. The noble sequence of spaces, lavish mural decorations, and the tranquillity of the ample interior courtyard convey the feeling that books deserve to live in palaces. Nobody would deny the validity of the assumption underlying the design. Even after many years and many visits, the Great Hall and Main Reading Room of the Library of Congress still stir responses to their magnificent spaces and decoration. And in Europe, even more venerable structures strike the same notes of delight and awe.

Yet the very success of these monumental buildings in aesthetic terms may cause problems for those approaching such a structure for the first time. The initial step in library wayfinding for researchers is distinguishing the building from surrounding monumental structures, if no inscription or sign exists. For example, tourists often ask about the identity of the Library of Congress, since no clearly visible sign designates its main building.

A second element that causes confusion is large size. The first sensation on approaching not only an unfamiliar but a vast structure may be a sinking heart. Often short of time, the visiting scholar realizes that the adage "knowledge is power" clearly applies to an environment in which wayfinding may prove troublesome as a prelude to accomplishing a set task. After the researcher has established that the building *is* the library, the next step usually involves ascending a monumental staircase—itself often preceded by a vast courtyard offering a bewildering choice of entrances. Once safely inside the building, where to go next is not always obvious. After one goes through the main doors of Harvard's Widener Library, the only visible sign says merely ENTER. In contrast, at the two entrances to the Boston Public Library, one sees an excellent plan (Fig. 16-1) giving on one side directional information to the general library opened in 1972, and on the other to the old McKim and White structure, now serving as a research library.

FIGURE 16-1   Directional information brochure for the Boston Public Library gives brief historical information about the research library, including a photograph that identifies the facade and distinguishes it from the adjoining general library. It also summarizes the scope of the collections and lists in readable form materials, services, facilities, locations, and points of interest. Numbers of the facilities correspond to the floors on which they are situated. Floor plans are shown at the right of the brochure, and verbal material on them corresponds to the listings on the opposite side. An important feature of the brochure is the inclusion of those facilities connected with users' physical needs and ways of entering and leaving the building at different levels.

Initial Orientation and Admission Rules

In addition to a well-designed floor plan, an even more satisfactory device is a prominently placed information-reception desk clearly visible from the main entrance. Here a staff member not only can distribute directional material, but can also answer basic questions regarding the use of the library, especially access to the collections. If special passes or readers' cards are required, signage, floor plans, and personal instruction should clearly direct the researcher to the registration office. Otherwise, stumbling about vast institutional spaces in search of crucial information puts one at a considerable psychological disadvantage. Unfortunately, the monumental spaces of great libraries were not necessarily designed to help the new user of the building find the way with ease. As a corollary to the difficulties caused by spaces and scale, administrators seem reluctant to "litter" the splendid architecture with signs that might debase the building. Although great sensitivity is necessary to coordinate signage with architecture, ignoring the need for directional information produces not only confusion, but various ad hoc signs incongruous with the setting and ineffective as clear directional signals.

Once having found the registration office, the researcher may fill out simple forms to receive the required pass or card. Sometimes, however, despite prior correspondence in which the researcher requested rules for admission, a few unpleasant surprises lie in store. In one library one is expected to produce three photographs; at another, a driver's license and two credit cards. In a third, there was a two-day delay before issuance of the card. Needless to say, these kinds of surprises are extremely jarring to a researcher who has made a special journey to use a particular collection. Often the visitor confronts unsympathetic staff seemingly unconcerned that these demands not only mean a waste of time, but also indicate the library's lack of concern for the researcher. One possible solution is a general information brochure that includes *all* essential admission requirements, plus the hours of service for the office handling these procedures. Available through the mail or at the entrance desk, the brochure should clearly state hours when the library is open *and* dates on which it is closed.

Information on Physical Requirements

An information brochure should also tell researchers about security rules. Readers may be relieved to learn that they must leave coats (and presumably luggage) in checkrooms or lockers. Often readers will come to the library en route to another destination, and prior knowledge of checkroom facilities will solve the problem of storing baggage safely. Mandatory checking of coats has, however, a negative side. In fall or winter, or in year-round "climate-controlled atmospheres," particularly prevalent in rare book or manuscript rooms, lack of heat can cause the scholar acute discomfort, sometimes ending in the "blue-hands" syndrome. New readers should learn in advance from the brochure of any extraordinary temperature conditions so they can dress appropriately.

New researchers should also learn whether briefcases or handbags are allowed in reading rooms. Such knowledge permits them to arrange their research materials before arrival and relieves the feeling that they are suspected of criminal intentions. Otherwise, such unexpected requirements can make the library environment appear uncomfortable or hostile to the newcomer.

Information about the location of facilities, such as water fountains and telephones, should be available in signs and floor plans. Researchers frequently mention particular difficulties in finding toilets. These facilities should be identified on all floors and locations in the library. This problem can be particularly acute for women doing research in older structures that were once "male only" preserves. A prominent female scholar once located the unmarked ladies room in the Vatican Library by following a nun, thus creating for herself a "living visual sign."

Also vital to researchers is knowing the location of eating facilities. To the researcher in a hurry, a cafeteria or snack bar on the premises is a blessing. New researchers sometimes have difficulty finding eating places in old buildings because they are often placed in obscure and depressing corners of the basement. An open setting, as in the rooftop cafeteria of the Bibliothèque Royale in Brussels, is always a most welcome contrast to the windowless reading rooms.

In short, wayfinding both from the outside and the inside of the library presents psychological barriers that can impede the researcher's ability to work effectively. Good signage and printed aids would help readers to find their way in an unfamiliar and sometimes bewildering environment. Recognizing the human as well as the intellectual needs of the visiting scholar will make the library work better for staff and readers alike.

THE LIBRARY — A SETTING FOR RESEARCH

After learning the admission requirements and where to find certain facilities, the new researcher may next face problems in locating and using the basic materials that are the reason for the visit. At this stage, identifying the reading room, catalog, and reference materials plays a crucial role in the researcher's experience. Yet some libraries do not even provide clear directions for finding the main catalog in relation to the reading room, or vice versa. Appropriate signage and floor plans surely can avoid this complication.

Help with the Catalog

In large research libraries, the placement and arrangement of the most important single research tool—the catalog—can also cause problems if signage is inadequate or explanatory material is confusing. Until fairly recently, the location of the main catalog of the Library of Congress and detailed verbal information regarding its use were not visible at the principal entrance to the Main Reading Room. A research guidance office, to be discussed later, has obviated these problems. At Widener Library, new researchers must find their way into the reading room, where at a largely unidentified reference desk they receive detailed information about how to use the catalog in a publication entitled *The Research Services of the Harvard College Library*. Advice on where to go for help is placed rather inconspicuously on a small sign at the end of a catalog case. Of course, at Widener, as at other older libraries, the spread of

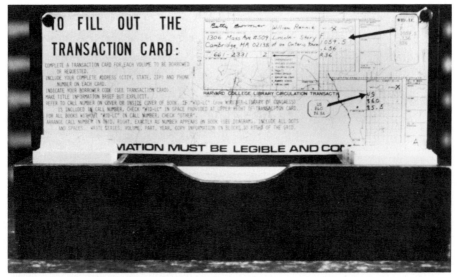

FIGURE 16-2 The confusing typography and layout of this sign make the instructions appear more complicated than they actually are.

the catalog into an original entryway shows the problems of finding space engendered by the "knowledge explosion."

Effective signage and detailed printed material would be a great improvement in aiding scholars with the initial use of the catalog. Furthermore, staff members—whose function in supplying catalog information ought to be immediately identified—should sit in close proximity to the various parts of the catalog when it spreads over several rooms or spaces. A brochure such as *Catalogs, the Major Access Tools to the Collections of the Library of Congress* must be available at all appropriate points. This publication not only explains the workings of the main catalog, but also points to its limitations. It discusses specialized catalogs in other collections and locations in the library, as well as automated catalogs, book catalogs of other major libraries, and the National Union Catalog.

Although experienced scholars have considerable knowledge about how to use catalogs generally, variations do occur from library to library. Filling out request slips for books is one obvious example. The typography of this example (Fig. 16-2) obscures rather than informs because of its densely written and messy format. And what comfort or enlightenment does the visiting scholar receive from the following message, inconspicuously placed at the end of a catalog bay in a major research library: "For recently published books not represented in this catalog, inquire in the Collection Development Office, Room 197"? In another library, researchers read this baffling phrase: "A separate catalog of serials adjoins the Main Catalog." Here the verb "adjoins" does not point the reader to an exact physical location, nor does the sign indicate placement of this catalog. Perhaps an even more confusing situation occurs at another major research library where the letters of the alphabet handwritten on the back of each catalog bay fail to conform to the beginning and ending entries of that particular section. Needless to say, this kind of inaccurate signage can only result in intense frustration to the researcher.

Finding Periodicals, Serials, and Newspapers

The location and use of periodicals, serials, and newspapers also present great difficulties both for libraries and researchers. Again, wayfinding applies to the location of the periodicals reading room. At Widener Library, no sign identifies the room or reference desk. At the Library of Congress and at the Boston Public Library, the distance between the main catalogs and periodical-newspaper rooms is both a psychological and a spatial barrier to their location and delivery.

The eternal difficulties of finding the call numbers of periodicals in their bound form demand the most explicit written information about how to locate them in the library. Once again, a separate brochure dealing with bound and unbound periodicals, serials, and newspapers is a good solution. Essential information in such a brochure includes a detailed list of periodical indexes and their specific locations within the library. Honesty remains the best policy concerning the length of time required before periodicals return from the bindery. Researchers should also receive an estimate of the approximate time necessary for new periodicals to appear on the shelves from date of issue, and they should be informed how long periodicals remain on the shelves before they go to the bindery.

A brochure on periodicals should tell the reader about the scope of holdings, procedures for calling for materials, and the length of time necessary for delivery. The greatest boon to the scholar is to find a wide variety of current periodicals clearly and prominently displayed, alphabetically or by subject, on open shelves in a space equipped with comfortable chairs and good lighting. Whether current periodicals should remain in one room or be divided among special collections depends on the size and facilities of the individual library. Easy access to current scholarly periodicals greatly encourages the researcher to keep abreast of new work in a particular field.

Finding the Books

Obviously the library and the researcher both share the goal of obtaining materials quickly and easily. The difficulties in achieving this aim vary considerably. One important factor involves the question of open or closed stacks. If the researcher has a choice, personally retrieving the books seems far more attractive and reliable. Getting books oneself may result in additional, unexpected, and exciting discoveries on the shelves next to the desired volumes. Also, a scholar can usually locate or identify on the spot any material that may be useless. It is impossible for the scholar to detect such material from any catalog listings.

Of course, the researcher must start with an adequate diagram of the book stacks indicating their points of access and the precise location of classes. The stacks themselves might carry clear signs identifying their number and compass direction, such as Eight North. In addition, signage at entry points should identify the classes by subject, assigned numbers, and precise location. Thus, when the researcher gets off the elevator, a sign such as the following should be clearly visible: Fine Arts—N—Deck 6, South. Each book row should in turn bear large, readable labels identifying the first and last numbers of the volumes it contains. Also helpful would be large signs, hung from the ceilings, that would break down by categories subdivisions within classes by subjects and numbers. For example, Sculpture, *NB*; Painting, *ND*, etc. The location of oversize volumes especially needs to be designated by prominent signage, because folios may reside in odd corners of the stacks not immediately apparent to the researcher. Indeed, staff and scholars alike would profit from a detailed diagram of each class at the entry point to the particular stack. Good lighting would certainly be of great value, and a few portable stools on which users might perch while examining books would greatly enhance the enjoyment of the hunt.

If, on the other hand, the researcher must depend on the library for delivery of materials, wayfinding involves a different set of experiences. Usually diagrams of call slips showing the information necessary to assure delivery appear both in the general information brochure and on signs in catalog locations. As we have noted, poor typography can confuse the new reader on this score. In some libraries, books come directly to the researcher's desk; in others, to a book delivery room that also serves as the drop-off location for request slips. These areas are not always clearly identified by sign or floor plan, and sometimes are situated at a considerable distance from the main catalog. Often the spaces where one must wait or place call slips look like detention camps; poorly lit, with few and uncomfortable seating areas. Adding to the physical and psychological gloom of book delivery rooms or issue desks may be the unpleasant surprises awaiting the new researcher. The first concerns the length of time necessary for a book to arrive. Sometimes handwritten signs, signifying desperation on the part of staff arising from constant repetition, convey this information at the issue desk. On other occasions, a question to the staff on duty will yield the unhappy fact. A sign giving the time required for receiving a book should be placed next to, or above, the deposit box for request slips. This practice will enable the scholar to use waiting time in other kinds of library work.

Another unpleasant surprise, sometimes first revealed at the issue desk, is a limitation on the number of books the researcher may use at any given time. If a scholar needs to examine a large amount of unfamiliar material within a short period, this constraint is a severe blow. Prior warning of this practice in rush periods should be included in the information brochure and posted in appropriate locations within the reading room and catalog areas. I recall my shock at receiving about eleven o'clock in the Bibliothèque Nationale a call slip marked *Terminé*, meaning "finished." On inquiry, I learned that with the third volume ordered I had exhausted the authorized number of five daily book requests allowed in the Manuscript Room. I had not understood that the total included two reference books reserved the day before, and thus "charged to my account."

Researchers should know whether they can reserve books for more than one day. This information should appear both in the general information brochure and at the issue desk on a sign placed close to the deposit box for call slips. The number of books, the length of time they can be held, and the place where they are kept should be specified.

Finding Reference Materials
and Reference Librarians

Another crucial element in wayfinding within the library is locating reference materials and their invaluable guides, reference librarians. An information or reception center should be set up at the principal entrance to the library. Its function can be primarily to give directions, or, as in the case of the Research Guidance Office at the entrance of the Main Reading Room of the Library of Congress, it can also supply basic research information. All the brochures prepared by the different divisions of the library are collected there for distribution, as is visual orientation material. If ample space exists in this type of area for the librarian and the new user to sit down while speaking, an initial interview allows for a more personal, one-to-one exchange. This atmosphere encourages the visitor to explain research needs and receive information not only on spatial orientation, but also on basic use of library resources. Staffed by sympathetic personnel familiar with the workings of the various divisions and collections of the library, a research guidance office can bridge an important psychological and intellectual barrier between the new user and the unfamiliar setting.

The Research Guidance Office at the Library of Congress directs scholars to the location of reference librarians who deal with specific questions on catalogs, bibliographic and reference materials, and all kinds of problems involving research. A librarian specifically designated to deal with catalog information is stationed in the corridor that connects parts of the main catalog. Another reference librarian gives instruction to new users of the automated catalog. An effective signage system must lead the researcher to the various parts of the catalogs and to the reference librarians. Thus, a combination of directional guidance by signs, effective posting of librarians, and specific printed material enhances the scholar's chance of successful wayfinding at a crucial point of introduction to the library environment.

Locating reference materials poses a difficult problem within the large spaces of major research libraries. Usually one has to walk considerable distances within the main reading room before finding where different types of reference materials are located. The large signs installed above the various alcoves of the main reading room of one large library do help in this respect. Also, the catalog of reference materials and a two-page guide to materials posted outside the central reference section are attempts to clue the scholar to available materials. Yet these devices do not clearly show the specific locations where one can find them. In one university library, signs inappropriate in scale and material are placed over sections of reference materials along the walls of the reading room. One must march down and around the length of this considerable space before locating the general subject area, to say nothing of individual works. At another institution, reference service has been split into three separate divisions—humanities, social sciences, and science. Since these sections are placed at considerable distances from one another, researchers must wander about before finding specific materials; no consistent sign system informs them where to locate particular types of information.

Large research libraries need to adopt an effective sign system to indicate the location by subject area of reference materials. Better still would be a published guide to reference materials, with a diagram or floor plan giving geographical locations. The guide would include under subject area the most frequently used works available and their call numbers.

Another type of reference assistance that scholars welcome is a directory of specialists within the library who might help with specific or technical problems of research. I have found that in European libraries, curators or staff in special collections—such as manuscript rooms—are a great help in solving vexing puzzles on the spot. Information about such a directory could form part of a general brochure on the library, or of a more specialized guide to research.

There remains another facet of locating material that deserves particular attention. The researcher needs to know what steps to take if the required books or other library resources are not found in their assigned places. How to clarify whether the items in question are in use elsewhere and the time necessary for retrieval should be indicated in the general information guide and at the issue desk. Other provisions, such as special searches, should also be described.

Special Collections

Special collections have long presented particular problems within the large research library. Finding these divisions is sometimes tricky; they are often tucked away in obscure corners or wings of the structure, or even in locations separate from the main building. Again, the informational brochure, with a map and printed directions, should accompany prior correspondence or be available at the reception desk. Even better, as already noted, would be a separate brochure for each major special collection. Contents should include hours of service, general scope of the collection, reference and photoduplication services, interlibrary loan and microfilm possibilities, and a brief bibliographical outline of finding guides to the holdings. The name of a specific staff member to whom one could address queries would be useful. These guides also would be available at all reference and information centers within the library.

Other Research Tools

Once the scholar has become familiar with the library environment and located the desired materials, certain research tools also may be necessary to make the visit successful. Obvious examples are typewriters or tape recorders. Rules for their use and the possibility of rentals should be part of the general information brochure.

Also essential, particularly to the researcher with limited time, is access to photocopy machines. Their location must be clearly indicated by signage, and their effectiveness as a research tool requires a sufficient number of machines, regular maintenance, and reasonable prices. Too often these conditions do not exist. This photograph (Fig. 16-3) indicates that obscure and unpleasant locations, limited numbers of machines, and a poor state of repair can contribute to unpleasant surprises for scholars.

Equally important for the researcher are knowledge of cost, availability, and length of time necessary to procure other types of visual materials, such as maps, slides, and photographs. If a central photoduplication service exists for the entire library, signs, floor plans, and the general brochure should mark its location and hours of service.

FIGURE 16-3   This gloomy basement setting, with uncoordinated signs and lack of seating facilities, too often characterizes the atmosphere and frustrations associated with the grim but essential task of photoduplication.

RECOMMENDATIONS

The best means to assist wayfinding in the research library setting calls for a coordinated strategy of effective signage, specific brochures, and the stationing of informed and friendly librarians at crucial junctions in the building. The use of the main catalog and its automated or microform supplements requires special attention. Clearly written materials and "trouble-shooters" placed at appropriate locations in the catalog area are needed. Separate material on finding and retrieving periodicals, including the location of indexes and guides, also merits careful consideration. Far more thought should be given to the effective placement of reference librarians in easily identifiable and spacious settings that provide the opportunity for a real exchange between them and researchers. In addition, a detailed listing by subject matter—including call numbers and locations—of major reference tools should be a separate compilation.

It also seems feasible to compile several types of programs describing the research facilities within the library, in particular, a brochure aimed at the advanced scholar, keeping in mind the kinds of information discussed in this chapter. Another possibility is a specialized daily tour for visiting researchers. A third option would involve an orientation film. The Library of Congress is considering a plan to insert into a specialized brochure for researchers separate pages listing reference materials in a specified class. The insert would list the major types of material located not only in the central reference section, but also throughout other areas of the library. The format would constitute a checklist on which the librarian would indicate collections and texts. Included in either the specialized brochure for researchers or in the brochure on reference collections ought to be notice of a directory of subject specialists available for consultation.

This chapter has tried to show that, for a scholar, wayfinding in an unfamiliar library environment involves a complex set of responses to the whole setting, including physical and intellectual needs. Recognizing the various steps in the wayfinding process is the first stage in making the library a more humane and efficient setting for research and scholarship.

ACKNOWLEDGMENTS

I wish to thank Stanley M. Sherman for taking the accompanying photographs and for showing me the connections between the architectural environment and signage problems. For their sympathetic responses and helpful recommendations, I am most grateful to Linda Arret and Peter Petcoff, reference librarians at the Library of Congress.

Part
4

*Visual Guidance and
the Library Building*

17

Coordinating Graphics and Architecture

BRUCE DANIELS GARRET EAKIN

A library needs physical space to house its services and graphics to advertise those services and facilitate their use. Together, graphic design and architectural design can become the visual means of orienting people to areas and services of the library. By planning the graphics with the architecture (instead of tacking on the graphics after the structure is built), the total design can announce the library's presence, amplify its image, and broadcast its services.

Design involves identifying and arranging a series of elements to serve a definite purpose. In a building, it means organizing certain areas, or spaces, as the architect refers to them, in a way that permits, encourages, or bars access. Functional areas, well-organized patterns of movement, and ready access all depend on how well the architect planned the arrangement of the spaces to serve the needs of the users. One might say that a library building uses certain architectural elements in order to "look" and "work" like a library.

In the case of signage, design means creating a systematic series of meaningful graphic elements. A *signage system* is simply a coordinated set of directions that provides all the

FIGURE 17-1 The Lake County Public Library's new addition is a compact, metal-skinned, three-story square building with limited glass for energy conservation. Furnishings and signage will pick up the bright exterior accent colors used at the entry, staircase, and building corners to create a cohesive image for the library complex.

information needed to use a facility efficiently. Signs clarify the ways to use a library by funneling information to the user in simple, immediate forms. At the same time, signs enrich the environment in which they are placed. For example, graphics can highlight the architectural elements and their organization by repeating shapes, colors, and textures used in the building design. Design also creates an image. The shape, color, and quality of both the graphics and the building reflect the nature and purpose of the organization they serve. An architectural and graphic style subtly characterize a library's atmosphere and the nature of its services.

As new and more complex environments are created and as older facilities are rehabilitated for new and different uses, signs and graphics become increasingly important in making our world understandable. Perhaps in part as a reaction against the complexity of modern technological society, graphic design in recent years has become more visual, less verbal, and less linear. Contemporary graphic design transmits information clearly and directly by eliminating unnecessary, nonfunctional visual elements. Designs employ flat planes of solid, highly contrasting colors. One-word messages and commonly understood symbols allow for immediate communication. Simplicity, economy, and clarity are the guidelines. This is not unlike contemporary architectural design, which has become cleaner, crisper, and more compact. Newer buildings tend to be simple geometric shapes designed for function, economy, and access. Accompanying graphics spotlight function and image expressed in the architecture by restating the same design concepts in a different visual mode.

The Lake County Public Library in Merrillville, Indiana, is an example of the purposeful harmonizing of graphics and architecture to provide a modern, efficient library building and create a new, fresh image (Fig. 17-1). The old building suffered from "image deficiency." The original square, gray, concrete library is coarse, faceless, lackluster—in a word, drab. It sits among the car lots, hamburger stands, neon signs, and gas stations typical of many a suburban city, lost in the flash and roar of a society on wheels.

When congested reading areas, overflowing shelves, and expanding administrative needs demanded an addition, the library board decided that revitalizing the library's image was as important a requirement as providing more space. The board wanted a bright, shiny, attractive library complex that would reflect, yet stand apart from, its suburban, auto-oriented surroundings.

The architects and the graphic and interior designers carefully chose shapes, colors, textures, and materials that would produce a vibrant, twentieth-century image. Plans called for sheathing the new, three-story, practically windowless, metal-skinned addition in neutral-toned panels, which would blend in with the gray color and contrast with the rough texture of the existing building. Panels of bright red, yellow, and blue would spotlight the entry, grand staircase, and corner "pods" that housed permanent systems such as plumbing or mechanical equipment.

The panels were designed to give the addition a shiny, metallic look to harmonize with the metal and glass commercial buildings ringing its site. The drive-in entry, drive-up book drops, and expanded parking areas further tailor the library to the needs of the mobile community it serves.

Everything about the library is designed to be simple, functional, and flexible. The new building is a square with the top two floors organized around a naturally illuminated atrium. There is seating in the middle with the book stacks wrapped around the perimeter, similar to the manner in which stores face a central mall in an enclosed shopping center. Each floor has a separate function—a central hub of activity, including reference and service desk at mid-level, a place for quiet reading and study above, and high-traffic areas below, such as public meeting rooms, a listening room, the slide library, and the children's library. The interior has minimal, movable walls and is structured so that every square foot can accept fully loaded shelves.

Access to the library's services is simplified by the organization of the functional spaces, direct traffic routes, and clear, strategically located signage. Signs are designed to transmit information clearly, using simple, one-word messages or arrows superimposed on solid backgrounds. Like the building, they are planned to allow for future change. Sign faces are printed on removable inserts and set into fixed mounts.

Outside, a huge exterior sign, projecting from the walkway that intersects the original building, advertises the library to motorists passing on the expressway. An extensive system of exterior signage directs users from various points in the community to the library's front door.

Inside, corridors to all areas of the library radiate from the midlevel lobby or hub. All signage starts from this hub, too. A kiosk, commanding a central point, serves as a kind of road sign and central information source, offering space for posting bulletins and notices of special events. Kiosk arrows guide users in one of three directions: straight ahead, to the link connecting the new and old buildings; to the right, the service and information desk; or to the left, to the elevator and stairs leading to the upper and lower levels. Figure 17-2 graphically identifies elevator and conference doors in the library.

Directional information is packaged so that users receive only enough information at one point to move them one step toward their ultimate goal. The

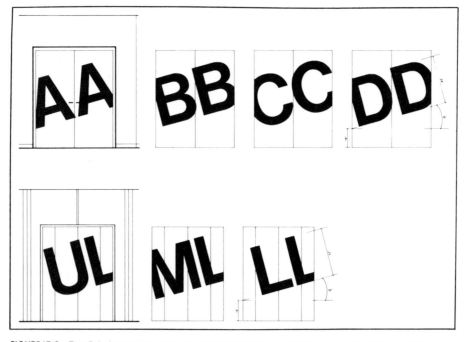

FIGURE 17-2 *Top:* Exterior conference door elevation (Sign Type 10 Supergraphics). *Bottom:* Exterior elevator door elevation (Sign Type 11 Supergraphics). Graphic image for both: 42 inches tall, placed on a 15 degree angle. Letters for both: hand-cut vinyl, white, applied directly onto outside of doors. From Lake County Public Library.

kiosk is the first decision-making point. From there, colorful plastic banners suspended from the ceiling identify areas on each floor, and then smaller, changeable signs on book-stack ends provide the next level of information needed to find a book. The entire system is a refining process, gradually "stepping the user down" to more specific information.

The three primary colors used as exterior accents are reinforced throughout the design so that the whole library becomes identified with these colors. Signs, flags, banners, stationery, carpeting, furniture, and even the bookmobiles borrow colors, shapes, and textures from the building design. Both the logo and the signage play off elements of this design (Fig. 17-3): signs stationed blocks from the library, announcing its presence in the community, have softly rounded corners and thin fiberglass faces that recall the sculpted metal panels covering the new addition. The "inwardness" of a windowless library built around an atrium is emphasized by using a positive design (colored lettering on a white background) for nearby exterior signage and a negative design (white lettering on a colored background) for interior signage. The logo, consisting of monogram letters set inside each other on a white background, also recalls the building's shape and inward orientation.

Use of bright primary colors is intended to invoke an aura of childlike wonder and discovery, and thereby regenerate the excitement of the early learning experience. The flags, banners, and supergraphics painted on the ends of the book stacks in the children's library carry this idea further, creating a lively environment for readers.

FIGURE 17-3 The logo, used to create an identifying mark for the library, mimics the library's inward orientation and round-cornered square shape by setting the library monogram letters inside each other to form a square, as shown on the library truck.

All external visual communications instruments—stationery, signage, flags, and bookmobiles—carry this same visual excitement into the community, adding to the users' perception of the library and its services. At the same time, the signs, graphics, and banners expand the community's awareness of the library as a multiple resource center that is also an exciting, vital place.

18

Architectural Techniques for Wayfinding

AARON COHEN ELAINE COHEN

Many people look on signs and signboards as forms of clutter, discards of pop culture—in a word, junk. During the Johnson Administration, Lady Bird Johnson spearheaded an American beautification project, which resulted in the removal of signboards from the rights-of-way adjacent to the nation's interstate highway system. Signs were viewed (and are viewed still) as the very antithesis of the natural beauty of the American countryside.

This dislike of signs is often shared by those in charge of the construction and maintenance of public buildings. In some buildings only the most essential signs, or those mandated by law—such as EXIT— can be found; there are no direction or identification signs. Even the location and exterior of a public building may not be designated. To find such a building, the first-time visitor may query several passersby, who may never have heard of the place anyway. On other buildings, the camouflage technique is used: gray letters, for example, may be affixed to gray granite so that the message blends in with the surrounding decor. In a nutshell, the message is hard to find and, once found, even harder to read.

Building designers—architects, interior designers, and others—tend to look down on graphics, although they would not admit it. For some reason, print messages in particular are viewed as a direct attack on the unity of design. These professionals see their own works as art, but print messages as anything but art. There are also some architects who believe in personalizing space, that is, in creating public buildings in which people are comfortable and at home. That is why they leave out signs. After all, few of us hang signs in and around our homes—except, of course, for the numbers on our front doors and our names on the mail boxes (as well as the notes on the refrigerator warning that the chocolate cookies must be saved for tonight's dessert or that *somebody* better remember to take out the garbage).

Unfortunately, by disdaining good graphics, architects make their buildings anything but personalized. In fact, the opposite is the case. Some public buildings, libraries especially, turn into confusing, mazelike structures—the exact opposite of the architects' original intent. Think about it: few architects would dream of designing a confusing structure to handle hundreds, or perhaps even thousands, of people each day. It goes against the basic techniques of architectural education. Architecture is supposed to provide shelter and aid people in their daily activities. Good traffic flow, well-thought-out building interrelationships, and flexibility of design are more in tune with proper architectural practice. In fact, when asked, most architects claim that they design buildings in which it is relatively easy to find one's way, and that their designs aid building orientation.

So why is the opposite so often the case? Most architects want to design interesting buildings, and the more interesting a building is, the more unconventional it is. Because the design is unconventional, no matter how good, visitors are not certain how the spaces are supposed to interrelate. A fine example is the academic library bounded by a sunken plaza, the rage of the last few years. These plazas often are ten or even fifteen steps below street level, and lead directly to what looks like an imposing main entrance. Most of these very same buildings have been outfitted with street-level doors—at the side of the building—if for no other reason than to provide access for the handicapped. But first-time visitors are often unaware that such access points exist. There are no identifying signs pointing to them, and the exterior pathways leading to the doors are not well defined. How annoying it is to walk down slippery steps to enter a library building in the wintertime only to find there are no library services on that floor. One has to take an elevator or stairway to the main floor—and once there, one realizes, with even more annoyance, that the main floor was approachable through a nicely appointed, but well-hidden, street door in the first place.

This is what is known as architectural disorientation, a condition not only annoying but potentially serious. (A handicapped or elderly person could have fallen down those slippery steps.) Of course, this can be prevented by thinking out the problem and using architectural techniques along with a system of signage. Architecturally, the problem could have been handled by downplaying the plaza entrance and making the side doors stand out through the use of awnings, lights, or other eye-catching details. In addition, a well-written signboard or two indicating the easiest way in for people approaching the building could have done the trick.

ARCHITECTURAL ORIENTATION NEEDS

Architectural orientation, or wayfinding, needs can be divided into five cate-gories—identification, direction, prohibition, information, and status. Some can be aided by designing the building to promote wayfinding, not only around the periphery, but inside the building as well. Others cannot be handled archi-tecturally at all, and need a good deal of help from print or symbols.

Identification

Orientation needs in building identification can be handled architecturally to some extent, although at times the problem is difficult. Some may try to find a library by looking for a building that looks like a library. But all libraries do not look like the public's conception of a library—but just what *is* the public's con-ception of a library? Just displaying the library reading room with a glimpse of the book stacks through a window facing a busy street aids building identifica-tion. The view of this function announces that this is indeed a "library."

Direction

Building direction is more easily dealt with by using architectural guideposts. Traffic flow is often anticipated by forming paths of texture, color, and form. Most architects try to do this naturally. For example, when one enters a building the lobby may be distinguished by one type of wall covering, while the corri-dors and other areas feature another type. Floor coverings and ceiling motifs change as well. Then, too, in most buildings one easily finds the stairway or the elevator, because both are in full view immediately upon entering the structure. Those libraries shackled with architecture that hides elevators and stairwells in the depths of the buildings constantly have to deal with direction questions from users.

Architects know that people instinctively gravitate toward light. Walkways are often formed by using pools of light to draw people along. In the field of retailing, the opposite technique is used—lighting for events. Here, only the events (or displays) are lit, and the corridors and walkways depend on the spillover for illumination. When one walks into a store, one makes a beeline for the display first in view, and then the next and the next. Some libraries have appropriated this technique. One library consultant, who believes that the infor-mation desk should be the hub of all user activity, counsels librarians to light that desk to a higher degree than the surrounding area. The desk stands out like a beacon: it is the first thing seen on entering, and in the smaller facilities it is visible from all access points.

Libraries are furniture-intensive buildings—the furniture and equipment take up a lot of floor space, more than in the average structure. In fact, many libraries have no interior walls at all except for those around the rest room facilities and perhaps one cutting off the technical processing area from the rest of the building. Furnishings form all corridors and walkways. By manipulat-ing the furnishings, clear lines of movement, as opposed to a haphazard con-figuration, can be formed. Walls of furniture acting as barriers direct people at predictable angles, forming pathways through the building.

Obviously, the librarian can more easily manipulate furniture placement than building elements. People tend to take shortcuts, and if a librarian sees that a small space is becoming a main corridor, with flexible furnishings a better walkway can be made simply by moving the piece of equipment out of the way. (Removing a wall usually means construction with accompanying noise, dust, and dirt.)

Color as well as light can be used as a direction aid. Not only do people gravitate toward areas that are well lit; they are attracted to those that are more colorful as well. In some of the newer public libraries with very nicely appointed children's areas, the librarians often have to guide adults who inadvertently wander in, attracted by the bright decorations. Many of us color library lounges more intensely than the rest of the facility, because the lounge is a place of relaxation, and color lends a feeling of informality. And it turns out that if the lounge is more attractive in terms of color than the rest of the place, it is heavily used. Some libraries use color coding instead of printed signs to denote direction. One large academic facility has color coded the stacks so that the reader understands "Orange = 800s." It works. Others have simply changed the decor from one major area to another, thus defining each area's limits.

Prohibition

Even more successful than those defining direction are the architectural techniques for prohibition, or warning. True, a sign helps, but a clear barrier is even better. Not many people pay attention even to the most interesting graphics (unless they want to), even when danger is near, but a locked door clearly says "Do Not Enter."

Everyone has seen examples of architectural techniques that imply warning or prohibition in libraries. Leaving some of today's security-conscious libraries can be accomplished only by walking through a turnstile or an electronic checkpoint. But there are more subtle ways of handling some of the same problems. For example, if the library does not wish an area to be used by the public, a much lower lighting level than that used in adjacent spaces may help dissuade users. Another method is simply to place an area out of sight in a quiet backwater of the facility. This is constantly done, although most users are not aware of it. The boiler room, for example, is a place that most libraries do not want users or even staff members to frequent. For that reason it is usually hidden below stairs in the depths of the building, far away from everything else. To find it, a person actually has to know where the room is. So if the library does not want the children to play on the loading dock, is it not possible when designing the building to place the dock in an area far away, hidden from easy view?

Building Information

Although prohibition and warning are relatively easy to deal with architecturally, the third orientation need—building information—rarely is. Without print, it is nearly impossible to deliver the message that this is the third largest library in the United States, or that here, on this very spot, George first spied Martha. For that matter, it is difficult in a large facility to indicate architecturally that the classrooms are on the fifth floor, at the back of the building, without a directory and/or a diagram. The library can use special decor. In the case of the third largest library, the building could have been made of grandiose materials to indicate its importance. In the case of George and Martha, use of the colonial style could show that the library stands in an area of historical significance. Still, without a signboard, the message will not get through. As for the location of the classrooms, without signs to lead the way, the best one can hope for is that there will be a staff member on hand to give the proper advice.

Status

The fifth type of orientation—status—is often displayed architecturally. Like warning or prohibition, it is commonly found in libraries. By using the so-called wealthy materials—wood, marble, gilding, special moldings, expensive fabrics, costly furnishings—importance can be made evident. Often all we need to do is glance at the size of the building, its extensive gardens, and its big double doors to know how fine it is. Once inside we can discern the status of a staff member by the size of the office, the furnishings, or even the presence of a nearby window. The importance of certain books is emphasized by placing them in locked cabinets or in special rooms. In our so-called classless society, these things connote a higher level or two, and they certainly are more pervasive than a few signs affixed to a wall.

SIGNS AND ARCHITECTURAL ORIENTATION

So far we have examined several architectural techniques that aid building orientation and we have indicated that some techniques are better than even the best system of signage. However, in the end, the very best methods employ a combination of the two.

In the design of a system of graphics to aid building orientation, or wayfinding, wherever applicable all signs should display a mixture of print and symbols. Symbols are fine and were used long before the alphabet was developed, but today most people are oriented to a print world. The president of the American Institute of Graphic Arts (AIGA) has written that symbols can be used only in a limited manner and that the combination of symbols with print is best.[1]

Even some of the simplest symbols are not easily recognized by everyone. AIGA developed a signage program for the government,[2] and included representations of a man and a woman separated from one another by a vertical bar. To graphic artists, the drawing was a clear indication of rest room facilities— both men's and women's—nearby. However, in the United States the two sexes generally do not use the same facilities, and although the symbol did denote two different rooms, the context of the message was confusing to some. The word TOILETS inscribed below aided the message considerably.

Unfortunately, many architects, interior designers, and even graphic artists gravitate toward designing signs that display symbols only. These people are practitioners of the visual arts and do not always see the sense of print. Especially in libraries, where print is still king, signs should usually convey messages in both symbols and print.

When one is drafting sign messages, it is best to use simple words. In the library of a prestigious law school, the sign in front of the information desk was changed to read HELP. Foreign students in particular seem to read and understand the smaller word more easily, and more students approached the desk than did before.

If long words are used, they must be printed in as clear and direct a manner as possible; otherwise they are difficult to read. This suggestion, in effect, cuts out supergraphics as far as the dissemination of messages is concerned. Although supergraphics are fine for decoration, they are not particularly good where one wishes the message to be read. Designers have been asked once too often, "How could they have missed the sign? The darn thing was nearly half the wall!" *That is the whole point!* The sign was too long and too intricately written to be well understood.

Librarians often ask about sign shapes, colors, and messages. Faber Birren (one of the foremost experts on color use) and the famous artist Wassily Kandinsky, without ever having met, developed almost identical systems of shapes and colors. These same shapes and colors reoccur together from time to time in various cultures throughout the world. Although there is something to be said for a universal consciousness, Americans seem to be more in tune with the shapes, colors, and messages that appear on the highways (some of which use the same shape and color system as Birren and Kandinsky), simply because they see them all the time. If a library wants to employ a system of shapes, colors, and messages that have specific meaning for users and staff, the system commonly used on highways should be taken indoors. In other words, a red octagon will always say STOP, and a yellow diamond, CAUTION.

When developing a graphics program, many librarians wait until everything else in the building is completed—not only the construction, but the interior design and installation of furnishings as well. Sometimes they even wait until opening day. This is never advisable. Some furnishings have to be constructed with places for signs. Book stacks, for example, need slots for identifying cards for the numbers of the library's classification system. Then, too, if supergraphics are part of the system, they have to be applied to the walls. Why paint a corridor one color only to repaint it a few weeks later with a supergraphic logo? Furthermore, some signs, particularly lighted and directional ones, require special construction or electrification. It certainly would be better to know in advance where to place wall outlets before wires are hidden in raceways.

When one is designing a system, a series of drawings, each done on tracing paper, is a helpful technique. The first overlay may contain furnishings, the next lighting, and the next graphics. Not only the placement and height of the signs should be indicated (whether they are to be affixed to the walls, freestanding, or hung from the ceiling), but also the distances from which they are best seen. This is important so that the height of the letters can be worked out.

Before the whole system is designed, a mock-up should be tested if possible. If the library is moving from a small building to a larger one, the mock-up can be tried out in the old space. Granted, that is not a perfect solution, but for people who are not particularly visual in their approach to things, it is the only answer at the moment. If the library is simply renovating its space, the mock-up can be tried out where it will eventually be used. It will indicate if a sign is improperly drawn, too small or too big, or if it has legibility problems during certain times of the day. This is particularly true of signs that are to be affixed to the exterior of the library. When the sun is shining brightly, can the message be read? What does it look like in the rain? At twilight? Lighted signs also cause problems. If the sign is too bright, a halation effect can occur around the letters, making them difficult to read. This often happens to signs that stand close to a bright window wall. Because of the sunlight condition during the day, the sign is lighted to a high degree. However, at night the background of the sign is much too bright and has to be toned down.

Some library supply companies sell lighted directories that depend on a button system to show users where they are at the moment and how to get to where they want to go. These systems are fairly expensive, but very popular. Whether or not these are used, the library should display several directories throughout the building at major access points—usually near stairwells, entrances, elevators, and similar places. Well-thought-out directories do a good job of eliminating most of the extraneous questions asked of the staff all day. However, these techniques will not eliminate all such questions. There will always be someone standing under the sign that indicates the historical collection asking for the location of the historical collection.

The architectural and signage techniques described in this chapter can contribute a great deal to successful wayfinding in libraries. However, an effective visual guidance system is a complex blending of many elements—architecture, signs, symbols, directories, printed guides, and helpful human beings.

NOTES

1. Thomas Geismar in *Symbol Signs*, prepared by the American Institute of Graphic Arts for the U.S. Department of Transportation, 1974 (DOT-OS-40192).

2. Ibid.

Designing Open-Stack Areas for the User

Large, open-stack libraries frequently have no staff assistance in the stack areas. Once users leave a service point, they are on their own to succeed or fail in locating books. Signs and printed materials alone may not provide enough direction, especially in large or complex buildings. However, the design of the space itself[1] can greatly aid the user.[2] This chapter describes the way in which stack design as a means of aiding users was considered in planning for the expansion and remodeling of the University of Houston (UH) Central Campus Library building, and the way in which stack design factors were identified and applied in the final stack arrangement.

Before the renovation of the UH Library building, stack areas on different floors were arranged in several different patterns. The library staff was aware that users frequently encountered difficulties in locating books in some stack areas, whereas other areas were relatively trouble free. It was apparent that space arrangement influenced user success in locating the proper stack area, and in locating the desired book or books within the area. It also appeared that user difficulties due to poor arrangement would be compounded as the library and the student body grew.

page 195

INITIAL STUDIES

Because of the variety of stack arrangement patterns in the original building (see Figs. 19-1 *left*, 19-2 *left*, and 19-3 *right*), UH had a good opportunity to gather data about the areas that assisted or hindered users. Queries from the suggestion box revealed that many users failed to find whole areas of the stacks. Reference/information staff responses suggested possible causes for the failures, and also possible solutions. The staff reported user problems in detail and contributed analyses and comment based on experiences—for example, difficulties users had when first attempting to find books in the stacks, and successful or confusing features users noted in the design of UH stacks and those in other libraries.

An analysis of all this information led to the identification of several design factors that appeared to contribute to user success. These factors and their application are described below. Most of the design requirements could have been met by any one of several solutions. Although solutions, or specific arrangements, appropriate to any given library will vary, the overriding design considerations can be applied to any open-stack area. The study process at UH resembled that described in Deasey[3] and Heimsath:[4] collecting data, creating verbal descriptions of the processes and goals to be achieved, and translating the descriptions into a spatial arrangement.

DESIGN FACTORS AND APPLICATION

Organize the collection according to a comprehensible pattern. The collection may be arranged in call number order from the top to the bottom floor or from the bottom floor to the top, or the library may be arranged by subject division.[5] It is important to first have a system,[6] and then to communicate the system[7] to the user through book location charts, building diagrams, and other means.[8] If users can see that there is a logical pattern to the book arrangement, they can more readily accept the logic of, and follow, the call number arrangement.[9]

The UH library collection originally had been arranged to accommodate a divisional reference structure, with the stacks for each subject on the floors nearest to the appropriate reference desk. When the divisional reference areas were consolidated into a central reference service on the first floor, there was no longer any meaning to the stack arrangement.

The objectives in planning a new stack arrangement in the expanded building were to place the collection in call number order and to keep the major subject divisions of the Library of Congress (LC) classification together on the same floor and wing. In such a building, with book stacks on more than one floor and stack floors of two or more adjoining wings, there are four possible arrangements that place a collection in call number order: beginning the call number sequence on the upper or the lower floor, and in the left- or right-most wing. To select the arrangement that would minimize the physical division of major subject classifications, data was gathered on the present size and projected rate of growth of the collection as a whole, and on the size and growth of each major subject division of the collection. These figures were compared with the book capacity available in each stack area for each of the possible call

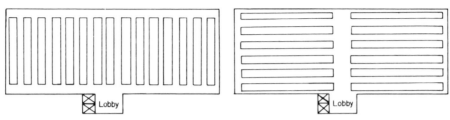

FIGURE 19-1   (left) Main aisle with stacks on only one side—the least confusing stack arrangement; (right) main aisle with stacks on both sides of aisle.

number sequence arrangements. The best arrangement was selected by choosing the one that minimized the physical separation of major subject divisions of the collection. In the UH library, analysis revealed that only one of the four possible arrangements met the second objective of keeping major subject divisions together on the same floor and wing. Other libraries may find that there is more than one arrangement that meets both of these major objectives, or that there is no ideal choice, i.e., the book collection of one or more subjects will be physically separated by any possible collection arrangement. In such cases, additional questions should be asked and answered in selecting a final collection arrangement: Are the books of some subjects more heavily used? Are the users of some subject collections more skilled in finding their materials? Would some of the possible arrangements divide subjects by a greater distance? Is it more important for some subject collections to be near a reference desk?

After the overall stack arrangement for the building is determined, the arrangement of smaller areas should be considered.

Arrange each stack area according to one scheme.   All floors or stack areas should be arranged in the same pattern, or in as few patterns as possible. Even users who do not succeed in developing a cognitive map of the entire building may learn the pattern of a stack area and be able to "predict" the pattern of other stack areas if the pattern is repeated.[10]

The book-stack arrangement may be consistent even if the stack floors are of different sizes and shapes. For example, the shelving can be arranged so that users arriving on a floor go straight ahead down a central aisle, or so they turn left or right down an aisle along the wall (Fig. 19-1).

The ideal is, of course, not possible in all buildings, especially those with many small spaces or with very large rectangular spaces. At UH, all stack floors could be arranged as shown in Figs. 19-1 (left) and 19-2 (right). Repeating the same stack arrangement in all stack areas was particularly helpful, since the building itself is complex and many users never succeed in developing a cognitive map[11] of the building as a whole. The library staff had observed that some users requested floor maps as an aid in finding library materials, and other users preferred step-by-step directions. Therefore, two types of book location guides were developed, one with floor maps and one with only a map of the first floor (with which users are verbally directed to the elevator for each wing), and a printed list of book locations by floor and wing. This list encourages users to learn a basic route from the first floor card catalog area to the elevator for each stack wing. On reaching the stack floor, users find the same stack pattern in each.

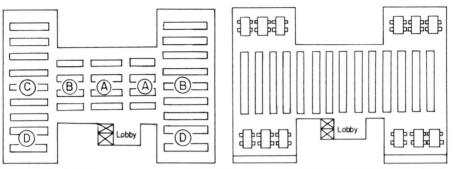

FIGURE 19-2 (left) This floor plan produced the highest rate of user failure before remodeling. Users regarded the aisle between the two ranges labeled A as the main aisle for the floor, and had progressive difficulty locating books in ranges B through D; (right) same floor rearranged, with the main aisle along elevator wall, secondary aisles eliminated, and architectural nooks converted to study areas.

Eliminate "hidden aisles." Aisles that are not visible from the floor lobby are frequently not located by users. Hidden aisles were the main problem with the original UH stack arrangement. Even though a large floor plan was prominently displayed in each stack area, user feedback indicated that a substantial percentage of users failed to find whole areas of the collection.

Hidden aisles may be eliminated by rearranging the shelving to create one main aisle in each stack area with the ends of all ranges facing this aisle. In large spaces, it is best to arrange the shelving so that it runs across the short dimension of the area, creating a main aisle along the long dimension (Fig. 19-2).

If even the short dimension is too long for an unbroken range, it will be necessary to have cross aisles. However, cross aisles are confusing to users and should be avoided if possible. Maximum range length for any given library is determined by considering range length together with the level of use of the collection, and the aisle width.[12] In the one-million volume UH Central Campus Library, with a campus community of 30,000 students, the library has standard-ized 32-inch aisles and 51-foot ranges. This is longer than ranges in most similar libraries, yet UH users are much less confused by the present arrangement, and congestion in the stacks has not become a problem.

When cross aisles are necessary, books should be shelved as though the cross aisle did not exist (Fig. 19-3), a practice recommended by Ellsworth.[13]

ARRANGING THE STACK SECTION

Once the library's planning group began to view the arrangement of library space as a means of communicating with users and facilitating desired behavior, space arrangement suggested a solution to another user problem that had not been solved with signs alone.

To lower the percentage of misshelved books, the library wanted to minimize reshelving of books by users. To encourage the desired behavior, clearly marked book return shelves were provided at the end of each range, and the center shelf of each stack section (at counter height) was left empty throughout the stacks. Signs encouraging users not to reshelve books are more effective

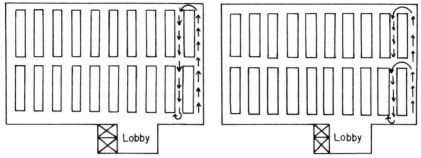

FIGURE 19-3   (left) Correct flow of cross aisles; (right) incorrect flow of cross aisles.

now that a handy place is available for unwanted books. The "consultation shelf" also allows diagonal lines of sight. After one stack wing was arranged in this manner, a university security study recommended that all stack areas be arranged to provide diagonal lines of sight.[14] The university security office reported that user harassment has significantly decreased since all stack floors were rearranged in this way.

Solving Problems by Arrangement or Signage

Locating oversize books is an example of a potential user problem that can be solved by space arrangement or by card catalog/book directory information. Oversize books in the original UH Library building were shelved in an oversize section on each floor. In the card catalog, oversize books were designated by the letter q, which had no meaning to most users. Consequently, user failure to locate oversize books was a major problem.

The problem was solved by shelving all oversize books in their call number location. An entire shelf was provided when necessary so that large books could lie flat. The largest books were accommodated by placing two shelves, on opposite sides of the stack section, at the same height, thereby providing a double-width shelf. An alternative solution would have been to designate these books in the card catalog by a meaningful word, such as "oversize," and to give directions for locating these books in the book location guide. Another alternative, suggested by Mehrabian, is the color coding of the catalog cards to denote unusual book locations.[15]

Special Locations

Once users reach the stacks, they are looking for books only and frequently fail to notice a wooden or plastic dummy or to realize that it contains useful information. At best, users resent being directed to a stack location, then redirected (by the information on the dummy) to another site. All UH stack information is now provided by the card catalog and the serials list.

Psychology of Book Stacks

Stack areas of large libraries are frequently designed as storage areas, with little consideration given to the user's need for a comfortable, low-load environment in which to perform the frequently difficult task of searching for books. The original UH Library stacks were rather typical, with drab metal shelves, tile floors, and few study areas.

One of the major goals of the architect and designer of the UH Library's building addition and renovation was to turn the stack areas into "people spaces," not just areas for book storage. Principles of architectural psychology (as described by Mehrabian[16] and other authors) were applied to produce a hospitable, cheerful, and less stressful environment. Areas of personal space (study areas) were created, warm colors and some carpeting were used, and some novel stack accessories, such as trees and couches, were introduced.[17] The goal was to produce an environment in which users could concentrate on study or research without environmental threats and distractions. Although users may not find books more readily in tree-lined stacks, the library has experienced a tremendous increase in the number of users entering the building, and circulation figures and in-house use of books have increased significantly.

CONCLUSIONS

Signs alone will not compensate for a poor stack design. Successful open-stack operation is facilitated by giving the user all essential location information in the card catalog area. Users at this point need to acquire the information necessary to find books. Once they leave this area, their goal is to obtain the books, and they are seeking primarily direction information. The format and placement of book location signs and charts should be standardized in each stack area throughout the building. Book location information should be readily distinguishable from other directional messages. The stack areas themselves should be as accessible as possible, and should indicate traffic patterns, limit options, and require few decisions.

NOTES

1. C. M. Deasey, *Design for Human Affairs* (New York: Wiley, 1974).

2. R. J. P. Carey, *Library Guiding: A Program for Exploiting Resources* (Hamden, Conn.: Linnet, 1974), pp. 104–112.

3. Deasey, *Design for Human Affairs,* pp. 89–123.

4. Clovis Heimsath, *Behavior Architecture: Toward an Accountable Design Process* (New York: McGraw-Hill, 1977).

5. Stephen Langmead, *New Library Design: Guide Lines to Planning Academic Library Buildings* (New York: Wiley, 1970), pp. 66–68.

6. Carey, *Library Guiding,* pp. 103–107.

7. Dorothy Pollet, "You Can Get There from Here," *Wilson Library Bulletin* 50 (February 1976): 456–462.

8. Herbert Spencer and Linda Reynolds, *Directional Signing and Labelling in Libraries and Museums: A Review of Current Theory and Practice* (London: Readability of Print Research Unit, Royal College of Art, 1977), p. 66.

9. Carey, *Library Guiding,* p. 104.

10. David Stea, "Architecture in the Head: Cognitive Mapping," in *Designing for Hu-*

man *Behavior: Architecture and the Behavioral Sciences*, ed. by Jon Lang (Strouds-burg, Pa.: Dowden, Hutchinson and Ross, 1974).

11. C. C. Trowbridge, "On Fundamental Methods of Orienting and Imagery Maps," *Science* 38 (1918): 883.

12. Keyes D. Metcalf, *Planning Academic and Research Library Buildings* (New York: McGraw-Hill, 1965), pp. 144–145.

13. Ralph E. Ellsworth, *Planning the College and University Library Building: A Book for Campus Planners and Architects* (Boulder, Colo.: Pruett, 1968), pp. 86–87.

14. Richard Davis, "A Physical and Operational Security Analysis of the M. D. Anderson Memorial Library, University of Houston" (unpublished, July 1977).

15. Albert Mehrabian, *Public Places and Private Spaces: The Psychology of Work, Play and Living Environments* (New York: Basic Books, 1976), p. 165.

16. Albert Mehrabian, "Libraries," in his *Public Places and Private Spaces*, pp. 162–173.

17. Betty Raymond, "University Library Remodeling and Expansion: A Friendlier Facade and Personal Space Make the M. D. Anderson Library at University of Houston a Student Sanctuary," *Contract Interiors* 138 (September 1978): 92.

Effective Library Signage: A Pictorial Study

INSTITUTE OF SIGNAGE RESEARCH

Information is basic in our society. Without it we cannot function or grow. People look to the environment for information on services or products to meet their needs. Libraries are a primary source of information. Library signage systems must be designed to help people obtain that information effectively and efficiently.

In library signage, specific goals must be met. Signs identify and locate the building for the user, provide information on the services available and how to use them, direct the flow of traffic, and generally create an atmosphere of welcome.

The photographs in this chapter are examples of effective library signage. They are arranged to display the signs as the library patron would see them: exterior signs first, followed by interior signs to guide the way to specific information. These signs are effective because they are legible and visible. Their content is readily understood. It is hoped that these examples will help library planners to create signage systems that will meet the needs of the public in an aesthetically pleasing way.

EXTERIOR SIGNS

Signs locate and identify the library for the patron. They attract attention and direct people into the library. Exterior library signage serves as an advertising or marketing medium to attract potential users.

Signs enhance the vitality of an area. Modern architectural practices and regulations enforce a sameness on the visual impact of buildings. Signs can help to overcome the deadening effects of standardization. They can make a building stand out from the environment, soften architectural lines, and renovate, enhance, and give character to less-than-ideal structures.

The exterior sign helps to create an image for the library. It introduces a theme to be carried out in the interior signage. Lettering and graphics offer visual clues to the services available.

Exterior signs must be clearly visible if they are to function effectively. Low-profile signs, for example, must be placed close to the street to be readable to passing motorists.

1   Canada Institute for Scientific and Technical Information. Exterior sign complements and enhances architecture. Type is clear, simple, and visible. The lettering style suggests the printed technical information inside.

2   Moffitt Library, University of California at Berkeley. Entrance sign. The library is introduced with the same typeface and materials as those used in other signs throughout the University library system.

3   McLaughlin Library, University of Guelph, Ontario, Canada. Exterior identification sign, engraved aluminum block mounted on concrete plinth, at main entrance. A campus office coordinates the signage for all buildings on campus. This type of exterior identification sign is common to all building identification on the Guelph campus. The standard lettering for all interior and exterior signs is Helvetica Medium.

4   Fairbanks North Star Borough Public Library, Fairbanks, Alaska. Exterior signage composed of individual letters. The letters are approximately one foot high, and are easily visible from the street.

5 Public Library of Columbus and Franklin County, Columbus, Ohio. This contemporary exterior sign conveys the image of the modern and efficient services this public library provides to the community from its old and dignified structure.

Exterior signs are not always permanent. Temporary signs can be used to advertise specific displays or library programs. These signs can create a feeling of excitement and portray something out of the ordinary.

6 Metropolitan Museum of Art, New York City. Temporary exhibit banners present a lively image of exhibits that a library may have or of some theme the library is communicating. These nonpermanent signs dress up the building and enhance the streetscape.

7 Lincoln Center, New York City. Banners attached at four points to light poles announcing programs. The banners are printed on both sides for maximum exposure.

8 Metropolitan Museum of Art, New York City. Posters of museum information enclosed in glass cases.

Electronics and space-age technology make possible sophisticated signs with changeable copy, such as time and temperature units, message centers, and scoreboards. Such advanced signs can become part of the landscape design and utilize space that might otherwise have been little more than decorative. Libraries can use these signs effectively for public service announcements and for providing timely information on special programs, exhibits, or collections.

9   California State University Union, Los Angeles. Electronic message center. Electronic information can be updated easily and quickly by typing on a keyboard. This saves the time and materials involved in manufacturing a new sign.

10   Madison Square Garden, New York City. Electronic signage vividly gives information of present and upcoming events. Library directories, central information signage centers, and temporary exhibit signage can be electronic.

11 Idaho State University, Pocatello. These electronic message signs, operated by means of a computer, can portray graphics, foreign language, and other forms of visual communication. There is a great potential for electronic signage in libraries.

INTERIOR SIGNS

Once inside the library, patrons need directions to locate the information or services they require. Signs can provide direction through symbols, maps, or written communication. Immediate information assures library users and makes them feel at ease. The visual guidance system also ensures that valuable librarian time is not expended in directing traffic.

12 Firestone Library, Princeton University, New Jersey. Information center located in foyer adjacent to main library entrance. Bold Helvetica letters, white on black background, are used to tie together all aspects of the signage system. On entering this library, the user encounters a staffed information desk and directories providing both general and specific information.

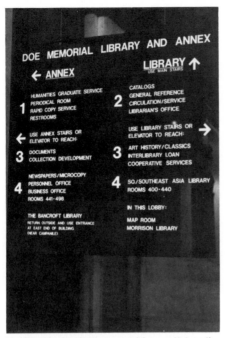

13 Doe Memorial Library and Annex, University of California at Berkeley. Main entrance directory. The Doe Memorial Library is very complex architecturally. A well-planned signage system helps to guide the library patron.

14 Doe Memorial Library, University of California at Berkeley. Secondary entrance directory. Directory is made of component parts for flexibility. Individual panels can be removed to change any portion of the directory.

15 Undergraduate Library, University of Tennessee. The library is a five-story building combining stacks and four service points — one on each of the first four floors. This picture shows entering users' perspective at second-floor entry. Bold numbers indicating floors are in different colors. The graphics and signage on each floor are coordinated with the colors of this directory.

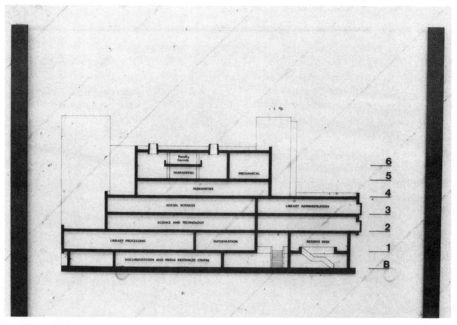

16   McLaughlin Library, University of Guelph, Ontario, Canada. Horizontal plan of library. This type of map is easier to read than most floor plans. Seeing the whole building's functional arrangement in cross section effectively orients the library user.

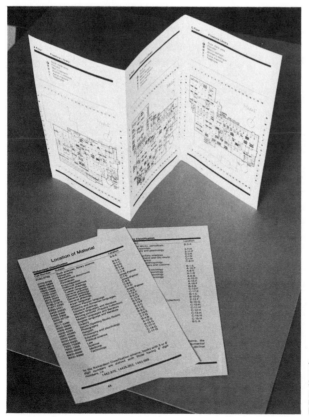

17   Firestone Library, Princeton University, New Jersey. "Portable Signage": Handouts of library floor plans and guides to material. This material supplements Firestone Library's signage system.

Signs inform the library patron regarding what services are available, where they can be found, and the hours they are open to the public. Information signs should be located in such a way that the viewer's attention is drawn to them. Lettering must be large enough to be read easily.

18   McLaughlin Library, University of Guelph, Ontario, Canada. On entering the library on the main floor, the user is centered in an area of information services. Clear white letters against a red background draw immediate attention. Letters are silk screened onto desk.

19   Doe Memorial Library, University of California at Berkeley. Librarian time is saved through use of this electronic sign in the reading room. Book request numbers light up on the board when the book has been delivered to the reference desk.

20 McLaughlin Library, University of Guelph, Ontario, Canada. Window sign of pressure-sensitive letters applied by library staff. Pressure-sensitive letters are available in kits for easy application to surfaces.

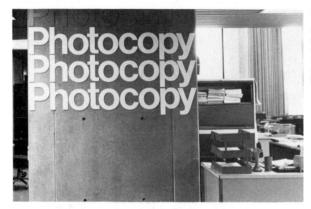

21 The D. B. Weldon Library, University of Western Ontario, Canada. Photocopy sign uses repetitive pattern as both a decorative and attention-getting device. This pattern illustrates the sign's functional meaning (duplication of originals).

Signs inform users concerning what is expected of them. Regulations should be clearly posted so as to leave no unanswered questions.

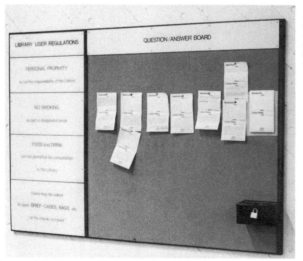

22 McLaughlin Library, University of Guelph, Ontario, Canada. Users' regulation and question-and-answer board, located at entrance to library. The more important phrases are printed in red; the others in black.

Signs explain how to use certain services or features of the library. Information explaining what the sign tells should be set in bold type to attract attention. Once users are cued that the information they seek is located on the sign, they can then read further to find specific details.

To use the Card Catalogue
There are two parts to the Card Catalogue, an Author-Title Section and a Subject Section.

Look in the Author-Title Section for a particular book if you have the author's name and the title, or the title only. Look there also to see what books the Library has by a particular author or in a particular series. Author, editors, titles, series and other entries are interfiled in one alphabetical arrangement.

Look in the Subject Section of the Card Catalogue for material on a particular subject, including material on a person. For example, critical and biographical works on the poet Shelley are brought together in the Subject Section under his name, while in the Author-Title Section they are scattered, each being listed under its own author.

Subject headings are as specific as possible. For example, for material on Canadian politics look under 'Canada – Politics and government' not under 'Political science.'

Subjects are interfiled in one alphabetical arrangement. Under certain subject headings there are period subdivisions, which are in chronological order.

List of Subject headings
Use the book Subject headings used in the dictionary catalogs of the Library of Congress and its supplements to find cross references from the first heading you try to other headings which might yield the material you want.

For example, 'Economics sa Agriculture-Economic aspects' means that you should see also the subject heading 'Agriculture-Economic aspects.'

Copies of the book are placed near the card catalogue.

Ask at the Catalogue Information Desk or Information Desk, if you cannot find what you want.

23 McLaughlin Library, University of Guelph, Ontario, Canada. Instructional signage located near card catalog and information desk. The text is in black, silk screened on white Plexiglas.

24 McLaughlin Library, University of Guelph, Ontario, Canada. Engraved molded plastic form can be placed on desk tops and counters and used for identification of various parts of the card catalog and as name identification for personnel. This sign is not attached to the surface. McLaughlin Library has no interior support walls. All furnishings can be moved at will. The signage system must be flexible to accommodate the changing needs of users and the growth of the collection.

Once users have learned the location of materials they need, signs can guide them along the way.

25 Firestone Library, Princeton University, New Jersey. Close-up of "A" floor directory with floor plan and notice of changes. A special place reserved for changes can save the time and expense of constructing new signage. Alternatively, flexible signage is available that allows for changes while maintaining overall design quality.

26 Firestone Library, Princeton University, New Jersey. "C" floor, bay 13F marker. The number 13 and letter F correspond to grid markings on the library floor plans. They help users to locate the specific bay where a call number is found.

27 Firestone Library, Princeton University, New Jersey. Elevator on "A" floor, bay 14F. Floor plan is on the right of elevator and floor compass gives north/south orientation.

28 Firestone Library, Princeton University, New Jersey. On the second-floor landing of stairwell, information sign directs the user to further library floor plans and guides. Signage should anticipate the user's needs and questions.

Supergraphics are an eye-appealing way to present directional information. They can provide color and a sense of design. Care must be taken, however, to ensure that the letters are not too large to be read easily.

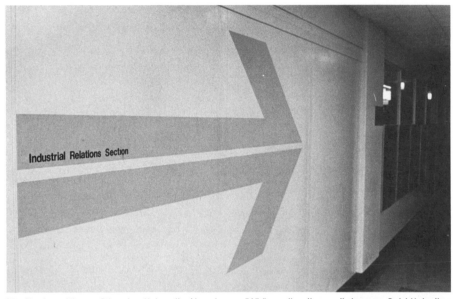

29 Firestone Library, Princeton University, New Jersey. "A" floor direction wall signage. Bold Helvetica letters continue to be used, with variety of design. If the words "Industrial Relations Section" were set on the wall without the arrow, they would probably be lost in the expanse of wall space.

30 Undergraduate Library, University of Tennessee. Wall Identification signage. The background is color coded according to the floor number. Placement adds a touch of visual humor.

31 Undergraduate Library, University of Tennessee. Direction signage continued on escalator. Color again indicates floor.

Color-coded signage systems help display information so that it can be perceived quickly.

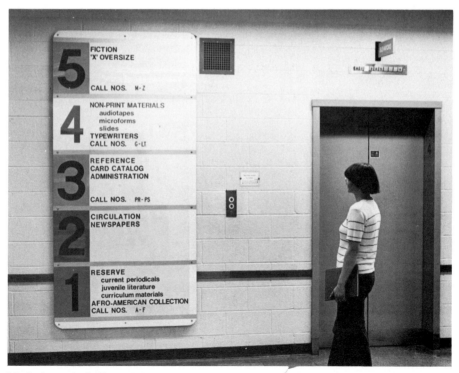

32 Undergraduate Library, University of Tennessee. Color coded wall directory displayed on each floor adjacent to elevator.

Overhead and wall signs are practical for easy identification of library areas, stacks, or services available. These signs must be bold to attract attention and must be easily visible. They should be readable from a distance.

33   The D. B. Weldon Library, University of Western Ontario, Canada. Location of elevators and check out desk are clearly identified.

34   The D. B. Weldon Library, University of Western Ontario, Canada. Main reference desk, first floor.

35 The D. B. Weldon Library, University of Western Ontario, Canada. Northwest exterior of the library. Large numerals placed opposite elevators indicate floor numbers. (Numerals are affixed directly to windows, and thus appear reversed in this photograph.)

36 The D. B. Weldon Library, University of Western Ontario, Canada. A view of the first floor and lower concourse. Identification and direction signs are bold and clear and can be read at a great distance. They serve two functions: signage and design.

37 Canada Institute for Scientific and Technical Information. View of the main floor (reference area) and second floor. Suspended signage along user route (second floor) is very effective, especially in the open-spaced architecture where wall or projecting signs would be impossible.

38 Canada Institute for Scientific and Technical Information. Signage design echoes design of ceiling, integrating signage with the interior. (Interior signage integrates messages with lighting fixtures.)

39 Canada Institute for Scientific and Technical Information. Suspended signage carries overall design into specific areas.

40 Fairbanks North Star Borough Public Library, Fairbanks, Alaska. The signage strips are consistent in size and large enough to contain the longest words in the series. Words are flush with the left-hand side of the signage strip.

41   Undergraduate Library, University of Tennessee. Escalator leads directly to the reference desk.
Wall signage is painted on brick. The design element is emphasized over legibility, yet the sign
commands attention.

Signs can correct deficiencies in architecture or spatial planning. They
help to provide a feeling of continuity and flow.

42   Firestone Library, Princeton University, New Jersey. Main Floor foyer direction signs. White letters
silk screened on black Plexiglas. A diagonal arrow indicating stairs could not be used where there
is also a choice to move diagonally forward through a hallway or room. The positioning of this sign
over the steps helps to clarify the distinction between horizontal movement and movement up the
stairs.

43   San Jose Public Library, California. Vertical sign indicating career file. In some situations, vertical positioning of signs is more effective than horizontal.

44   The D. B. Weldon Library, University of Western Ontario, Canada. Letraset letters on plaster walls. In this case, if the word had been positioned horizontally, it could not be seen from as many locations. Vertical signage is also popular for its contemporary design.

45 The D. B. Weldon Library, University of Western Ontario, Canada. Letraset stencils with orange paint are used on a cream plaster background. The legibility of signage that cannot be viewed in a plane parallel to the user depends on the angle of vision and the size of the lettering. In this case, the relatively large oblong column and the large letter size together ensure legibility.

Small information signs tell users that they have found the locations they were seeking.

46 McLaughlin Library, University of Guelph, Ontario, Canada. Stack end signs. Call numbers are stenciled on white paper that is held within a plastic frame. The frame is inserted into a mount permanently attached to the stack.

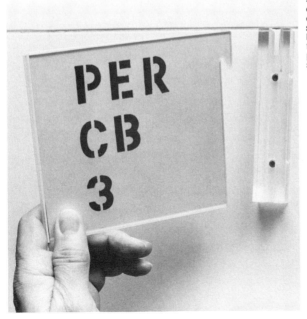

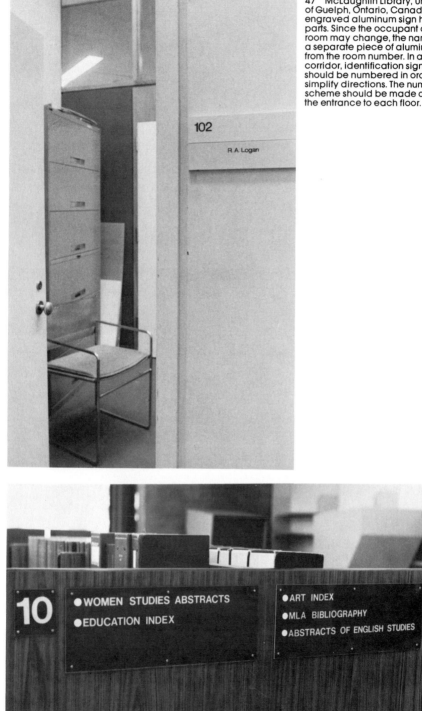

47   McLaughlin Library, University of Guelph, Ontario, Canada. This engraved aluminum sign has two parts. Since the occupant of the room may change, the name is on a separate piece of aluminum from the room number. In a corridor, identification signs should be numbered in order to simplify directions. The numbering scheme should be made clear at the entrance to each floor.

48   Doe Memorial Library, University of California at Berkeley. Specific identification signage. Sign has clear protective piece of Plexiglas. Both parts are bolted to board.

49 San Jose Public Library,
California. Numbered stack with
special category identification.
Suspended sign identifies same
area from different directions.

SUMMARY

Library signs serve a multitude of functions. They identify and locate the library for the patron. They advertise specific events and programs. They tell of services available and explain how to use them. They direct traffic and help use space efficiently. They create an image and encourage the library patron to feel welcome.

Library signage systems must be well planned if they are to function efficiently and effectively. It is hoped that this chapter provides not only examples but also incentives for creative and thoughtful library signage.

ACKNOWLEDGMENT

Photographs and captions compiled by Leslie Reininger Elkus.

Appendix: Technical and Psychological Considerations for Sign Systems in Libraries

INSTITUTE OF SIGNAGE RESEARCH

This appendix, adapted from *The Sign User's Guide*,[1] provides technical and psychological considerations for effective sign system design in libraries. Although not intended as an in-depth discussion of all technical criteria, it points out some of the more important factors in acceptable sign design.

The elements of sign design are interactive. To be effective, signs must be readable, legible, and visible. *Readability* is the quality that enables the observer to grasp correctly the content of the sign message. *Legibility* refers to the differentiation of one letter or symbol from another. *Visibility* refers to whether the sign can be distinguished from its surroundings. Color, lettering, sign shape, materials, and lighting all have important psychological connotations in viewer perception. All technical criteria for sign construction, such as type of sign, copy, and size, should receive attention. Sign placement and maintenance requirements also deserve consideration.

Library administrators should first determine their priorities in developing a signage system. Once limitations are known, such as placement or budgetary constraints, a balanced system can be developed through the planned use of other design elements.

ENVIRONMENTAL VISUAL COMMUNICATION

Signs are a communication medium. They convey a visual message from a sender to a receiver. As with other media, signs influence the way in which a message is perceived and can subtly convey a message while creating a mood or feeling of atmosphere.

Sign Placement

To communicate effectively, signs must attract the viewer's interest. Since signs are only one part of a shared visual environment, the surrounding area must also be considered. The type of sign and its placement must work together to compete effectively for viewer attention.

Techniques developed by highway and traffic engineers may be applied to the effective placement of library signage. Highway engineers are aware that drivers are constantly processing information and making decisions. Certain sections of road may be particularly demanding. The landscape, trees, buildings, hazards, weather or other conditions, all claim a share of driver perception. Traffic engineers avoid placing excess information in these areas.[2]

Signs are most effective, then, when they are placed in areas where they do not compete with other visual stimuli. Careful observation of site characteristics will enable the library administrator to choose good locations for signs. Signs placed outside the library building require extra considerations: the speed of passing traffic, for example, and the angles from which the sign will be viewed from the street.

Any sign at an angle suffers distortion in the eyes of the viewer. This distortion is related both to the speed of approach and to the angle of the sign: the closer the viewer comes to the object, the greater the effect of distortion. Eye-level highway advertising signs should not be angled more than 20 degrees from the normal position of facing oncoming viewers; when the angle must be greater than 20 degrees, the widths of the letters should be increased accordingly.[3]

For signs above eye level, for example, on tops of buildings, it should be remembered that the apparent height will shrink when viewed from below. Signs placed on the side of a building and at an angle will seem narrower.

Types of Signs

In designing library communication systems, sign structures must be chosen that will best inform the library user. Additionally, each library has specific signage needs. A careful assessment of those needs will help the administrator choose the types of signs that will function best in the particular environment. First, however, the administrator must have a clear idea of the types of signs that are available.

Banner signs are made of lightweight materials such as cloth, paper, or nonrigid plastic, not enclosed in a rigid frame. They are often used as temporary announcements of special exhibits.

Canopy signs are mounted on and supported by an architectural canopy.

If the sign hangs beneath the canopy, it is called an *undercanopy sign*. Under-canopy signs generally must be small in size to comply with height limitations imposed by the building or by the municipal sign code.

Changeable-copy signs are signs that allow written copy to be changed manually. They consist of a panel on which individual letters or pictorial panels are mounted. These signs are used when frequent copy changes are required, such as on building directories or theater marquees.

Electronic message centers, displaying copy on a lampbank, are a fairly recent development in signage. The centers can be programmed, allowing copy to be changed quickly and efficiently. Several messages may be programmed in a sequence. Many businesses use such centers to display public service messages.

Floor signs are painted on or set into the floor, such as lettering or symbols in tile flooring. These signs should be as brief as possible. Symbols or codes are preferable to written copy. Written messages on floors can be difficult to read and easily obstructed. Floor signs have the advantage, however, of graphic appeal and effectiveness in guiding users to hard-to-find locations.

Freestanding signs are located on the premises of the library and are not attached to the building. They are supported by one or more columns, uprights, or braces in the ground or on the floor. The poles on which these signs are mounted are often tall, enabling the message to be seen from a distance. Because they offer great visibility, they are effective in exterior signage for reaching people passing the library in motor vehicles. Freestanding signs used for interior signage are most effective in large open spaces. In libraries they can designate sections, categorize stacks, and mark service areas. A recent trend incorporates the pole of the sign into the overall design. Probably the most widely known such example is the freestanding sign used by American Motors in which the structural elements are part of the sign itself. The subway line for Washington, D.C., utilizes the structural system as part of the sign, as do lobbies of some large shopping complexes.

Projecting signs are attached to and project from a wall, either exterior or interior. They are usually at right angles to the wall and are double-faced, enabling the sign to be read from either direction.

Roof signs are erected on or above the roofline of a building and are supported by the building. This type of exterior sign is aimed primarily at the motoring public.

Suspended signs are used almost exclusively for interior signage. They are hung from the ceiling by chain, wire, cord, or other material. When positioned in strategic points along the direct route of the library user, suspended signs may attract attention more effectively than wall signs. Suspended signs can also be used in areas where wall signs or freestanding signs would not integrate with the architectural design of the building. They can be highly visible in areas where one's view of the walls is obstructed.

Wall signs can function as either interior or exterior signage. They are affixed parallel to the wall of a building, projecting not more than 18 inches. They have only one face, and are often box-type signs—the letters are mounted against a sign cabinet or board. In other cases, they are composed of individual letters, which are affixed directly to the wall. Wall signs may be more difficult to read than some other types of signs since they may not directly face the viewer. These signs can often be integrated into the overall architecture of the building.

Window signs are placed on the inside of windows for outdoor viewing. They can be made of paper, cardboard, or similar materials. Vinyl architectural letters, available in kits, can also be applied to the window and can serve as a window sign. Care must be taken to ensure that a hand painted or stenciled sign is of professional quality. The sign must be clear and readable, and should reflect the professional image of the library. Not only are window signs inexpensive, but they can be made and installed quickly, making possible quick communication of specific information about special programs or collections. They may be effective for providing information in situations where large numbers of people walk past the library. A disadvantage, however, is that they usually cannot be seen by the motoring public.

Choosing an Effective Sign

Exterior signs, those outside a building, generally serve as information/direction devices. They inform the public of the library's location. The library administrator, however, must define the purpose of the particular exterior signage in order to choose the type of sign that will function best. The needs of the library user must also be considered. If, for example, the library is located on a university campus, the exterior sign will generally act as an information device. It needs only to tell the students where the library is located. For this purpose, a wall sign might be selected. On the other hand, if a public library is located on a side street of the community, the library administrator may wish actively to draw people to the library. In this case, the sign functions to advertise the library, so a freestanding or roof sign might be selected. A changeable-copy sign or electronic message center would be most effective for informing the public of specific events or displays at the library.

Interior signs, those inside a building, generally guide library users to specific information or services. The most important factor in interior signage is that the sign be readable. Signs that face the viewer directly are most effective. Consideration must be given to the physical layout of the building so that signs will be visible from the necessary distance and the view will not be obstructed. Wall signs, floor signs, and suspended signs could be used effectively for interior library signage.

CRITERIA FOR DETERMINING SIGN SIZE

Sign size is one of the few elements of sign design incorporating objective, quantifiable data. Questions such as whether the lettering of a sign is appropriate for the architecture of a building or whether the colors create the desired atmosphere are subjective: there are no scientific standards for evaluating performance. In determining sign size, however, scientific data can offer specific suggestions based on the amount of time required by the average person to read a message and the size of lettering dictated by normal visual acuity.

Processing Visual Information:
Visual Acuity

If the eye were to be compared to a fabricated instrument, it might be compared with radar: constantly scanning the environment and charting what it sees.[4] The brain processes this flow of information, interpreting the signals and making order of the visual stimuli. The process is limited by a viewer's visual acuity.

Visual acuity, the sharpness or clarity of normal vision, is usually measured under optimal conditions. Snellen letters are most often used, and the recording method charts visual acuity as a fraction, e.g., 20/20. The first or upper figure is a notation in feet of the distance from the viewer's eye to the letter. The lower figure represents the size of the letter to be seen. Table 1 shows minimum sizes of Snellen letters and the distances from which they can be read by people with varying levels of visual acuity. Although the table was drawn for exterior signs, it can also be used to calculate visual acuity for interior signage.

It is important to remember that such considerations as the influence of color, other visual competition, or the speed of a viewer's motor vehicle are not a part of the standard visual acuity measurement. These factors imply that letter size for signs should be larger than statistics on visual acuity suggest. Adjustments must also be made for the angle from which the sign will be seen. On the other hand, words are more immediately recognizable than the individual, unrelated letters used in measuring visual acuity.

Calculating Exterior Sign Size

In highway sign design, the visual acuity standard for letter size is 1 inch of letter height for each 30 to 50 feet of distance. This figure accounts for the fact that highway signs generally face the viewer directly and are easy-to-read white lettering on a green background. Other factors to consider in on-premise signage are the speed of traffic past the sign location and the fact that a driver may not be specifically looking for a sign. In these situations and where the sign is not at an ideal viewing angle, or there is considerable competition for viewer attention, a lettering size ratio of 1 inch to 25 feet is practical.

TABLE 1   Minimum Resolvable Snellen Letter Size for
Eyes with 20/20, 20/40, and 20/60 Visual Acuity at
Distances between 100 Feet and One-quarter Mile

Distance (Feet)	Letter Size (Inches) Minimum Resolvable		
	20/20	20/40	20/60
100	1.8	3.5	5.2
200	3.5	7.0	10.5
400	7.0	14.0	20.9
600	10.5	21.0	31.4
800	14.0	28.0	41.9
1000	17.5	35.0	52.4
1320	23.1	46.1	69.1

TABLE 2   Three Basic Design Criteria for Calculating Area of Freestanding Signs for Vehicular Traffic

1. Reaction distance based on speed
2. Number of words in message
3. Size of letters

Basic formula for calculating total sign area (in square inches):
No. of letters × (letter ht.)^2 + 40% no. of letters × (letter ht.)^2 = Total area (sq. in.).

Example: A message of 10 words with approx. 7 letters per word = approx. 70 letters.

Reference Table

SPEED (MPH)	REACTION DISTANCE (FT.)
30	470
45	700
55	825

Recommended height to distance ratio for letter 1 inch
to 25 feet (optimum viewing conditions).[a]

Required sign size example in 30 mph traffic zone
1. Reaction distance = 470 ft.
2. 470 ft. requires 18.8 in. letter using 25 ft. to 1 in. proportion
3. Area per word = 18.8 in. × 18.8 in. × 7 = 2474.08 sq. in.
4. Area per sign = 2474.08 × 10 = 24740.8 sq. in.
5. Copy area = 24740.8 ÷ 144 = 171.81 sq. ft.
6. Borders and margins 40% greater than copy area = 68.72 sq. ft.
7. Total sign area = 171.81 + 68.72 = 240.53 sq. ft.

Required sign size example in 55 mph traffic zone
1. Reaction distance = 825 ft.
2. 825 feet requires 33 in. letter using 25 ft. to 1 in. proportion
3. Area per word = 33 in. × 33 in. × 7 = 7626 sq. in.
4. Area per sign = 7623 × 10 = 76230 sq. in.
5. Copy area = 76230 ÷ 144 = 529.375 sq. ft.
6. Borders and margins 40% greater than copy area = 211.75 sq. ft.
7. Total sign area = 741.125 sq. ft.

[a]See Karen E. Claus and R. James Claus, *Visual Communication Through Signage*, Vol. 1, *Perception of the Message*, Chapter 1 (Cincinnati, Ohio: Signs of the Times Publications, 1974).

Reaction distance is also important in on-premise library signage. Viewers need not only to see the sign, but to brake and stop their cars. Typical reaction distances are shown in Table 2 as part of the formula for calculating sign size.

This formula uses three basic criteria for determining the size of a sign: reaction distance based on speed of a motor vehicle, the number of words in the message, and the size of letters. Lettering size is based on the 1-inch to 25-foot ratio. The formula is meant only as a guideline.

In areas of potential hazard or places demanding driver attention such as intersections, interchange exits, lane drops, or railroad crossings, the anticipatory sight distance figure might be substituted for the reaction distance table of the formula. Anticipatory sight distance is reaction distance with added time for selecting an alternative when it is known that a decision is required. For example, if a driver is moving at the rate of 30 miles per hour, the anticipatory sight distance will be 600 feet; if driving at 40 mph, the anticipatory distance is 800 feet; at 50 mph, 1100 feet; and at 60 mph, 1500 feet.

Calculating Interior Sign Size

Interior signs can be more wordy than exterior signs since the viewer has a chance to stop and read them. The size of the lettering can be based on the 1-inch to 25-foot ratio. No calculations are necessary to account for reaction time, although the angle at which the sign is placed remains important. Sometimes the size of an interior sign may be adjusted to form part of the overall interior design concept, such as in the use of supergraphics. In these cases, however, care must be taken that the letters are not too large to be read easily.

CRITERIA FOR DETERMINING SIGN COPY

The copy on a sign will depend on the sign's function. The sign may act as an identification device, information/direction aid, or advertising cue. In some cases it might be sufficient to include only the name of the library on the sign. In other cases words will be used that invite specific action.

Information Processing

Sign users often wonder how much information can be put on a sign. Recognizing that a sign is a powerful communication medium, sign users want to advertise as extensively as possible without presenting more information than the average person can comprehend.

The sign industry has developed the rough estimate of seven words to a sign. Although this estimate does not strictly apply to interior signage, which a viewer can take time to read, it is interesting to note that the experience of the sign industry is now validated by research of perceptual psychologists.

Scientific data have been accumulated to prove that, in a certain time span, humans can usually process about seven "chunks" of information.[5] A "chunk" is necessarily a loosely defined term. It is not synonymous with letters or words and varies according to the previous experience of the viewer. Miller[6] uses the example of the Coca Cola slogan—Drink Coca Cola—to explain chunks. There is no way of determining the number of chunks this phrase contains merely by looking at the number of letters or words. The number of chunks depends on the previous experience of the viewer. A person who knows the English alphabet, but no words of English, will have to treat it as containing 13 chunks of information. Someone who understands English, but has been completely shielded from this advertisement, will treat it as containing 3 chunks of information. The vast majority of people, however, who have seen this slogan many, many times, comprehend it in its entirety and see it as one chunk of information. The same physical stimulus has different numbers of chunks for different people.

Other factors, also used in determining sign size, are of importance in selecting copy. If, for example, the sign is placed at an angle to the viewer and is difficult to read, less copy should be used. If the lettering is not clear and not immediately readable, fewer words may make the sign's message easier to comprehend.

Brevity and Use of Key Words
Signs must have sufficient information to serve their function. There is a danger, however, in having too much copy. Vital information can be lost in a clutter of words.

It may be wise to display one or two key words in larger type on the face of the sign. In exterior signage, for example, the library name might be set in large, bold type with additional copy in smaller type. In interior signage, e.g., a directory or sign providing extensive information, key words denoting the nature of the sign may be set in bold type. Once viewers have been cued that the information they are seeking is located on the sign, they have an opportunity to stop and read it.

Changeable-Copy Signs
Advertising effectiveness can be increased through the use of changeable-copy signs. Not only does such a sign prevent viewer habituation, it allows the library staff to provide timely information on specific events or displays.

Changeable-copy signs, however, do require maintenance. In order to be effective, the copy must be changed. Signs with letters missing detract from a professional image.

PSYCHOLOGICAL SIGNAGE CONSIDERATIONS

Cultural Factors
Signs communicate in many ways. Some of the information they convey is direct and to the point. A sign that says "Return Overdue Books Here" gives direct, concrete information. However, signs do more than provide information. They also create a mood, enhance the attractiveness of a building, and project an image.

Culture plays a large role in our understanding of sign design. An example of the subjective nature of one's culture is seen in the interpretation of an ink-blot test. In the past, certain colors might have been viewed as indications of masculinity or femininity. With growing changes in human roles, however, there is now far less correlation between color preferences and sexual orientation.

Cultural influences are seen in almost every facet of sign design. The shape of the sign, lighting, materials, colors, and lettering all convey subtle messages. These factors can be used in combinations to repeat the message, another way of making the sign more effective. The red octagonal stop sign, for example, communicates its message not only through wording but also through shape and color.

Sign Face Layout

Layout refers to the overall arrangement of letters, symbols, and other graphic elements of a sign. These elements should be used to draw the eye to the most important part of the message first. There should be empty space on a sign. If an attempt is made to crowd too much copy into a small space, the result will be clutter and confusion. Adequate room must be given to borders and spaces between words and symbols.

The human brain responds readily to pictorial concepts. Symbols and pictorial graphics also communicate beyond language and cultural barriers. Government design agencies are demonstrating a growing interest in the standardization of symbols for universal use. Library signage systems can be developed to take advantage of this trend.

Sign Shapes

Shapes of signs offer certain psychological connotations. A rectangular shape implies solidness; an oval shape suggests stability. Sign shape may be limited by budget or technical constraints. Rectangular signs, for example, are generally less expensive than other shapes. Electrical sign shapes are limited by the size of fluorescent lamps, ballasts, and plastic sheeting. Unusually shaped signs for libraries, however, may be worth the added expense. A study correlating the shape of a sign and a subject's ability to recall specific signs concluded that unique shape appears to be an essential factor in remembering a sign.[7]

Sign Materials

The three primary materials used in sign construction are wood, metal, and plastic. Each offers different qualities and design features.

Wooden signs have grown in popularity due to the "natural" trend of recent years. When displayed outdoors, wood is more vulnerable to the elements than plastic or metal. Only exterior illumination can be used with wooden signs.

Metal is not used as commonly as plastic or wood in signage. However, metal does suggest stability and modernism. It is durable, but lacks the versatility of other materials. Indirect lighting is required to avoid glare.

Plastic is the most commonly used material for electric and interior sign systems. Plastic signs can be back-lit or illuminated from the inside, giving a high degree of visibility. Plastics are available in a wide range of colors and can be designed to look like any other materials. Almost any desired typeface can be utilized with plastic.

Sign Lighting

Illumination enables signs to be effective at night as well as during daylight hours. Lighted signs draw attention and work well in dimly lit areas.

Several types of illumination are available for signage. However, it is important to first understand the principle of irradiation, the phenomenon in which illuminated bright areas look larger than they actually are. The greater the viewing distance, the more pronounced this effect becomes. In signage, careful attention must be given to sign illumination so that irradiation does not make the lettering illegible.

Exposed lighting refers to lighting in which the light source is directly visible as part of the sign. It can be divided into two categories: incandescent lamps and luminous tubing. Exposed lighting offers flexibility in color, motion, and brilliance and can be highly visible.

Incandescent lamps were the earliest form of electrical sign illumination. Today, incandescent lighting is used almost exclusively to create an image reminiscent of that era.

Luminous tubing is commonly referred to as neon. Technically, however, neon is only one of the gases used to produce luminous lighting. Luminous tubing offers many advantages in sign lighting. It is highly efficient: a pure neon tube radiates five times as much red light for a given amount of power as an incandescent lamp. It is also versatile. The flexibility of heated glass allows the tubing to be formed into different designs and shapes. Luminous tubing can be used to create animation and on-off displays, or to superimpose one message upon another to be shown in an alternating sequence. Luminous tubing is not effective, however, in highly illuminated interior spaces or during daylight hours. The range of colors is not as wide as the range available in plastic signs.

Luminous panel signs are lit from the interior. The light source is concealed behind a translucent face, usually of plastic or fiberglass. This common electric sign is relatively inexpensive. Luminous panel signs require less maintenance than incandescent or luminous tubing signs. They offer the greatest flexibility for choices of color, type style, and use of graphics.

Silhouette signs are illuminated from behind so that the letters stand out as dark images against a lighted background. Generally, these signs are created by concealing luminous tubing behind opaque letters, a valance, or cornice. Care must be taken so that the effects of irradiation do not render the sign illegible, and distracting shadows or reflections must be avoided.

Sign Colors

Color has a powerful psychological effect, which can be used advantageously in signage. For example, colors are often associated with emotions. To "see red" describes anger, to be "blue" indicates depression or sadness, to be "yellow" means cowardice. The color red is frequently used for warning signs because people have been taught to associate red with immediacy and importance. Color coded sign systems can be a powerful use of color.

Some color combinations are difficult for the eye to perceive. Studies on readability and color in signage conclude that the most important consideration is the contrast between the background color and the color of the lettering. The following list ranks color combinations from the most visible (1) to the least visible (16).

1 Black on yellow	5 Yellow on blue
2 Black on white	6 Green on white
3 Yellow on black	7 Blue on yellow
4 White on blue	8 White on green

9 White on brown

10 Brown on yellow

11 Brown on white

12 Yellow on brown

13 Red on white

14 Yellow on red

15 Red on yellow

16 White on red

Orange on white, red on green, and black on purple are combinations not recommended for use in signage.[8]

Boldness of color is important. Color can be used subtly in paintings, photographs, or other media that will be seen close up. In signage, where the object will be perceived quickly from a distance, a bold contrast is required.

Sign color can be an effective aid in reinforcing the message that the sign is designed to communicate. Certain attributes are associated with some colors. Although these considerations can be incorporated into sign design, more concern should be given to graphic appeal and aesthetics.

Red suggests boldness, quickness, efficiency.

Yellow creates an atmosphere of brashness and suggests positiveness.

Green is associated with living things and, therefore, with freshness and purity.

Blue connotes serenity and quiet.

Purple is associated with royalty, pomp, and luxuriousness.

White is the traditional color of purity and innocence; in signage it suggests cleanliness and neatness.

Black creates an impression of low-keyed crispness and sedateness.

Subtle shifts in tints or tones of color can make a difference in how the color is perceived. Pale yellow, for example, can suggest daintiness, while deeper yellow can be quite powerful. Red might be used in a limited area successfully, but it can be overpowering if used in large quantities.

Other psychological effects of color deserve consideration. Older people tend to prefer blue. Men tend to respond to deep shades of colors; women generally prefer more delicate tints.

Lettering

Lettering is generally the most important communicating element of a sign. It not only presents a straightforward message; effectively done, it enhances the image of the library.

A myriad of typefaces is available for use in signage. They fall into five main divisions: roman, gothic block, text, italic, and script. An easy-to-read typeface should be selected for use on signs. Plain block lettering is the most common.

As with color, lettering offers a wide variety of psychological interpretation. Several factors are involved:

1 *Slope.* Lettering written upward is associated with positive attributes. A downward slope may indicate depression or negative feelings.

2 *Slant.* Letters that are straight up and down or slanted to the right generally do not convey any specific emotion. Backward slants indicate coldness or even calculation;

forward slants tend to be associated with positive emotional attributes. Extreme forward slants may indicate nervousness.

3 *Letter thickness.*   Thin lettering may indicate simplicity, modesty, refinement. Thicker lettering suggests self-confidence and solidness. Generally, the thicker the letter, the stronger the will or dominance conveyed.

4 *Letter compression.*   Compression refers to spacing between letters. Highly compressed words indicate clannishness and reserve. Extended and large lettering indicates a friendly, open nature.

5 *Capital letter height.*   Low capital letters, approximately the size of the lowercase letters, indicate humility and simplicity. Slightly raised capital letters give the impression of self-respect and pride.

6 *Shape.*   Pointed or triangular-shaped letters convey an image of energy and quick thinking. Rounded letters indicate a more passive and gentle atmosphere. Letters that are overly pointed may create an impression of aggressiveness. Overly rounded letters may convey laziness and indolence.

Spacing between letters is a particularly important concern in signage. If equal space is allotted for all the letters of a word, the result will not have a smooth professional look because letters take up differing amounts of space. This factor, a concern in all typography, is emphasized in signage. Since the lettering is so large, any imperfection is accentuated. Vertical lettering presents unique problems in spacing. The letters must not appear to spread out or to be of unequal weight.

Although sign lettering is often comprised solely of capital letters, recent studies have shown that greater legibility can be achieved through the use of upper- and lowercase lettering.[9] Words are recognized more by their general shape, size, and position than by the characteristics of each individual letter. Lowercase letters have more recognizable shapes than uniform uppercase letters.

Sign lettering should harmonize with the architecture of the building, a particularly important consideration in wall signs. A delicate or slanted script on a massive square building, for example, especially if placed on the lintel, could seem to weaken the soundness of the structure. Lettering can be designed to maintain a feeling of strength in a load-bearing architectural element.

NOTES

1. R. J. Claus and K. E. Claus, *The Sign User's Guide: A Marketing Aid* (Palo Alto, Calif.: Institute of Signage Research, 1978).

2. D. B. Miller, "Traffic Engineering Applied to On-Premise Signage" (paper presented at the ISR Conference, Chicago, Illinois, 1976).

3. J. H. Prince, "Height of Sign and Speed of Approach Affect Visibility," *Signs of the Times,* March 1958, p. 79.

4. S. Wechsler, "Vision, Visual Acuity, and Sign Size Standards" (paper presented at the ISR Conference, Chicago, Illinois, 1976).

5. G. Miller, "The Magical Number Seven, Plus or Minus Two: Some Limits," *The Psychological Review,* March 1956, pp. 81–97.

6. Ibid.

7. C. R. Patty and H. L. Vredenburg, "Electric Signs: Contribution to the Communication Spectrum" (Fort Collins, Colo.: Rohm & Haas, 1970), 52 pp.

8. K. E. Claus and R. J. Claus, *Visual Communication Through Signage,* Vol. 1, *Perception of the Message* (Cincinnati, Ohio: Signs of the Times Publications, 1974), p. 34.

9. R. M. Oliphant, K. E. Claus, and R. J. Claus, *Psychological Considerations of Lettering for Identification* (Cincinnati, Ohio: Signs of the Times Publications, 1971).

Annotated Bibliography on Visual Guidance Systems

WILLIAM W. PRINCE

This selective annotated bibliography includes primarily English-language materials relating to visual guidance systems. The majority of the references are to journal articles published after 1970 and books published after 1960. For ease of use, the bibliography is divided into four categories: Theory and Research, Materials and Techniques, Visual Guidance Systems in Libraries, and Visual Guidance Systems in Other Institutions. (Readers are also referred to the more specialized "Notes" sections in many of the chapters.)

THEORY AND RESEARCH

Altman, Irwin. *The Environment and Social Behavior: Privacy, Personal Space, Territory, Crowding.* Monterey, Calif. Brooks/Cole, 1975, 256 pp.

Designed as an introductory text for undergraduate and graduate students, this book is well documented and readable; includes a 17-page bibliography.

American Institute of Graphic Arts (AIGA). *Symbol Signs: The Development of Passenger/Pedestrian Oriented Symbols for Use in Transportation Related Facilities.* Washington, D.C.: U.S. Dept. of Transportation, 1974, 172 pp.

AIGA, in cooperation with the Department of Transportation, "has created 34 passenger and pedestrian oriented symbols for use in transportation related facilities." The purpose of the project was to create a symbol system that could "simplify basic messages at domestic and international travel facilities." AIGA attempted to utilize symbol forms widely in use and introduce new forms where none existed. "The report includes detailed descriptions of the process employed to create the symbols as well as guidelines for their use" (abstract, p. 1). The guidelines section (pp. 119–131) is most useful for librarians, covering such aspects as legibility criteria; proper lettering size; fabrication; and types of signs. Selective bibliography included. The complete report is available from the National Technical Information Service, Springfield, VA 22151, contract no. DOT-OS-40192.

Bechtel, Robert B. "The Study of Man: Human Movement and Architecture." *Transaction* 4 (May 1967): 53–56.

Bechtel examines the potential impact of the hodometer (an instrument that indirectly measures patterns of movement by electrically recording the number and location of footsteps across a floor) on the ability of the architect and social scientist to better understand "man's behavioral responses to his architectural environment" (p. 56).

Bell, Paul A., Fisher, Jeffrey D., and Loomis, Ross J. *Environmental Psychology.* Philadephia: Saunders, 1978, 457 pp.

In this textbook, the authors discuss perception and evaluation of the environment, a theoretical approach to environment-behavior relationships, the effects of environmen-

page 243

tal factors (noise, temperature, personal space, crowding, etc.) on behavior, adaptation to environmental settings, the design of environments to influence behavior, and ways of changing behavior to save and preserve the environment. Chapter summaries and references, an extensive bibliography, and an author/subject index enhance usefulness. Includes brief discussions of library design features (pp. 330–331) and orientation to the library (p. 241). Many of the topics discussed relate to the development of a library sign system.

Best, G. A. "Direction-Finding in Large Buildings." Msc. thesis, Univ. of Manchester, 1967.

Examines the behavior of pedestrians in the Manchester Town Hall, and uses these observations to formulate proposals for improving methods of sign posting in complex buildings.

Blake, John E., ed. *A Management Guide to Corporate Identity*. London: Council of Industrial Design, 1971, 100 pp.

Considers design programs as a way for businesses to improve their standing in the market (p. 7). Articles (with case studies) explore uses of opinion research, role of the designer, costs of design, and application of corporate identity programs. Librarians could learn methods of establishing a positive identity for the library, thus improving its image.

Britt, Stewart Henderson. "An Experiment on the Perception of Signs." *International Journal of Symbology* 3 (March 1972): 9–15.

Reported are methods, results, and implications of an experiment conducted at Northwestern University to determine whether signs communicate their messages to the public and which type/styles do so most effectively.

Cahill, Mary-Carol. "Interpretability of Graphic Symbols as a Function of Context and Experience Factors." *Journal of Applied Psychology* 60 (June 1975): 376–380.

Ten of the graphic symbols designed by Henry Dreyfuss Associates for Deere and Company are tested for ease of interpretation in context and in isolation (p. 376). Research indicates that a symbol cannot stand alone and must be validated by the user. Includes a nine-item bibliography.

Carpenter, Edward K. "Travelers' Aid, Courtesy DOT and AIGA." *Print* 29 (March/April 1975): 25–31.

Carpenter describes the joint effort of the American Institute of Graphic Arts and the Department of Transportation to develop "a coordinated set of symbols to guide people . . . through . . . travel facilities" (p. 26). (Also see American Institute of Graphic Arts, *Symbol Signs*.)

Claus, Karen E., and Claus, R. James. *Visual Communication through Signage*. Cincinnati: Signs of the Times, 1974–1976.

The authors of this three-volume series propose that "the use of information available from industry sources might enable decision makers in the public forum to reach a valid and intelligent basis for judgements and policy decisions concerning the visual environment" (foreword, vol. 1). The series is meant to serve as a link between industry and people in need of information. Although predominately concerned with highway sign systems, because it deals with areas common to interior and exterior sign systems this set is of value to the librarian. Brief bibliographies in all volumes. Volume 1, *Perception of the Message*, deals with technical considerations in achieving legibility, information processing from the viewer's standpoint, and the relationship between signage and highway safety (foreword, vol. 1). Volume II, *Sign Evaluation*, deals with the "communications value of both on- and off-premise signs and their replacement costs." It includes site location variables, signage appraisal, and marketing factors (foreword, vol. 2). Volume III, *Design of the Message*, looks at the essential characteristics of a good sign system—lettering, color, shape, lighting, and architectural harmony (foreword, vol. 3).

Claus, R. James, and Claus, Karen E. *Signage: Planning Environmental Visual Communication.* Palo Alto, Calif.: Institute of Signage Research, 1976, 68 pp.

Prepared for the Open Forum on Urban Signage sponsored by the Department of Housing and Urban Development and developed by the Clauses and the Rohm and Haas Company, this publication probes the basic concepts of designing signs to meet environmental requirements. The principal subjects are functions of signs in the environment, determining the effectiveness of signs, and signs as a land-use planning tool (120 illustrations).

Claus, R. James, Claus, Karen E., and Oliphant, Robert M. *Psychological Considerations of Lettering for Identification.* Cincinnati: Signs of the Times, 1971, 47 pp.

This work deals with the psychology behind lettering for identification, and should be read by anyone involved with lettering.

Dandridge, Frank. "The Value of Design in Visual Communication." *Curator* 9 (1966): 331–336.

Emphasizes the educational function of design in visual communication. Discusses helpful and adverse design factors, including the design function in relation to seeing and the process of learning from the viewpoint of visual behavior.

Dean, Andrea O. "Graphics in the Environment." *AIA Journal* 63 (October 1975): 19–31.

Addressing the problem of insufficient and excess signage in environmental graphics, Dean provides numerous innovative examples of supergraphics, including outsized wall paintings and three-dimensional graphics.

Directional and Informational Signs for Educational Facilities: A Selective Bibliography. Madison: Univ. of Wisconsin, ERIC Clearinghouse on Education Facilities, 1970, 14 pp. ED040511.

Lists materials dealing with physiological, psychological, sociological, and visual design considerations.

Downs, Roger M., and Stea, David. *Maps in Minds: Reflections on Cognitive Mapping.* New York: Harper, 1977, 284 pp.

This study is an important contribution to the theories of wayfinding and cognitive mapping. The authors have defined cognitive mapping as "an abstraction covering those . . . mental abilities that enable us to collect, organize, store, recall, and manipulate information about the spatial environment. A cognitive map is a product—a person's organized representation of some part of the spatial environment" (p. 6). The authors explain the link between the world in the head (cognitive mapping process) and spatial behavior (response to spatial problems as we move from location to location). Includes name, place, and subject index, and a nine-page bibliography.

Downs, Roger M., and Stea, David, eds. *Image and Environment: Cognitive Mapping and Spatial Behavior.* Chicago: Aldine, 1973, 439 pp.

This interdisciplinary sourcebook of selected papers presents an overview of cognitive mapping, including sections on theory, cognitive representations, spatial preference, development of spatial cognition, geographical and spatial orientation, and cognitive distance. Section introductions and the summary paper in the theory section discuss ease of use. Includes subject, name, and place name indexes, and an extensive bibliography.

Dreyfuss, Henry. *Symbol Sourcebook: An Authoritative Guide to International Graphic Symbols.* New York: McGraw-Hill, 1972, 292 pp.

Dreyfuss's work is based on a world data bank of 20,000 symbols from which he selected only those giving instructions, directions, and warnings. These symbols have been grouped by: (1) discipline and subdiscipline, e.g., agriculture is subdivided into agronomy, livestock, and forestry implements, (2) graphic form, thus enabling the user to identify the symbols out of context, and (3) meaning—an alphabetical index including what Dreyfuss calls a "Design Category," which makes it possible to find symbols related to a basic design concept (introduction). A 15-page bibliography, subdivided by discipline, and an 18-language index make this book helpful to a wide audience. Although comprehensive, it includes no signs that relate to specific library functions.

Easterby, Ron. "Clash of Symbols?" *Design* (London), no. 281 (May 1972): 72–75.

Discusses *Symbol Sourcebook* (above) by Henry Dreyfuss and *Glossary of Graphic Signs and Symbols* by Walter Shepherd (New York: Dover, 1970). The author suggests that effective use of symbols must account for the often opposing forces of pictorial quality vs. simplicity and the designer's concept vs. the user's concept. Because graphic design and experimental psychology are relatively new areas of concern, Easterby suggests that people should be patient with the proliferation of symbols.

Elliott, Pamala, and Loomis, Ross J. *Studies of Visitor Behavior in Museums and Exhibitions: An Annotated Bibliography of Sources Primarily in the English Language.* Washington, D.C.: Smithsonian Institution, Office of Museum Programs, 1975, 36 pp.

Books, articles, dissertations, studies, reports, and some unpublished works on visitor response to museum materials and environments are included in this 204-item annotated bibliography.

Gallagher, C. C. "The Human Use of Numbering Systems." *Applied Ergonomics* 5 (December 1974): 219–223.

The role of short-term memory in relation to the manipulation of numbers and letters is considered. Summarizes guidelines for developing an optimal number and letter series in conjunction with short-term memory, and cites a number of studies. Most applicable to quickly observed signs such as library labeling.

Herdeg, Walter, ed. *Archigraphia: Architectural and Environmental Graphics.* Zurich: Graphis Press, 1978 (distributed in the U.S. by Hastings House, N.Y.), 235 pp.

A lavishly illustrated overview of architectural and graphics signage (pictograms, traffic signs, visual guidance systems, graphics and lettering on buildings, and supergraphics and animated walls), with introductory comments by prominent designers. Helpful as a state-of-the-art review. Text in French, German, and English.

Kneebone, Peter, et al. "International Signs and Symbols: Special ICOGRADA Issue." *Print* 23 (November/December 1969): 25–89.

A seminal collection of articles by sign specialists. Kneebone, Peter, Introduction, p. 25, "Finding the Right Exit: An Introduction," discusses the complexities of designing signs (pp. 26–27). Carr, Richard, "The Legibility of Signs" (pp. 28–31, 78). Easterby, R. S., "The Grammar of Sign Systems" (pp. 32–35, 78). Clipson, Colin, "The Uses and Abuses of Signs" (pp. 36–39). Jacob, Heiner, and Katzumie, Masaru, "Sign Systems for International Events: Munich, Sapporo, Osaka & Co" (pp. 40–49). Mead, Margaret, "Anthropology and Glyphs," glyphs are symbol signs (pp. 50–53). Spencer, Herbert, untitled article on arrows (pp. 54–55). Vanmalderen, Luc, "Semiotics and the Graphic Sign" (pp. 56–58, 89). Krampen, Martin, "The Production Method in Sign Design Research" (pp. 59–63). Bliss, Charles K., "Semantography: One Writing for One World" (pp. 64–65). Modley, Rudolf, et al., "More About Sign/Symbol Coordination" (pp. 66, 68, 85). de Majo, W. M., "Bibliography" (pp. 70, 72). "Notes on Contributors" (pp. 74, 76, 82, 85).

Krampen, Martin. "Signs and Symbols in Graphic Communication." *Design Quarterly* 62 (1965): 2–32.

Summarizes some of the theoretical and experimental work in visual and graphic communications. The theoretical discussion includes topics of perception, signs, symbol surrogates, and pictic analysis as it relates to graphic communication. Special problems imposed by a low literacy group, a sophisticated audience, and a multilanguage audience are addressed, as well as picture languages already developed. A summary, with some suggestions for applications of theory, and a glossary and 22-item bibliography conclude the article.

Lang, Jon, et al., eds. *Designing for Human Behavior: Architecture and the Behavioral Sciences.* Community Development Series, vol. 6. Stroudsburg, Pa.: Dowden, Hutchinson, and Ross, 1974, 353 pp.

These selected papers, written from the viewpoint of the practicing architect, introduce social and psychological issues to be faced in designing better environments. The work describes issues in architectural theory and practice, the aspects of environmental psychology in architectural theory, and ways in which to obtain and use behavioral data for architectural programming and evaluation. Includes an extensive bibliography divided into categories approximating the outline of the book.

Mehrabian, Albert. *Public Places and Private Spaces: The Psychology of Work, Play, and Living Environments.* New York: Basic Books, 1976, 354 pp.

The author is involved with three levels of analysis: the person and his or her emotions; the person interacting in small groups, for instance, in the work environment; and the person interacting with the macrocosm of cities, suburbs, and dormitories. The interaction of a user with the library is briefly discussed (pp. 162–173), but sign systems are omitted. Includes a 12-page bibliography.

Modley, Rudolf. "Speaking of Sign Language." *Industrial Design* 23 (July 1976): 60–63.

Modley covers the value and potential of pictorial signage systems, universal graphic symbols, and corporate logos. Includes theoretical steps in developing a symbol and a brief discussion of professional symbols. Revised and updated version of his article "World Language without Words." *Journal of Communication* 24 (Autumn 1974): 59–66.

Modley, Rudolf, with the assistance of William R. Myers. *Handbook of Pictorial Symbols: 3,250 Examples from International Sources.* New York: Dover, 1976, 143 pp.

Part one contains 1,300 pictorial symbols grouped in subject categories ranging from children to household equipment. Part two contains public symbols arranged by facility (telephone, bar, shops, transportation, etc.) and by system (National Park Service, Olympic Games, Air Transport System, etc.). Since there are variations on a number of symbols, one can choose the particular version that is felt to be the most effective. Only one symbol specifically relates to libraries. A detailed index and a 25-item bibliography are helpful.

Papademetriou, Peter, and Hester, Paul. *Icons and Eye-Cons: Signs in the Houston Landscape.* Houston: Houston Public Library, 1978, unpaged.

A photographic essay with text, focusing on the implications of signage for the future form of cities. Includes a brief and helpful annotated bibliography on the "landscape of information." Of especial interest to public libraries considering aspects of exterior signage.

Passini, Romedi Eugenio. "Wayfinding: A Study of Spatial Problem Solving with Implications for Physical Design." Ph.D. dissertation, Pennsylvania State Univ., 1977, 317 pp.

Intended primarily for the design profession, this dissertation attempts to identify behavioral characteristics of wayfinding and to develop a notation system in which users' behavioral characteristics can be incorporated into design planning. Of particular interest to the librarian is the discussion of design shortcomings of signs and maps, and the operation of information booths.

Porteous, J. Douglas. *Environment and Behavior: Planning and Everyday Urban Life.* Reading, Mass.: Addison-Wesley, 1977, 446 pp.

Porteous explores the interaction of human behavior and the environment designated as MER (man-environment relations). This study examines human spatial behavior, human behavior in a number of settings, and ways that planning may influence behavior and environment (preface). Problems of spatial management such as seating arrangements are discussed in the context of the library (pp. 54–56). Knowledge of the MER concept is useful in the development of an effective sign system (but sign systems per se are not covered). This textbook has an extensive bibliography (pp. 381–425) and chapter summaries.

Schulitz, Helmut C. "The Message as an Architectural Medium." *Architectural Forum* 132 (May 1970): 44–49.

Schulitz thinks that lettering and graphic communications as shown in such areas as commercial signs and billboards should be considered an integral part of architecture (examples shown). He states that because of the decreasing relationship between the architectural form (building) and its function, orientation through graphic communication will become increasingly important.

Screven, C. G. "Exhibit Evaluation—A Goal-Referenced Approach." *Curator* 19 (1976): 271–290.

This text details a systematic evaluation process for assessing the value of a display or exhibit, in relation to a measurable learning or performance objective, thus enabling the evaluator to make future decisions. A detailed flowchart and a description of the main steps and decision points are shown. Bibliography included.

Screven, C. G. *The Measurement and Facilitation of Learning in the Museum Environment: An Experimental Analysis.* Publications in Museum Behavior 1. Washington, D.C.: Smithsonian Institution Press, 1974, 91 pp.

Screven addresses the problem of finding the most effective way to "motivate the productive observation of noncaptive, voluntary museum visitors given the practical and aesthetic considerations of the public museum environment." He places a strong emphasis on the virtues of instructional technology as a way of establishing specific learning objectives, and the specific behavior expected as an indication that these objectives have been fulfilled. In the context of an anthropological exhibit in a museum, various techniques for improving instructional effectiveness are compared. The visitor is involved in some form of interaction with the exhibit by providing feedback through question-answer techniques, self-paced automatic-stop audioguide tapes, portable self-scoring devices tied to exhibit questions, and built-in pushbuttons tied to differential feedback for correct-incorrect answers to exhibit questions. Bibliography included.

Shlechter, Theodore M., and Campbell, David E. "Ecologically-Oriented Methods in Evaluation: An Illustrative Example." Paper presented at the American Educational Research Association Annual Conference, Toronto, Canada, March 1978, 15 pp.

The authors address the need to evaluate the effects of settings on student behavior. Using the interview method, behavioral mapping, and diaries, the impact of a library's physical milieu on its users' behavior is assessed (abstract). Bibliography included.

Sommer, Robert. *Personal Space: The Behavioral Basis of Design.* Englewood Cliffs, N.J.: Prentice-Hall, 1969, 177 pp.

Sommer emphasizes the architect's need to account for all people using a building. Part one covers spatial behavior; part two examines the relationship of interior design to user behavior and attitudes in such settings as classrooms, dormitories, restaurants, and hospitals. Concludes with a chapter on behavioral research and environmental programming.

Wools, Roger, and Canter, David. "The Effect of the Meaning of Buildings on Behaviour." *Applied Ergonomics* 1 (June 1970): 144–150.

Wools and Canter explore the relationship between physical environment and public behavior, concluding that in some cases "the appropriateness of a building for its purpose may be measured" (p. 149). By using semantic scales, buildings may be described in "precise user-oriented terms." A number of studies are cited, and a bibliography is included.

Wurman, Richard Saul, and Katz, Joel. "Beyond Graphics: The Architecture of Information." *AIA Journal* 63 (October 1975): 40, 56.

The authors show that, through effective design, the environment can be self-explanatory and self-revealing.

Zeisel, John. *Sociology and Architectural Design.* Occasional Publications, no. 6. New York: Russell Sage, 1975, 57 pp.

"User needs research in architectural design has established methods and procedures to help bridge the gap between the architect and his or her user client" (p. 47). Areas for the future application of social research to architectural design are user analysis, design guidelines, design analysis, and design-use relationship (summary, p. 47). Organizations, journals, and sourcebooks on this subject are listed.

MATERIALS AND TECHNIQUES

"Architectural Spaces That Communicate." *Print* 28 (January 1974): 66–70.

The design firm of Propper/Elman integrates "functional reality" (the real world) with "graphic imagery" in two-and three-dimensional settings. Through what Propper terms "archmedia," their designs communicate a message by the special treatment of architectural elements and spaces (p. 66). Examples are used to illustrate the concept.

Ballinger, Raymond A. *Lettering Art in Modern Use,* student ed. New York: Van Nostrand Reinhold, 1965, 96 pp.

This primer, which contains examples and a description of Roman, Modern Gothic, script, and other styles of lettering, is designed to provide instruction in lettering techniques. The section on stenciling would be helpful in preparing information brochures.

Canadian Standards Association. *Signs and Symbols for the Occupational Environment.* Ontario: Canadian Standards Association, 1977, 35 pp.

A short handbook on the design and placement of signs "with the emphasis on messages related to safety and/or health" (p. 9). Includes guidelines useful in the fabrication of any sign system.

Claus, R. James, and Claus, Karen E. *The Sign Users Guide: A Marketing Aid.* Palo Alto, Calif.: Institute of Signage Research, 1979.

An introduction to signage in a marketing context, this guide shows how to plan a signage program by comparing signage with other forms of advertising and using standard advertising effectiveness measures, such as cost per 1,000, reach, and frequency. Contains detailed information on determining business signage needs, selecting appropriate size and type of sign, and sign design criteria. The guide is written for the businessperson, so that he or she can make informed decisions regarding signage needs and work easily with sign company representatives.

Crosby/Fletcher/Forbes. *A Sign Systems Manual.* London: Studio Vista, 1970, 76 pp.

With helpful illustrations and concise text, this publication serves as a guide to the design of a basic signage system applicable to public service environments. Includes background information on typography and printing terminology, spacing (of letters, words, lines, and margins), letter sizes, layout, symbols, categories of signs, and additional planning considerations. An excellent source of basic information for libraries beginning to design a signage system.

Environmental Graphics Sourcebook—Part One: Materials and Techniques. Chicago: Society of Environmental Graphics Designers, 1978, 52 pp.

Includes brief descriptions of the wide range of technology available, including adhesive film, plastics, wood, metal, neon, paper, stone, imprint, coatings, and illumination. Part Two will list sign manufacturers and their capabilities; Part Three will be related to elements of the design process (contracts, fees, etc.).

Follis, John. "Vital Signs." *Interiors* 135 (June 1976): 74–77.

Follis addresses problems in properly designing a signage system, discussing off-the-shelf versus custom graphics, planning and budgeting for signs, and processes and techniques. Included is a concise description with illustrations of cutout, fabricated, and die-cut vinyl letters, built-up plastic signs, subsurface printing, screen processing, flags and banners, and hand-painted and illuminated signs. Provides an excellent overview of how to plan a sign program.

Follis, John, and Hammer, Dave. *Architectural Signing and Graphics.* New York: Whitney Library of Design, 1979, 224 pp.

This work, containing 24 color and 300 black-and-white illustrations, is written for the design professional. All phases of designing a sign system are described in detail, including project analysis and planning, design, documentation, and installation supervision. Guidelines are established for solving aesthetic and functional problems, with emphasis on integrating signing and graphics with the architecture. Technical subjects include contract and specification writing, fabrication techniques and materials, and alphabets and symbol usage.

Harney, Andy L. "Signage: Fitting Letter Forms to Building Form." *AIA Journal* 64 (October 1975): 34–39.

Harney feels that lettering on the building's facade should "reflect the building's nature and reinforce its character" (p. 36). Several examples showing appropriate and inappropriate use of lettering, particularly the Helvetica style, illustrate this thesis.

"Ideas by Design: Symbols and Silhouettes." *Nation's Schools and Colleges* 2 (April 1975): 21.

Hoffman/Saur and Associates used student silhouettes at DeMun Elementary School, Clayton, Missouri, while KMM Associates used stylized symbols at Columbia Central High School, Brooklyn, Mississippi, to guide students through the school.

Knight, Robert S., et al. "Special Section: Signage Systems." *Signs of the Times* 201 (February 1979): 35–47, 98.

Articles related to the interchange between fabricator and designer. Introduction, p. 35. Knight, Robert S., "A Place in NESA," explains the objectives of a new Architectural and Graphics Division of the National Electric Sign Association (p. 36). Corbin, Jeffrey, "A Place in SEGD," describes goals of the Society of Environmental Graphics Designers and the role of the designer in the sign system design process; includes a step-by-step chart of the design process itself (pp. 37–40). "The Design Process at Work," interviews with designers (pp. 41–45). Horsley, Peter B., "Working with the Architect," advice for the sign manufacturer (pp. 46–47, 98).

Ryder, Sharon L. "Interior Architecture: A Sign of the Times." *Progressive Architecture* 57 (May 1976): 70–77.

Ryder states that a signage system should identify a place or direct a person to his or her destination as well as convey the character of the building. The author has photographed signs on glass and building facades, signs as sculpture, and neon signs. Illustrates a hospital sign system by Christopher Klumb and an airport facility sign system by AIGA.

Seng, Mark. "Signmaker: Photo-lettering You Can Do in Your Classroom." *Audio Visual Instruction* (Learning Resources Supplement 1) 19 (January 1974): 10–13.
The construction of a signmaker, which uses a photographic process, and the printing of signs are described in detail.

Signage Quarterly. Palo Alto: Institute of Signage Research, 1978– .
A monographic quarterly featuring articles on topics from marketing and design to installation and maintenance, of particular interest to people in the sign industry. Vol. 1, no. 1, *The San Diego Study,* is a comprehensive look at one city's signage policy and system; no. 2, *The State of the Industry,* provides an up-to-date picture of the sign industry; no. 3, *A Glossary of Terms,* is an attempt to standardize the language of the industry and to provide a common base for communication within and about the industry; no. 4, *The Energy Report,* provides an overview of sign industry policy and its use of energy.

"Signs." *Design Quarterly* 92 (January 1974): 1–39.
All the major categories of outdoor signage—"signs made in plastic, metal, and neon, signs with interior or exterior light sources, printed decals and stencils"—found on a selected street in Philadelphia are studied by a graphic design class at the Philadelphia College of Art in terms of "materials, manufacture, and application." The section on plastics is particularly helpful, describing in detail the physical characteristics of plastics and the fabrication processes, including methods of framing and mounting individual letters and coloring of plastic signs. This is a nuts-and-bolts article.

Signs of the Times. Cincinnati: Signs of the Times, 1906– .
Aimed at the outdoor advertising industry, this monthly periodical includes extensive advertising, as well as short articles on manufacturing, construction, and installation processes; trends in the design of signs; outdoor sign legislation; and conference news. Photographs.

Smith, Charles N. "Sign Systems." *Interior Design* (New York) 46 (October 1975): 148–153.
Describes in detail five phases in developing a sign system when using an interior designer. This process includes project requirements, conceptual design, design development, contract documents, and contract administration. For a layperson this article is helpful in learning the process of developing a well-designed sign system.

Thompson, Philip. "Do You See What I Mean?" *Design* (London), no. 347 (November 1977): 33–39.
Reasons for the present "polluted sea of information" are discussed. Includes some excellent examples of depicting ideas graphically rather than in written form.

Topalian, Alan. "The Why and How of Design Decisions." *Design* (London), no. 335 (November 1976): 43–45.
Topalian believes that design decisions are similar to other management decisions. He describes his approach and anticipated results in a projected two-year study, including "nature of design projects," "client responsibility and contribution," expectations of the client and resultant impact on the project, and the final evaluation. Charts client and designer responsibilities in the preproject, project, and postproject stages.

U.S. General Services Administration. *Manual on the Design of Sign/Symbol Systems for Federal Facilities.* Washington, D.C.: U.S. Government Printing Office, 1979, ca. 141 pp.

The General Services Administration started a "series of sign system demonstration projects," which culminated in a loose-leaf format manual of uniform standards for the interior and exterior sign requirements of federal facilities. The objectives of the project were to (1) write a "how to" instructional manual for developing in-house sign systems, (2) develop standardized specifications, and (3) provide in-house capabilities to change and replace signs (annotation from the review article "Federal Facilities to Get Facelift," by Dave Meyer, in *Signs of the Times,* August 1978, p. 37). Appendix I. "Design Guidelines on Symbol Signs for Public Buildings" (39 pp., by Paul Arthur) could be most useful to anyone designing a sign system.

White, Jan V. "Architects and Graphic Designers: How to Make the Best of a Potential Partnership." *Architectural Record* 159 (February 1976): 57–58.

Emphasizes the importance of improving the visible image of a corporation through the development of a master plan by a graphic designer. The role of the graphic designer and his or her relationship with the client in developing this image are discussed.

VISUAL GUIDANCE SYSTEMS IN LIBRARIES

Beck, Richard J., and Norris, Lynn. "Communication Graphics in Library Orientation." *Catholic Library World* 47 (December 1975): 218–219.

Methods for producing an inexpensive, in-house library sign system through the use of signs, bulletin boards, banners, single-sheet handouts, posters, displays, directories, and floor plans.

Besant, Jane, et al. "Helping Users Find Their Way." *Wisconsin Library Bulletin* 73 (July–August 1977): 145–174.

A collection of articles suggests methods (orientation, media skills curriculum, instruction, tours, signs) for helping users find their way around a library media center. Jill S. Hartmann and Robert R. Hartmann, "Inviting Design Helps the User," discusses the importance of color and signs for improving the usability of a library. Avis Solon and Lare Mischo, "Ways Through the Library Maze," describes several ways to help orient the library user, including a directory, handouts, tours, and identifying areas through highly visible graphics and color coding.

Carey, R. J. P. *Library Guiding: A Program for Exploiting Library Resources.* London: Clive Bingley, 1974, 186 pp.

To increase reader accessibility, an effective guiding system must satisfactorily answer these three queries: what can the library offer? where is it to be found? how can it be used? This guiding system includes the following elements: (1) permanent visual information, e.g., standing signs and shelf labels, (2) sign information in printed or non-printed format at the point of use, (3) printed guides that supplement the sign systems and point-of-use guides, (4) colored guiding systems in which each geographical area is color coded, and (5) administrative routines to update the above information. Although this work was written from the perspective of the university library, it is applicable to all libraries. Numerous illustrations and examples enhance the work, especially the chapter on printed materials. The section on developing a plan for a sign system is sketchy, while the discussion of sign systems is limited to the do-it-yourself situation. Chapters include brief references. The major value of the book is its broad treatment of a guiding system of which a sign system is one aspect.

Dean, J. R. "Design Co-ordination and the Corporate Image of Libraries." *Library World* 72 (February 1971): 240–241.

Dean states that a coordinated design policy for a library will communicate a positive image to the public. He discusses the steps to implement such a policy and applies this process to his own library.

Dertien, James L. "Plexiglas Signs Put Pzazz in Library Directional Plan." *Unabashed Librarian* no. 3 (Spring 1972): 10–11.
  The cost, advantages, and use of plexiglas signs are briefly described and illustrated.

Ellsworth, Ralph E. *Academic Library Buildings: A Guide to Architectural Issues and Solutions.* Boulder, Colo. Colorado Associated Univ. Press, 1973, 530 pp.
  This sourcebook provides numerous illustrations depicting interior design aspects of library architecture. Of particular interest is the description of directories and floor plans (pp. 177–210).

Ellsworth, Ralph E. "How Buildings Can Contribute." In *Educating the Library User,* ed. by John Lubans, Jr. New York: R. R. Bowker Co., 1974, pp. 415–422.
  Discusses the attributes of a "good" library building, which contribute to its instructional value. Graphics are touched on. (Printed bibliographic aids, library tours, point-of-use aids, and other methods to increase the accessibility of the collection are also discussed in other chapters of the Lubans book.)

Grimley, Susan. "Signs and Graphic Displays: A Survey of Their Use in Public Libraries." Master's thesis, Univ. of Chicago, 1974, 128 pp.
  "The results of a pilot examination of the signs and graphic displays in use in thirty-nine medium-sized public libraries" are presented. Assumptions underlying the study are: an experienced library user entering the library for the first time can use its resources without a librarian's assistance, and the less-experienced library user can find his or her way to large categories of materials without the assistance of card catalog or librarian. "The results revealed that no library in the survey has a signage system supporting the two asumptions." However, Grimley did not test the effectiveness of the signs for users (abstract). Bibliography includes several citations to works on library signs.

Heathcote, Denis. "Public Relations and Publicity." In *Libraries in Higher Education: The User Approach to Service*, ed. by John Cowley. Hamden, Conn.: Linnet Books, 1975, pp. 39–64.
  Discusses the importance of library guides in publicizing the library and describes the attributes of a well-designed guide. Included is an analysis of three illustrated floor plans.

Kosterman, Wayne. "A Guide to Library Environmental Graphics." *Library Technology Reports* 14 (May-June 1978): 269–295.
  In addition to material excerpted in *Sign Systems for Libraries* (Chapter 6), the author discusses aspects of library interior signage, including planning considerations, sign categories, decision factors, consultants, and suppliers. Also includes an extensive list of sign manufacturers.

Lancaster, F. W., with the assistance of M. J. Joncich. *The Measurement and Evaluation of Library Services.* Washington, D.C.: Information Resources Press, 1977, 395 pp.
  Chapter 12, "The Effect of Physical Accessibility and Ease of Use," covers major studies of the library's physical accessibility and location of its materials in determining the ease of use. In Chapter 14, "Conclusion: Factors Affecting the Performance of Library Services," Lancaster summarizes factors affecting library performance in a known-item search, a comprehensive literature search, a request for factual information, and a search for books on a given subject. A well-written work with chapter references and index.

Langmead, Stephen, and Beckman, Margaret. *New Library Design: Guide Lines to Planning Academic Library Buildings*. Toronto, Canada: Wiley, 1970, 117 pp.

Langmead, the project architect, and Beckman, deputy and systems librarian, relate their experiences in planning and construction of the McLaughlin Library, University of Guelph. The signage program section in the chapter "Library Design and Construction" provides a succinct discussion of most aspects of a library sign system. Through reading the book, one can easily place the signage program in the perspective of the total architectural scheme for the library. Includes bibliography and index.

Lockwood, James D. "Involving Consultants in Library Change." *College and Research Libraries* 38 (November 1977): 498–508.

Lockwood discusses considerations for involving consultants in any library project: presenting a "decision model" for determining the need to use a library consultant; preparation for the consulting engagement; and selection of the appropriate consultant (article headnotes). An extensive bibliography on consultants is included.

Lushington, Nolan, and Mills, Willis. *Libraries Designed for Users: The Library Planning Handbook*. Syracuse, N.Y.: Gaylord, 1979.

Emphasizes the "information center" library design, as opposed to the traditional circulation library design. The author draws on the experiences of interior planners, lighting specialists, and others for program-oriented approaches. Discusses the impact of physical settings on the interaction of users with a variety of media and services.

Metcalf, Keyes D. *Planning Academic and Research Library Buildings*. New York: McGraw-Hill, 1965, 431 pp.

The most comprehensive work on library planning. Although the treatment of library signs is scant (in Appendix C, Metcalf reminds the library planner to include exit signs, floor plan charts, directional signs and door labels, and a building directory in the new building), the book is an indispensable aid in the planning of any phase of a library building program. An extensive selected and annotated bibliography by topical areas is included.

Pollet, Dorothy. "You Can Get There from Here: New Directions in Library Signage." *Wilson Library Bulletin* 50 (February 1976): 456–462.

Designer David Pesanelli, in a conversation with the author, covers aspects of library signage, such as: basic principles in designing a signage system, defining the library's user groups and their various missions, information desk role in the design model, use of color coding, "You are here" maps and directories, and some down-to-earth suggestions for librarians designing their own signage systems.

Schlitt, Gerhard. "Beschilderung als Benutzungshilfe" [Signs as instructional aids]. In *Bibliotheksarbeit Heute*, ed. by Gerhart Lohse and Gunther Pflug. Frankfurt, West Germany: Klostermann, 1973, pp. 272–280. "A Commentary on the Layout of Library Buildings."

The author discusses how the quality and usefulness of signs play an important role in the way a building is accepted by the public. During the planning stages, signs are as important as other details. Some points to be considered are: (1) the lettering of signs has a psychological effect; (2) a uniform graphic concept should be evident throughout the entire building; (3) there is a need to find a happy medium between too much and too little information; (4) positioning of signs is extremely important; and (5) sign systems must be flexible. The author also comments on various methods and materials used in in-house sign making. His main thesis is that better communication will result from an effective sign system (abstracted by Anita I. Malebranche, Virginia Polytechnic Institute and State University, Blacksburg, Va.). Text in German.

Seng, Mary. "Reference Service Upgraded: Using Patrons' Reference Questions." *Special Libraries* 69 (January 1978): 21–28.

Through the analysis of patron questions over a three-year period, it was found that changes in the library environment influence questions asked by patrons. In the directional question area, the statistics demonstrated that improved graphics designating book stack locations resulted in a decreased number of locational questions.

Spencer, Herbert, and Reynolds, Linda. *Directional Signing and Labelling in Libraries and Museums: A Review of Current Theory and Practice.* London: Readability of Print Research Unit, Royal College of Art, 1977, 117 pp.

Based on a survey of the relevant literature, in-depth interviews with graphic specialists, and an examination of existing signs, this work provides theoretical and practical guidelines for the design of signing, guiding, and labeling systems. A directional signing system helps guide the user to library materials and services. The functional categories of these signs are direction, orientation, identification, mandatory, warning, and informative (p. 15). The function of a library guiding system is to help the patron use the resources in the most efficient way possible; as defined here, it refers only to hard-copy displays of information (p. 61). Examples of a guiding system would include written procedures for using the card catalog, making photocopies, and borrowing materials (p. 65). Part I examines the state of the art in library and museum graphics and makes recommendations for future research. Part IIa, "Directional Signing in Libraries and Museums," covers the effects of architectural design, user and management requirements on signing, typography and layout of signs, use of symbols and color, choice of materials, and methods and placement of signs. Extensive topical bibliographies and a list of British manufacturers of sign and label materials are provided. The detailed table of contents, arranged by universal decimal classification, and concisely written sections make this a most useful book for those developing a graphic system.

Stevenson, Malcolm. "Progress in Documentation: Education of Users of Libraries and Information Services." *Journal of Documentation* 33 (March 1977): 53–78.

Stevenson provides a comprehensive review of user education literature, including a section on library guidance systems (pp. 64–65) and library guides (p. 65).

Wintermeier, Wolfgang. *Technik, Lay-out und Konzeptionsplanung der Beschilderung in Bibliotheken* [Techniques, layout and concept planning of library signs]. Köln, West Germany: Bibliothekar-Lehrinstitut des Landes Nordrhein-Westfalen, 1975, 59 pp.

Included in this work are chapters on techniques, materials and design, sign assembling, visual techniques (stenciling, letter press machine, etc.), planning a library sign system, special problems (cost, personnel, how to coordinate library signs), a list of manufacturers of sign equipment and materials, and an 18-item bibliography of German, British, and American sources. This paper was submitted as credit toward the examination for employment at the Bibliothekar-Lehrinstitut Scientific Library. Text in German.

VISUAL GUIDANCE SYSTEMS IN OTHER INSTITUTIONS

Abercrombie, Stanley. "Zoo Story." *Urban Design* 8 (Summer 1977): 40–41.

This description of the graphic design system of the Smithsonian's National Zoological Park in Washington, D.C., is illustrated. The author briefly discusses the problems of communicating information efficiently to a diverse audience through visual symbols.

American Hospital Association. *Signs and Graphics for Health Care Facilities.* Chicago: American Hospital Association, 1979, 70 pp.

This publication explains the need for a readily understandable and coherent visual information system, and the way to go about getting it. Written for administrators and designers, the book offers practical directions for planning, design, selection, purchase, installation, and maintenance. Includes 54 illustrations and an index.

Best in Environmental Graphics 1975– , The. Print Casebook Series. Washington, D.C.: R. C. Publications, 1975– .

The extensive illustrations in this work provide highly informative examples of environmental graphics systems.

Brutton, Mark, et al. "Design Evaluation: ICOGRADA in Chicago." *Design* (London), no. 354 (June 1978): 44–63.

The series of articles, drawn from papers at the International Council of Graphic Design Association's meeting, August 1978, offers accounts of four graphic programs and illustrates the application of design evaluation techniques. Brutton, Mark, "Why Designers Should Stop Worrying and Learn to Love Design Evaluation" (p. 45). Ferebee, Ann, "How a Brand New Metro Lost Its Way," explains why the sign system of Washington's subway was inadequate and the steps taken to improve it, with emphasis on the importance of testing the goals, tentative design solution, and the implemented solution (pp. 46–49). Best, Alastair, "Why the People Stay Away from a People's Culture Centre," covers the sign system in the Centre Beaubourg (Pompidou) in Paris as evaluated by ENFI Design; discusses the lack of quality in the programming as conceived and the failure to implement the recommendations set forth in the design manual (pp. 50–55). [No author] "How a Lump of Rock Failed to Make Its Point" tells how visitors knew no more about an archaeological exhibition in Victoria, Canada, after viewing it than before they went in; after C. G. Screven, psychologist, with selected museum staff members, determined the intended and real effects of the exhibition on visitors, the exhibit was redesigned based on the evaluation (pp. 56–59). Abercrombie, Stanley, "How to Aim Accurately at the Minds of Child Readers," describes the involvement of children in a pre-publication analysis of *Sesame Street Magazine* in order to ensure that the magazine's message matches the children's comprehension (pp. 60–63).

Corlett, E. N., Manenica, I., and Bishop, R. P. "The Design of Direction Finding Systems in Buildings." *Applied Ergonomics* 3 (June 1972): 66–69.

A direction-finding system for large university buildings, based on the findings of G. A. Best in his 1967 Msc. thesis, "Direction Finding in Large Buildings," is delineated in a step-by-step procedure.

Crompton, Dennis. "Centre Pompidou: A Live Centre of Information." *Architectural Design* 47 (February 1977): 110–127.

Paris's Centre Pompidou consists of the Museum of Modern and Contemporary Art, the Public Reference Library, and the Industrial Design Centre. Crompton describes some of the principles underlying the concept of a live center of information ("two-way participation between people and activities exhibits") and the techniques available for making this concept a reality. He then discusses the reasons for its failure.

DeNeve, Rose. "Signs and Symbols for a Children's Hospital." *Print* 26 (March 1972): 26–31.

Outlines and illustrates procedures used in developing a signage system for a children's hospital in Mexico. Separate sign systems were used for the staff, the general public, and the children.

Doyle, Brendan. "Underground Maps: It's Hard to Improve on Beck." *Design* (London), no. 349 (January 1978): 31.

The author compares the effectiveness of subway diagrams used in London and New York. The importance of adopting a diagram form compatible with the entire system's purpose is underscored. Illustrated. Based on the author's dissertation. The article may be useful to libraries attempting to direct the user in task-oriented patterns (how to find a journal, a book, etc.) via a diagram.

Gutman, James. "How Campuses Use Signage to Improve Communications." *College and University Business* 47 (November 1969): 85–90.
Discusses and illustrates aspects of the campus sign systems at Southern Illinois University, University of California, Santa Cruz, Syracuse University, and the University of Chicago.

"Hospital Graphics." *Industrial Design* 19 (April 1972): 58–61.
E. Christopher Klumb Associates developed a sign system for New York City health facilities, which Klumb hoped would "communicate effectively, help to create a friendly environment, and express the concern of the facility for its patients" (p. 60).

Hunt, Wayne, and Hammer, Dave. "JF&A for Sea World of Florida." *Industrial Design* 22 (May 1975): 60–63.
The sign system and graphics, as well as the educational exhibits, completed by John Follis and Associates for Sea World are discussed. The detailed outline for the phases in a design project and the graphics schedule are most useful.

Interior Space Designers, Inc. (ISD). "Campus Graphics: Designing a Campus Signage System." *College and University Business* 47 (November 1969): 79–84.
ISD outlines its signage program and discusses areas of special consideration when developing a signage system. The firm begins with consultation and progresses into the conceptual design stage. A third phase includes the accepted final design and implementation. Construction, fabrication, and installation constitute the final stage. Although the article deals with exterior signage, it is equally applicable to the interior.

Jensen, Robert. "Shopping Malls in Suburbia." *Architectural Record* 151 (March 1972): 113–121, 124–128.
The graphic designs of the mall at Columbia, Maryland, and the Eastman Regional Mall in San Jose, California, are discussed. Of particular interest is the discussion and illustrations for the Columbia Tenant Information Manual, which is primarily concerned with external signs.

Klumb, Eugene C. "Hospital Signs that Everyone Can Understand." *Modern Hospital* 120 (May 1973): 96–99.
Describes a hospital sign system using primary signs to direct patients and visitors, and secondary signs for staff use. According to the author, professional planning and a coordinated approach are necessary in creating a workable sign system. Considerations in the development of a sign system are discussed. Illustrations.

"Landside/Airside Traffic: Studies in Directed Motion." *Architectural Record* 148 (August 1970): 128–130.
The airport layout and graphic design for Jacksonville and Tampa airports are illustrated and briefly discussed. Jane Doggett, head, Architectural Graphics Associates, Inc., describes the importance of the graphic specialist for testing the appropriateness of traffic flow solutions to predict problem areas in the plans.

"Logomotives." *Design* (London), no. 314 (February 1975): 36–41.
The historical development of the Coca-Cola logo or trademark is discussed and illustrated. Coke is the "best example of a trademark using the name of the company as the symbol and then the symbol as an identity" (p. 41), according to David Bernstein.

Manella, Douglas. "Exxon Keeps You Moving." *Industrial Design* 20 (June 1973): 68–71.
 A sign system for a 30-floor office building that uses the elevator cores as the location of main floor signs is illustrated and described.

Manella, Douglas. "Packaging and Graphics, This Way In . . . You Are Here . . . This Way Out." *Industrial Design* 19 (May 1972): 67–77.
 Architectural signage for the University of Louisville's Health Science Center (including Research Library), the State University of New York at Stony Brook, the Greater Pittsburgh Airport, and Polaroid Corporation is illustrated and briefly discussed.

Manella, Douglas. "Sign Language." *Industrial Design* 20 (April 1973): 62–65.
 A corporate identity program for Hiebert, Inc., and signage systems for McCarran International Airport, San Diego Wild Animal Park, and Metromedia, Inc.'s People's Gallery all illustrate the approach taken by John Follis and Associates, an architectural graphics and signage firm.

Mangan, Doreen. "Design System Transforms Mass Retailer." *Industrial Design* 23 (September/October 1976): 42–46.
 Through a comprehensive design program in the areas of graphic standards, business forms, packaging designs, and advertising guidelines, J. C. Penney hoped to change the visual character of its company by projecting a new image. Plans for this are discussed and illustrated. The parallels between a consumer-oriented retail store and the patron-oriented library bear examination. An application of Penney's total design system might help to change the library's low-profile passive image into a more active patron-oriented one.

Noyes, Eliot. "Study for an IBM Sign Design Program." *Architectural Record* 127 (June 1960): 157–164.
 The development of a comprehensive external sign program for all IBM plants is described. Fifty-two examples of IBM signs illustrate both effective and ineffective uses. The ineffective examples bear some study.

"Planning, Flexibility, and Growth Enable Hospitals' Signage Systems to Meet Many Needs." *Hospitals* 51 (July 16, 1977): 54, 57–58.
 The importance of developing an overall signage system—consistent, efficient, economical, and flexible—is emphasized. The four phases of a consultant's services—planning, design, working drawings, and supervision—are enumerated. Aspects of each are described in four hospital projects.

"Signage System Eases Frustration." *Hospitals* 48 (April 16, 1974): 50–52.
 The problems and consequent development of a sign system for Mount Sinai Medical Center, which consists of separate but interconnected buildings, are described.

Smith, C. Ray. "Graphic Renovation Earns Dividends." *Industrial Design* 24 (July/August 1977): 44–47.
 Through a well-planned graphics and signage program, a bank's three basic messages (direction, service area identification, and promotion) were analyzed to improve traffic flow and the customer's understanding of the total environment. Eighteen illustrations with brief descriptions delineate the problem and projected solutions. The article is particularly applicable to a library having queuing problems.

Stevens, Richard, and Rose, Stuart. "To Identify a Corporate Giant." *Design* (London), no. 332 (August 1976): 43–45.
 The graphic design system for the British Postal System is discussed and illustrated.

Contributors

Milton S. Byam served as Director of the Queens Borough Public Library, New York City, following a directorship at the Washington, District of Columbia Public Library.

Aaron Cohen, A.I.A., is a library consultant from Croton on Hudson, New York, whose special interest is in the three-dimensional aspects of library space. He has consulted on the planning and design of a number of libraries.

Elaine Cohen, Croton on Hudson, New York, is a space planner, behaviorist, and writer. Together with Aaron Cohen, she has conducted a series of workshops on space planning and practical design for libraries.

Evelyn H. Daniel is a professor at the Syracuse University School of Information Studies, New York.

Bruce Daniels is a graphics designer for the Chicago architectural firm of Perkins & Will. He has designed numerous exterior and/or interior architectural signage systems, for such clients as the King Faisal Military Cantonment in Saudi Arabia, Yusuf A. Alghanim & Sons headquarters in Kuwait, and a public library expansion program in Indiana, as well as many medical facilities.

Roger M. Downs is Associate Professor of Geography at The Pennsylvania State University. His major research fields include environmental cognition, spatial thinking, and human wayfinding. Together with David Stea, he published *Maps in Minds: Reflections on Cognitive Mapping*.

Garret Eakin is an architect and resides in Chicago.

William Hamby is employed as staff designer for John W. Durgin Associates, a Portsmouth, New Hampshire, engineering and architectural firm. As well as designing several library interior and graphic systems, Hamby has developed logos and graphics for such organizations as the Academic Resources Center of Cornell University and the National Librarians' Association.

Peter C. Haskell is Director of the Library at Franklin and Marshall College, Pennsylvania. He has consulted on the planning of minimum cost sign systems at Indiana University and elsewhere.

Institute of Signage Research is a nonprofit educational organization that directs its efforts to improving the use and quality of signage through publications, information, programs, and assistance to all who are concerned with environmental visual communication. The Executive Director is R. James Claus; the office is located at 4020 Fabian Way, Palo Alto, Calif. 94304.

Hylda Kamisar is Head, Reference Section, National Library Service for the Blind and Physically Handicapped of the Library of Congress.

David Kaser, Distinguished Professor of Library Science, Graduate Library School, Indiana University, has consulted widely in the planning of academic libraries.

Wayne Kosterman, formerly Director of Environmental Communications for RVI Corporation, Chicago, directs Wayne Kosterman Design, in Roselle, Illinois. He has designed a number of major sign systems for stores, hospitals, banks, universities, and shopping centers.

John Kupersmith has worked with informational graphics as a reference librarian responsible for instructional service in the Van Pelt Library, University of Pennsylvania. He has also served as liaison with the design consultant developing a comprehensive sign system for that building.

Gary Kushner is a designer at Communication Arts, Boulder, Colorado.

Ross J. Loomis is Associate Professor of Psychology at Colorado State University, with a research and teaching interest in environmental psychology. Specific research activities have included studies about museum visitors and psychological properties of the museum environment.

John Lubans, Jr., writes about library users, most recently in *Progress in Educating the Library User* (1978), following *Educating the Library User* (1974), both from R. R. Bowker. He lives in Houston and is combining librarianship with graduate study in public administration.

McRay Magleby is an instructor of graphic design and illustration and Art Director of the Department of Graphic Communications of the Brigham Young University Press, Utah.

Jane Maienschein is Associate Fellow at Dickinson College, Pennsylvania. She has completed a Ph.D. in history and philosophy of science at Indiana University.

Barbara S. Marks, Reference Librarian at New York University, is editor of the *New York University List of Books in Education*, and has contributed the education titles to *Books for College Libraries* and *Serials for Libraries*.

Judy Myers is Head of Documents/Microforms at the University of Houston Library, Texas. During 1976–1977, she was also one of two building coordinators for the addition to and renovation of the library building. She planned the book stack arrangement and assisted the signage consultants in planning the signs for the building.

Margaret B. Parsons has lectured on the evaluation of museum environments since 1973. She works for the National Gallery of Art, Washington, D.C., in the area of extension program development.

Guest Perry is Librarian for the Library of the Houghton Mifflin Company, Boston, Massachusetts.

Dorothy Pollet is Educational Liaison Officer at the Library of Congress. She has written several articles for library publications, including "You Can Get There from Here" in the *Wilson Library Bulletin*, which was the starting point for this book.

William W. Prince is General Reference Librarian at Virginia Polytechnic Institute and State University.

Katherine M. Selfridge is Assistant for External Affairs at Radcliffe College, Cambridge, Massachusetts, and a sign systems consultant. During 1973–1978, she was head of the Publications and Graphics Department of The Architects Collaborative, Cambridge, where she directed the planning and design of sign systems.

Claire Richter Sherman holds a Ph.D. in art history from the Johns Hopkins University, Baltimore, Maryland. A specialist in late medieval manuscripts, she is the author of *The Portraits of Charles V of France (1338–1380)* and of various studies of manuscripts from the library of this bibliophile king.

Sheldon Wechsler, Professor of Optometry at the University of Houston, Texas, has done extensive research on signs and visual acuity.

Marvin E. Wiggins is Assistant Professor of Library Science and head of the General Reference Department of the Harold B. Lee Library, Brigham Young University, Utah. He is chairman of the library's sign committee and has eleven years' experience in developing and administering library use instruction for a student body numbering 25,000.

Lawrence J. M. Wilt is Assistant Professor of Library Resources at Dickinson College, Pennsylvania.

Index

process of, 19–23, 25
relation to library effectiveness, 18
spatial style, 24–25, 29–30
system design, 22, 25–28
See also Architectural design, graphics coordination; Behavior; Cognitive mapping; Color coding; Floor identification; Orientation

White light, 40
Widener Library (Harvard University), 146, 169, 171–173
Wiggins, Marvin E., 150
"World Language Without Words" (Modley), 112 n.8

Zeisel, J., 5